The Masonic Book Club

Vol. 10

Sufferings of John Coustos

Wallace McLeod

Westphalia Press
An Imprint of the Policy Studies Organization
Washington, DC

SUFFERINGS OF JOHN COUSTOS

All Rights Reserved © 2025 by Policy Studies Organization

Westphalia Press
An imprint of Policy Studies Organization
1367 Connecticut Avenue NW
Washington, D.C. 20036
info@ipsonet.org

ISBN: 978-1-63723-591-1

Daniel Gutierrez-Sandoval, Executive Director
PSO and Westphalia Press

Updated material and comments on this edition
can be found at the Westphalia Press website:
www.westphaliapress.org

The Masonic Book Club

The *Masonic Book Club* (MBC) was formed in 1970 by two Illinois Masons, Alphonse Cerza, 33°, and Louis L. Williams, 33°. The MBC primarily reprinted out-of-print Masonic books with scholarly introductions; occasionally they would print additional texts as "bonuses" (though none were marked specifically as such on the title pages); sometimes a reprint would be marked "Masonic Book Club Edition"; often an unnumbered bonus was published jointly with the Illinois Lodge of Research or the Supreme Council, 33°, NMJ, USA.

Most of the MBC volumes indicated on the title page, "Volume [*Number*] of the Publications of the Masonic Book Club," some were misnumbered, and some were unnumbered. Indeed, the numbering of the early volumes was inconsistent. For example, *A Serious and Impartial Enquiry* is "Volume Five" (1974) but *Masonic Membership of the Founding Fathers* is "The Masonic Book Club Edition" (1974). Then, *Masonry Dissected* is "Volume Eight" (1977), *The Trestleboard* is "Volume 8A" (1978), and *Anderson's Constitutions of 1738* is "Volume Nine" (1978). If nothing else, MBC books keep bibliophiles on their toes.

The first volumes had deckle-edged paper and pages of slightly different sizes, though eventually the MBC settled into a 6"×9" trimmed-page format for their books. The books were bound in a dark blue fabric with gold lettering. Listed below are the fifty-nine MBC volumes published 1970–2010 with bonuses. N.B.: A number and letter, e.g. "Volume 8A," is a numbering for this reprint series.

The club originally was limited to 333 members, but the number grew to nearly 2,000, with 1,083 members when it dissolved in 2010. In 2017 MW Barry Weer, 33°, the last president of the MBC, transferred the MBC name and assets to the Supreme Council, 33°, SJ, USA. Under the editorship of Arturo de Hoyos, 33°, G∴C∴, and S. Brent Morris, 33°, G∴C∴, the revived Masonic Book Club has the goal of publishing classic Masonic books while supporting Scottish Rite, SJ, USA philanthropies.

Publications of the Masonic Book Club, 1970–2010

1	1970	*The Regius Poem*	Masonic Book Club
2	1971	*The Constitutions of the Free-Masons*	Benjamin Franklin
3	1972	*Ahiman Rezon*	Laurence Dermott
4	1973	*Illustrations of Masonry*	William Preston
5	1974	*A Serious and Impartial Enquiry into the Cause of the Present Decay of Free-Masonry in the Kingdom of Ireland*	Fifield D'Assigny
5A	1974*	*Masonic Membership of the Founding Fathers*	Ronald E. Heaton

6	1975	*The Signers of the Declaration of Independence*	David C. Whitney
7	1976	*The Signers of the Constitution of the United States*	David C. Whitney
7A	1976*	*Masonic Symbols in American Decorative Art*	Louis L. Williams & Alphonse Cerza
8	1977	*Samuel Prichard's Masonry Dissected, 1730*	Harry Carr
8A	1978*	*Trestle-Board (A facsimile of the original Trestle Board by the Baltimore Masonic Convention of 1843)*	Dwight L. Smith
9	1978	*Anderson's Constitutions of 1738*	Lewis Edward & W. J. Hughan
10	1979	*Sufferings of John Coustos*	Wallace McLeod
11	1980	*The Revelations of a Square*	George Oliver
11A	1980	*Biblical Characters in Freemasonry*	John H. Van Gorden
11B	1980*	*A Masonic Reader's Guide*	Alphonse Cerza & Thomas Warden
12	1981	*Three Distinct Knocks and Jachin and Boaz*	Harry Carr
13	1982	*Masonic Almanacs and Anti-Masonic Almanacs*	Plez A. Transou
13A	1982*	*Stephen A. Douglas: Freemason*	Wayne C. Temple
14	1983	*The Beginnings of Freemasonry in America*	Melvin M. Johnson
14A	1983*	*Bespangled, Painted & Embroidered: Decorated Masonic Aprons in America, 1790–1850*	Scottish Rite Masonic Museum & Library
14B	1983*	*Making a Mason at Sight*	Louis L. Williams
15	1984	*Masonic Concordance of the Holy Bible*	Charles Clyde Hunt
15A	1984*	*By Square and Compasses: The Building of Lincoln's Home and Its Saga*	Wayne C. Temple
16	1985	*The Old Gothic Constitutions*	Wallace McLeod

16A	1985*	Modern Historical Characters in Freemasonry	John H. Van Gorden
17	1986	The Rise and Development of Organised Freemasonry	Roy A. Wells
17A	1986*	Ancient and Early Medieval Historical Characters in Freemasonry	John H. Van Gorden
18	1987	The Lodge in Friendship Village and Other Stories	P. W. George
18A	1987*	Masonic Charities	John H. Van Gorden & Stewart M. L. Pollard
18B	1987*	Medieval Historical Characters in Freemasonry	John H. Van Gorden
18C	1987*	George Washington in New York	Allan Boudreau & Alexander Bleimann
19	1988	Records of the Hole Crafte and Fellowship of Masons	Edward Conder, Jr.
20	1989	A Candid Disquisition of the Principles and Practices of the Most Ancient and Honourable Society of Free and Accepted Masons	Wellins Calcott
20A	1989*	Freemasonry and Nauvoo, 1839–1846	Robin L. Carr
21	1990	Masonic Odes and Poems	Rob Morris
22	1991	Lessing's Masonic Dialogues	Gotthold Lessing
22A	1991*	ABC of Freemasonry: A Book for Beginners	Delmar D. Darrah
23	1992	The Folger Manuscript	S. Brent Morris
24	1993	Freemasonry and Christianity: Lectures from Two Ages	T. De Witt Peake & John J. Murchison
25	1994	The Constitutions of St. John's Lodge	Robin L. Carr
25A	1994*	The Mystic Tie and Men of Letters	Robin L. Carr
26	1995	Recollections of a Masonic Veteran	S. Brent Morris
27	1996	The Freemason's Monitor or Illustrations of Masonry in Two Parts	Thomas Smith Webb

28	1997	*The Masonic Ladder or the Nine Steps to Ancient Freemasonry*	John Sherer
28A	1997*	*Freemasonry and Democracy: Its Evolution in North America*	Allen E. Roberts & Wallace McLeod
29	1998	*The Masonic Harp: Collection of Masonic Odes, Hymns, Songs*	George Wingate Chase
30	1999	*Symbolic Teachings of Masonry and Its Message*	Thomas Milton Stewart
31	2000	*Freemasonry Its Meaning and Significance, An Exposition of its Ethics, Religion and Philosophy*	Otto Caspari
32	2001	*K. R. Cama Masonic Jubilee Volume*	Jivanji Jamshedji Modi
33	2002	*Caementaria Hibernica*	W. J. Chetwode Crawley
34	2003	*A Daily Advancement in Masonic Knowledge*	Wallace McLeod & S. Brent Morris
35	2004	*The Craftsman, and Templar's Textbook and, also, Melodies for the Craft*	Cornelius Moore
36	2005	*The Text Book of Freemasonry*	Retired Member of the Craft
37	2006	*Orations of the Illustrious Brother Frederick Dalcho Esq., M.D.*	Frederick Dalcho
38	2007	*Antiquities of Freemasonry Comprising Illustrations of the Five Grand Periods of Masonry from the Creation of the World to the Dedication of King Solomon's Temple*	George Oliver
39	2008	*Diogenes' Lamp or an Examination of our Present-Day Morality and Enlightenment*	Adam Weishaupt
40	2009	*Proofs of Conspiracy Against All the Governments of Europe*	John Robison
41	2010	*The Evolution of Freemasonry*	Delmar Darrah

* indicates a bonus book

Sufferings of John Coustos

THE
SUFFERINGS
OF
JOHN COUSTOS

THE SUFFERINGS OF JOHN COUSTOS

A facsimile reprint of the
first English edition,
published at London in 1746

with an introduction by
Wallace McLeod

VOLUME TEN

of the publications of
The Masonic Book Club

Published by
The Masonic Book Club
A Not-for-Profit Corporation of Illinois
Bloomington, Illinois
1979

[This page appeared in the original publication.]

This volume has been published
for Members of
The Masonic Book Club
in an edition of 1,250 copies,
numbered for Members of the Club,
this being

No. 307

© 1979 by The Masonic Book Club
Printed in the United States of America

Preface

Each new generation of Masons needs a new interpretation of Masonry,—its origin, its history, its traditions, its teachings. Among the several million Masons around the globe, there are many who are eager students,—anxious to learn the story of their beloved Fraternity. Among those thousands are many serious Masonic scholars, waiting for new light on the subject closest to their hearts. Yet, as we survey the present generation of Masonic scholars, there are probably no more than a score who could be called able *research* scholars. Rare indeed is the ability to investigate a problem, to get to the basic sources, and then to set it down clearly for the benefit of this and succeeding generations.

Fortunately for the members of the Masonic Book Club, and through us for the Masonic world at large, such a research scholar has been found. Dr. Wallace McLeod of the University of Toronto, the author of the following introductory study, is such a man. Quite modestly, he has requested that little be said about him, but for the record, the facts must be presented.

Dr. McLeod is Professor of Classics in the University of Toronto, where he specializes in Classical Greek language and literature. He was born in Toronto, and after preliminary studies there, received his A.M. and Ph.D. from Harvard.

Between the years 1957 and 1959, he studied archaeology in Greece, participating in excavations there and in Turkey. In 1970-1971, he studied the Crusader Castles in Greece. He has taught in colleges in Connecticut; Vancouver, B.C.; London, Ontario; and now in the University of Toronto. He has written numerous articles and reviews in his chosen field, and has had one book published, *Composite Bows from The Tomb of Tutankhamun* (Oxford, 1970).

Both his father and grandfather were Masons. He was initiated into his father's Lodge, Mizpah, No. 572, in 1952, and served as W.M. in 1969. He has worked on various committees of the Grand Lodge of Canada in the Province of Ontario, and is presently a member of the Board of General Purposes, and Chairman of the Committee on Masonic Education. He has edited several Grand Lodge publications, and has written numerous articles for various Masonic publications, including *A.Q.C.*

Such a brief biographical narrative cannot begin to describe Right Worshipful Brother McLeod's various interests and activities, but we can say without reservation that his capabilities in the field of research and writing are a rare combination; we, his readers, are the beneficiaries.

The story of John Coustos, which follows, is the definitive treatment of the subject. Many details have had to be omitted from the introduction to the book, such as a list of the members of Coustos' Lodge in London (No. 75, now known as Britannic Lodge, No. 33). They will all be incorporated in a much longer essay, to be published by Quatuor Coronati Lodge, No. 2076, in the 1980 volume of its *Transactions*.

Bro. McLeod's commentary raises many interesting questions, both for discussion and for further treatment. In Section 3.2, our author tells of some of the activities of the early Lodges during their meetings, with "a high premium on intellectual activities", with "debates on mathematics, or any other art or science such as medicine, architecture, and so on". In the early and middle years of the 18th Century, only about ten per cent of the English people were truly literate. Many members of the Lodges of that time had only the basic fundamentals of an education. Thus the Lodge meetings were looked upon as places where they could definitely improve their learning.

William Preston capitalized upon this need; and because he saw Freemasonry as an educational force in men's lives, he revised and rewrote the lectures of the degrees, and published them in his *Illustrations of Freemasonry* (reissued by The Masonic Book Club in 1973 as Volume IV of our publications). We will admit that much in the lectures of the first three degrees is elementary—such knowledge as is gained by any grade school student. But it was pertinent for its time and place, and bears the great hallmark of tradition. It *is* Ancient Craft Masonry, and therefore we have little sympathy with those ritualists of our present day, who confuse progress with change, and who would delete much of the present lectures. Most of those who favor alteration or deletion can offer no suitable substitute. But our lectures have the charm of antiquity, and should be retained for their historical value, if for no other.

Do not fail to read and enjoy Brother McLeod's translation of Pope Clement XII's Bull entitled "In Eminenti". It has been translated several times before, but nowhere more accurately and more readably. This is the papal pronouncement which, for the first time, prohibited members of the Roman Catholic Church from becoming members of the Craft. How fortunate for both sides that Pope John XXIII came along to foster understanding and good will! As a result of the new spirit he brought to the church, the question of Freemasonry was re-examined, and in 1974, a fresh interpretation of the laws of the church permitted its members to join the Craft in places where lodges are not opposed to the church or organized government. We can understand why this condition was attached, because unfortunately there have been groups calling themselves Masons who did not conform to the Landmarks of the Craft by being non-sectarian and non-political. This change will prove beneficial to both the church and to Freemasonry, as there has never been any fundamental conflict between the ideals of the two institutions. By making this book available to our members, we simply recall what happened many years ago, and the material should be read in the light of the conditions which existed at that time.

The Inquisition was a logical development of the Catholic

Church's intransigent attitude toward any form of heresy. It began in 1233 in France, and was established by Ferdinand and Isabella in Spain in 1478, whence it spread into Portugal. Torquemada was the most noted of the Spanish Inquisitors, and his name became a synonym for harshness and cruelty.

As pointed out in 7.2 of Bro. McLeod's commentary, the *auto da fé* (literally "act of faith") was the public denunciation of the heretics, following which they were usually burned at the stake; hence *"auto da fé"* is often associated with martyrdom by fire. In the second act of his opera, *Don Carlo*, set in Spain circa 1560, Verdi stages such a ceremony, and the scene ends with the flame of the funeral pyre lighting up the stage. But Coustos fared better than many others, and his *auto da fé* ended with a sentence of four years in the galleys (Section 9.6 of the commentary).

The substitute for the Lost Word has intrigued Masonic students from the day it was first incorporated into the ritual structure of the Third Degree, perhaps around 1725, when the Hiramic Legend first appears. The substitute word used in Coustos' Lodge (see Section 4.11) has gone through various changes before the final version used by us today. But all indicate the same origin. See the lengthy discussion of this point in the volume, *The Scottish Mason and the Mason Word* (Knoop and Jones; Manchester University Press, 1939), and the extended list of variants of the Word on pages 10-21 of Brother Roy C. Wells' new book on *Some Royal Arch Terms Examined* (published by A. Lewis, London, 1978).

In conclusion, we are proud to publish this book. It is for present day students, and it demonstrates how Masonic research may be both productive, rewarding and vitally interesting. There are still many fields in Masonry in which research remains to be done, and we may rest in the hope that perhaps our present author will see fit to continue his work of bringing further light to his brethren.

LOUIS L. WILLIAMS
ALPHONSE CERZA

Table of Contents

PREFACE ... v

INTRODUCTION

1. THE SETTING: TIME AND PLACE ... 1
2. LIFE OF JOHN COUSTOS ... 4
    - 2.1. The Flight of the Huguenots ... 4
    - 2.2. John Coustos: From Switzerland to London ... 5
    - 2.3. Masonic Career in London ... 5
    - 2.4. Paris ... 6
    - 2.5. Portugal: Lodge and Dungeon ... 9
    - 2.6. Release from Prison; The end of the Story ... 10
3. FREE MASONRY IN PORTUGAL 1733-1743 ... 12
    - 3.1. The Protestant Lodge, No. 135, E.R., Lisbon ... 12
    - 3.2. The Catholic Lodge: "Royal Lodge of Free Masons of Lusitania" ... 13
    - 3.3. Coustos's Lodge in Lisbon ... 14
4. MASONRY IN COUSTOS'S LODGE ... 15
    - 4.1. How do we know? ... 15
    - 4.2. Admission to the Lodge ... 15
    - 4.3. The Obligation ... 16
    - 4.4. Investiture ... 17
    - 4.5. Signs, Grips, and Words ... 17
    - 4.6. The Banquet ... 18
    - 4.7. The Form of the Lodge ... 20
    - 4.8. The Pillars; The Staircase ... 21
    - 4.9. The Death of Hiram ... 22

	4.10.	The Quest and the Discovery	23
	4.11.	The Raising of the Body	23
	4.12.	Opening and Closing the Lodge	24
	4.13.	The Bible; The Master	25
5.	Where did Coustos Learn his Masonry?		26
	5.1.	Sources of Information	26
	5.2.	Basic Uniformity of Practice	26
	5.3.	Features in which there is not Uniformity	28
	5.4.	Conclusion	31
6.	The Papal Bull "In Eminenti" of 1738		32
	6.1.	Introduction	32
	6.2.	Title and Salutation	32
	6.3.	Preamble: The Pope's Responsibility to the Faithful	32
	6.4.	Free Masonry and its evil Reputation	33
	6.5.	The Reasons for Banning Free Masonry	33
	6.6.	Detailed Prohibitions	34
	6.7.	The Charge to the Inquisitors and others in Authority	35
	6.8.	Closing Formula	35
	6.9.	Reasons for the Bull	36
	6.10.	Significance of the Bull	36
7.	The Inquisition		38
	7.1.	Introduction	38
	7.2.	Procedure	39
	7.3.	Torture	40
	7.4.	Comments	41
	7.5.	The Inquisition and Free Masonry	43
8.	Coustos's Book		44
	8.1.	The French Edition	44
	8.2.	The First English Edition	46
	8.3.	Contents: Preliminaries	46
	8.4.	Contents: The Book Proper	47
	8.5.	Other Editions	48

9. Coustos's Interrogation		50
9.1. The Inquisitorial Archives	50	
9.2. The First Two Sessions with the Inquisitors	50	
9.3. Third Session	51	
9.4. Fourth Session	55	
9.5. Later Sessions	59	
9.6. The End of the Case	60	
9.7. The Torture employed against Coustos and his Brethren	61	
10. Comparison between Coustos's Book and the Inquisitorial Records		62
10.1. The Denunciations	62	
10.2. Chronology of Coustos's Sojourn in Prison	63	
10.3. Similarities in the Two Accounts	65	
10.4. Discrepancies	67	
11. Significance of John Coustos		69
12. Bibliography and Acknowledgements		72
12.1. Abbreviations	72	
12.2. Chief Works on Coustos	72	
12.3. Additional References	72	
12.4 Acknowledgements	74	

THE FACSIMILE

The Author's Dedication	iii
A List of the Subscribers' Names	xi
The Editor's Preface	xxv
The Author's Introduction	1
Part I. The History of the Sufferings of John Coustos in the Inquisition at Lisbon	6

PART II. ORIGIN OF THE INQUISITION, AND ITS
 ESTABLISHMENT IN VARIOUS COUNTRIES   78
    Dawn of the Inquisition in France, with the
        farther Contests between the
        Emperors and Popes   88
    Establishment of the Inquisition in Italy   103
    The Inquisition Established in Spain   120
    The Inquisition Established in Portugal   125
    Attempts made to introduce the Inquisition
        into Germany and the Netherlands   128

PART III. A DISTINCT ACCOUNT OF THE INQUISITION,
 AND OF THE SEVERAL THINGS APPERTAINING TO IT   143

PART IV. EXAMPLES OF THE INJUSTICE AND CRUELTY
 OF THE INQUISITION   234

PART V. PRACTICE OF THE PRIMITIVE CHURCH, IN
 BRINGING OVER HERETICKS, COMPAR'D WITH THAT
 OF THE INQUISITION   364

           COLOPHON   401

Introduction

1. THE SETTING: TIME AND PLACE

". . . But (for God's sake) shall we seek Liberty amongst a lawless Rabble, the mountainous Men of the North, Men who from the Situation of their Country have all their Days been addicted to Rapine and Plunder? Who are as ignorant of the right Use of that glorious Blessing (Liberty) as brute Beasts, and like them live only in the Abuse of it? Surely no! We are not so far degenerated. Next, let us consider whom they assist: The merciless Sons of Rome, who will be so far from restraining their Fury, that they will exceed them in Cruelty, in Tyranny, in Oppression, and in every lawless Act, to all those who differ from them in Points of Religion, or in Notions of Liberty. Yet these are to be your mighty Deliverers, O Britons!" (*The Daily Advertiser*, London, October 11, 1745).

The year was 1745. The British throne was held by George II of the House of Hanover, sixty-two years of age, stupid, graceless, and Protestant; "snuffy old drone from the German hive," as Justice Oliver Wendell Holmes called him. On the continent of Europe, Great Britain was fighting the War of the Austrian Succession. Bonnie Prince Charlie, twenty-four years old, clever, fascinating, and Catholic, had landed in Scotland on July 23, and raised the Jacobite standard of rebellion. He routed Johnnie Cope at Prestonpans (September 21), and marched south into England, reaching Derby, a scant 120 miles from London, on December 4.

The English countered with the pen as well as the sword. The newspapers declaimed a litany of hatred against the Stuarts, and their Scots Highlander and Roman Catholic supporters. As early as September 7 a proclamation was issued "commanding all Papists, and reputed Papists, to depart from the Cities of London and Westminster, and from within ten Miles of the same; and . . . confining Papists, and reputed Papists, to their Habitations;" presumably the authorities were afraid that they would betray London to the invader. Printing presses flooded the country with shrill anti-Romanist propaganda, all duly heralded in the London journals: *A Faithful Portrait of Popery: By which it is seen to be the Reverse of Christianity*, by William Warburton; *The Papists bloody Oath of Secresy*, by Robert Bolton; *The bloody Cruelties of the Papists against the Protestants*, by "D.W.;" *Popish Intrigues and Cruelty plainly exemplified in the affecting Case and Narrative of Mrs Frances Shaftoe;* and dozens of others.

Two days before Christmas, *The Daily Advertiser* of London offered another book which seems cast from the same mould.

This Day is publish'd,

(Dedicated to the Right Hon. the Earl of HARRINGTON, one of his Majesty's Principal Secretaries of State)

THE Sufferings of JOHN COUSTOS in the Inquisition at Lisbon, from which he was not long since releas'd by the Interposition of his present Majesty King George the Second; containing, The Manner of his being seiz'd on Account of his being a *Free-Mason*; his several Accusations, and the Defence made by him, before the Inquisitors; his Confinement sixteen Months in their Prison; the Hardships he sustain'd in it, and various Tortures he was made to undergo. Likewise his walking in the *Auto da Fe*; with the Severities he labour'd under in the Galley at Lisbon.

To which is annex'd (as being presum'd more immediately necessary at this Juncture) An Account of the Rise and Establishment of the Inquisition; with several Examples of its Cruelty, &c. many of which are not to be found in any other Treatise on the Inquisition.

Embellish'd with Copper-Plates, design'd by Mr. *Boitard*, and engrav'd by Mr. *Truchy*, descriptive of the Tortures which the said *Coustos* endur'd.

Sold by Mr. Meadows, in Cornhill; Mr. Noon, in the Poultry; Mr. Rivington, in St. Paul's Church-Yard; Mr. Davis, in Holborn; Mr. Hawkins, in Fleet-Street; Mr. Stagg, in Westminster-Hall; Mr. Jolliffe, in St. James's Street, Mr. Dodsley, in Pall-Mall; and Mr. Chapelle, in Grosvenor-Street; And to be had also of John Coustos himself, at his Lodgings at a Peruke-Maker's, opposite the Red Lion Inn in Brownlow-Street, Drury-Lane.

Those Subscribers who have not had their Books, are desir'd to send their Receipts to the Author's Lodgings.

The author quickly became a hero, particularly among Free Masons. His book was republished twenty times during the next century, in two continents and three languages. Then he slipped into oblivion for a hundred years. In the past generation he has again begun to claim the attention of students. We are proud to offer to members of The Masonic Book Club a fresh reprint of *The Sufferings of John Coustos*. In the sections of the Introduction which follow we shall investigate the life and importance of the author.

2. THE LIFE OF JOHN COUSTOS

2.1. THE FLIGHT OF THE HUGUENOTS

On October 18, 1685, at Fontainebleau, Louis XIV, "Most Christian" King of France, signed the Revocation of the Edict of Nantes. With a stroke of the pen he cancelled the religious rights of the French Protestants (known as the Huguenots). Their churches were to be demolished, their religious services prohibited, their ministers banished, their children henceforth baptized as Catholics. And, the final crushing blow, Protestant laymen were forbidden to emigrate.

In defiance of the ban, a quarter of a million Frenchmen streamed across the border as best they could, in disguise, by stealth, to places where they could worship freely. The loss was incalculable, for most of them were hard-working merchants and artisans. Their skills they took with them. They taught the English to produce silk and fine white paper, the Germans to manufacture leather gloves and mirrors, the Dutch to make plush. To Denmark they introduced cabbages and turnips, and to Iceland hemp and flax.

Their posterity prospered and won fame. Huguenot families who sought refuge in New England are recalled by the names of Faneuil Hall in Boston and Bowdoin College in Brunswick, Maine. To South Carolina came Auguste Jay of La Rochelle and Benjamin Marion of Poitou—grandsires of Chief Justice John Jay and General Francis "Swamp Fox" Marion. Pierre Thoreau, a ten-year-old boy, escaped to the Channel Islands; from him sprang in due course Henry David Thoreau, of *Walden* fame. We are told that Jean Théophile des Aguliers was smuggled out of France in a barrel, as an infant; eventually he went to Oxford, took holy orders, and became third Grand Master of the Grand Lodge of England.

2.2. JOHN COUSTOS: FROM SWITZERLAND TO ENGLAND

Our particular concern is with a family called Coustos that fled to Switzerland. The name appears under various spellings in records of the time: Coustaud, Cousteau, Coustods, Custô, Custon, Custos, Goustaud, and Gousteau. It is pronounced "Koos-TOH."

Jean (John) Coustos was born late in 1702 or in 1703, in northwest Switzerland, probably at Bern. His parents were French exiles: Isaac Coustos, a medical doctor from Guienne in southwestern France, and Marie Roman, of Dauphiné in southeastern France. Both grandfathers had been Huguenot preachers, no doubt among those expelled in 1685.

When John was twelve his family left Switzerland, first going to Milan in northern Italy; then to Magdeburg, Germany; then to Holland (The Hague, Leyden, and Rotterdam). Finally they settled in London, England, in 1716. John was trained as a lapidary (that is, a worker in precious stones, particularly diamonds). When he grew up, he married Alice Barbu, who had been born in London of French descent, and they had four children; two died in infancy. Two, James and John, were still alive in 1743.

2.3. MASONIC CAREER IN LONDON

John Coustos was initiated into Masonry in London in 1728 or 1729, though we do not know his mother lodge. We do know that in 1730 he belonged to the lodge which met at the Rainbow Coffee House, York Buildings, London (No. 75; warranted July 17, 1730; still working today as Britannic Lodge, No. 33). It had sixty-three members—a very large number for those days; but it was not as rich, as aristocratic, or as powerful as some of the others on the register.

Another member of No. 75 was "Mr. Henry Price." This is thought to be Major Henry Price (ca 1697-1780), who on April 30 (or possibly April 13,) 1733, was named Provincial Grand Master of New England. Is it possible that the hero of our book actually sat in lodge with the founder of duly constituted Masonry in America?

Two years later, a new lodge was formed, meeting at Prince Eugene's Coffee House in St. Alban's Street, London (No. 98, warranted August 17, 1732). Most of its thirty founding members were French; eight or nine of them, including Coustos, had come over in a block from No. 75. There can be little doubt that they worked in French. In 1739, when the meeting place was changed to the Union Coffee House, Haymarket, the lodge took the name "Union French Lodge." Its brethren are given pride of place as the first entry in the List of Subscribers to Coustos's book.

A minute book in Paris says that Coustos "had been Master of five lodges in England;" and one of the witnesses told the Portuguese Inquisitors that "not only in France, but also in the Kingdom of England, the said Coustos had been Master of a Lodge." We can't be certain, but it is possible that at some date between 1732 and 1736 he actually became Master of Lodge No. 98.

2.4. PARIS

About 1736, Coustos tells us, a friend invited him to go to Paris, and he moved there, to practice his trade in the galleries of the Palace of the Louvre. He stayed for five years.

The eighteenth century encyclopedist J.J. de Lalande says that the second Masonic lodge in Paris was founded by one "Goustaud, an English lapidary," and other French sources give the date of its institution as June 12, 1726. This certainly sounds like our man; but at that early date he was still in London, and had not even been initiated. Clearly something is amiss with our information, and it may be simply an attempt to make sense of an early fragmentary tradition.

However that may be, Coustos *did* belong to a lodge in Paris. Its minutes survive from December 18, 1736, to July 17, 1737; they were seized in a police raid soon afterwards. Coustos was Master during the earlier part of the record.

Then, after February 17, when the Duke de Villeroy joined and was chosen Master, Coustos continued to occupy the Chair regularly as his deputy. The lodge is usually referred to as the Coustos-Villeroy Lodge.

It was a cosmopolitan group. Of sixty-eight names on the roll, perhaps as few as twenty-eight were French, thirteen were German or Austrian, nine may have been Italian, seven Scandinavian, six English, three from Eastern Europe, and two from the Low Countries. They came from the wealthier classes: the peerage, the diplomats, the professional men, the artists of the establishment, financiers, businessmen. Their economic status is reflected in the minutes of June 19, 1737, when the initiation fee was raised to eight *Louis d'or*, or the equivalent of a laborer's wages for six months.

Some of the members were men of note in their own time. Ch. J. Baur was a German banker, who later served as Substitute Grand Master of France, 1744. Count Czapski, a Polish nobleman, and cousin of the Queen of France, was later Master of a lodge in Paris. Jean-Pierre Guignon was the best violinist of the age. Pierre Jéliotte was the greatest tenor. Johann Daniel Krafft, a leather merchant of Hamburg, founded the first lodge in Germany, in 1737, and eventually became Grand Treasurer of the Provincial Grand Lodge of Lower Saxony, in 1743. Thomas Pierre Le Breton, a silversmith, was Master of another lodge in Paris. Prince Lubomirski was Grand Marshal of the King of Poland, and a member of the first lodge in Warsaw, 1744. Baron Scheffer introduced Freemasonry to Sweden, and served as Grand Master of Sweden from 1753 to 1774. The list goes on and on: Baron de Bousch; Philippe Farsetti, a Venitian nobleman; Count de Gatterburg; de Plessen and Wind, Danish gentlemen; Duke de Villeroy; Baron de Wendhausen. The lodge evidently played a pivotal role in disseminating Masonry to northern and eastern Europe. Clearly Coustos moved in exalted circles.

What is more, he was held in esteem, as we see from the lodge minutes of April 30, 1737.

Since an ill-founded slur had been cast on our W. Bro. Coustos, that he had not taken the usual Masonic obligation, he took it at the hands of Bro. Baur, S.W., and all the Brethren who constituted the perfect and regular Lodge; even though he had been Master of five lodges in England, and though he is the one, so to speak, who brought Masonry here, who has kept regular lodge, and established the Order on its present footing; since it is from him that we hold those admirable Masonic secrets which he possesses to perfection; and we are happy only insofar as we follow his instructions faithfully.

At the time there was a struggle going on in French Masonry between the "Jacobite" lodges, which were aristocratic, Catholic, and refused to initiate Frenchmen, and the "English" lodges, which were slightly less exclusive, tolerant in religious matters, and accepted Frenchmen. The Coustos-Villeroy Lodge was one of the latter, and had the temerity to bring a charge of innovation in the body of Masonry against the Grand Master, the Earl of Derwentwater (later beheaded by the English for complicity in the Jacobite uprising). The minutes of March 12 talk about the controversy, and show the quality of Coustos's leadership.

It was further proposed by W.M. Coustos, Deputy of the V.W. Duke, His Grace the Duke de Villeroy, Master of our Lodge, that the Masters and Wardens of the lodges should meet with the G.M. of France, to discuss some innovations which have taken place in the G.M.'s lodge; e.g., holding swords during Initiation, and finding more votes in the ballot-box than there were brethren present. Unanimously resolved by W.M. Coustos and the Brethren: that it is not in the power of any man to make new laws in Free Masonry; since the duty of the G.M., Master and Wardens, consists in observing only the ones which have been passed down to us by tradition. This uniformity distinguishes Masons from every other sect, and causes us to be respected throughout the whole of Europe. Without it, a Mason will not be recognized as such in a foreign country. And inasmuch as we are deprived of all metals at Initiation, the Brethren added that the Order is not an Order of Knighthood, but an Order of Society into which any man of virtue can be admitted even if he doesn't wear a sword; despite the fact that several Lords and Princes have been pleased to become members.

2.5. PORTUGAL: LODGE AND DUNGEON

Early in 1741 Coustos went to Portugal, in the hope of being permitted to go to the rich colony of Brazil, where diamonds had been discovered in 1729. The Portuguese authorities however kept a tight control on the immigration of aliens, and refused to grant him the necessary authorization. He contented himself with working in Lisbon. This was no particular hardship for a man of his training and ability, and he prospered. Fairly soon he was in touch with some other Masons who had been initiated in France, and they established a Lodge with Coustos as Master. Most of the other members were French Roman Catholics, many of them engaged in one aspect or another of the jewellery trade.

Masonry, alas, had been prohibited in Portugal since 1738. On October 6, 1742, the lodge was denounced to the Inquisition by Henrique Machado de Moura, who had a personal grudge against two of the brethren. Throughout the month of February 1743, the Holy Office gathered information, and then it acted. On March 14, 1743, Coustos was arrested and imprisoned; about the same time other members of his lodge were also taken into custody. Word of their detention was noised abroad, even as far as the New World.

We have Letters from Lisbon which say, that the Inquisitors having discover'd that there were Free-Masons in that City, found Means to take up about 18 of them; that they examin'd them about the Secret of the Society; but upon their refusing to reveal it, the Inquisitors declar'd to them, that they should remain in the Prisons of the Inquisition until they give satisfactory Answers on that Head (*Boston Weekly News Letter*, June 23, 1743).

Coustos remained in prison for over fifteen months, during which he was subjected to repeated interrogation and even to torture. On June 21, a mass public condemnation took place. One man was exiled for blasphemy, another was relegated to Angola for impersonating an officer of the Inquisition; seven were condemned for bigamy, and ten for witchcraft. One of the latter, a seventy-year old widow, was burnt at the stake. So were two Jews and five "heretics." Two of Coustos's Masonic associates were exiled from Lisbon for five years; and Coustos himself was sent to the Galley for a term of four years, "for introducing and practising the sect of the Free Masons." (The Galley was not a ship, as we might expect from the name, but a sort of workhouse, down by the river side.)

In due course word of this too reached the foreign press. The *Gazetin de Paris*, under date of August 1, 1744, reports as follows.

Letters from Lisbon say that the King of Portugal has taken drastic measures against the Free Masons. Though they had been forbidden to open lodge during Lent, they had the insolence during that season to hold festival, with rebellious ceremonial. At their head was a man named Coustos, the Master, whom we saw for a considerable time in Paris; along with him, two Frenchmen who, like him, are very good jewellers but very bad subjects. They have got just what they deserve.

And in the *Boston Post Boy* for December 17, 1744, we read:

London, August 14, 1744. We learn by Letters from Lisbon, that there has been lately Auto da Fe; after which several Jews were burnt, and some French Men, who were Free Masons, and have been two Years in the Prisons of the Inquisition, appeared in the S. Benito on that Occasion.

2.6. RELEASE FROM PRISON: THE END OF THE STORY

From the time that the Masons had been seized, diplomats of several countries had been exerting pressure for their release; to no avail, so far as Coustos was concerned. But he was a British subject, and in late October of 1744, by the intervention of the British Minister in Lisbon, he was set free, on condition that he leave the country. Getting home was a problem, however, because Britain was at war with France and Spain. Eventually he was able to take passage on board the *Damietta*, a Dutch man-of-war, and he arrived in London on December 14 or 15, 1744, "after a long and dangerous Voyage."

All that is known of his activities for the next year is reflected in a series of notices in *The Daily Advertiser* of London. On March 2, 1745, it announced the impending publication of a book on The Sufferings of John Coustos, and invited advance subscriptions. On August 1, Coustos begged leave to inform the subscribers "that the Publication . . . has been retarded by the Engraver's not being able to finish the Plates at the Time propos'd. . . ." On October 9 he advertised that the book would soon be delivered to the Subscribers. But it was not until December 23 that publication was finally announced; and the title page bore the date 1746.

Later sources say that John Coustos died that same year, 1746, at the age of 43, near Gainsborough in Lincolnshire.

3. FREE MASONRY IN PORTUGAL 1733-1743

3.1. THE PROTESTANT LODGE, No. 135, E.R., LISBON

On June 24, 1717, in London, England, the premier Grand Lodge was instituted. Within a few years Free Masonry spread to the continent. In 1725 a Jacobite Lodge, St. Thomas's, No. 1, was established in Paris, by immemorial right; that is, it had no warrant. Then, probably in 1727, a lodge was founded in Madrid, Spain, meeting at an inn called "The Three Fleurs de Lys;" it received warrant No. 50 from London on March 19, 1729. This was "the First Lodge warranted or constituted in Foreign parts by the Grand Lodge of England" (Lane's *Masonic Records*).

The Craft soon reached Portugal. The minutes of Grand Lodge for April 17, 1735, record the reception of "A Petition from several Brethren now residing in and about the City of Lisbon in Portugal humbly praying that a Deputation may be granted to Mr George Gordon for constituting them into a regular Lodge." The petition was granted, and warrant No. 135 was duly issued. This is the earliest official record of the lodge, but presumably it was working earlier.

Not long afterwards the *St. James' Evening Post* reported, under the date line of June 3, 1736:

They write from Lisbon that by authority of the Right Honorable the Earl of Weymouth, the then Grand Master of all Mason's Lodges, Mr George Gordon, Mathematician, has constituted a Lodge of Free and Accepted Masons in that city; and that a great many merchants of the Factory and other people of distinction have been received and regularly made Freemasons. That Lord George Graham, Lord Forrester, and a great many gentlemen belonging to the English fleet, were present at constituting the Lodge, and it is expected that in a short time it will be one of the greatest abroad.

The members were mostly Englishmen and Protestants, but the records are lost and very few of their names are known. Nor do we know how long they continued working; the warrant was erased in 1755, no doubt after some years of inactivity.

3.2. THE CATHOLIC LODGE: "ROYAL LODGE OF FREE MASONS OF LUSITANIA"

George Gordon, the founder of Lodge No. 135, subsequently founded another lodge, probably in 1735, possibly at the time when the British fleet visited Lisbon, in June of that year. It was called "The Royal Lodge of Free Masons of Lusitania," and seems to have worked without a warrant. We know the names of twenty-four members. None was Portuguese; at least sixteen were Irishmen resident in Lisbon; and sixteen (not the same sixteen) were Roman Catholics, three of them Irish Dominican monks. There were six businessmen of one sort or another, four ship's captains, three military men, two doctors, and two dancing masters. The lodge met in the house of Bro. William Rice, who kept a restaurant.

The lodge put a high premium on intellectual activities at its meetings. One member reported that "there was conversation, with debates on mathematics, or any other art or science such as medicine, architecture, and so on, singing and playing of instruments according to their abilities." Another said, "What does take place is discussion on various matters, some relating to economic Government, others to the public, whenever convenient to do so and whenever anyone should wish to improve his knowledge of such subjects. There is also that of Architecture, about which they have discussions and researches."

The Worshipful Master in 1738 was Colonel Hugh O'Kelly. That year Masonry was banned in Portugal, and the lodge voluntarily suspended activities. Several brethren were called before the Inquisition to tell what they knew. In due course the Holy Office decided that "nothing took place offensive to the Faith or to good morals;" since the lodge had voluntarily ceased to meet, "by which the persons composing it have shown that they are fearful and obedient to the Church," no further action was taken.

3.3. Coustos's Lodge In Lisbon

Early in 1741, soon after John Coustos arrived in Lisbon, he set about forming a Masonic lodge. These were casual times, and he needed no warrant from any superior authority. He enlisted the support of two Brethren who had been initiated in Paris, and they proceeded to recruit new members from the foreign population of Lisbon. We know the names of twenty-seven members; nineteen were French, five English, two Dutch, and one Italian. There is not an aristocrat among them. As many as fourteen were associated in one way or another with the jewellery trade—goldsmiths, silversmiths, engravers, watchmakers, diamond cutters, and the like. Another nine were classified simply as businessmen or merchants. There are two tailors, one book-keeper, and one ship's captain. The lodge met in various houses, chiefly those which belonged to its members. It worked in the French language.

In March and April of 1743 the Inquisition arrested four members of the lodge: John Coustos, the W.M.; Alexandre Jacques Mouton, the J.W.; Jean Thomas Bruslé; and Jean Baptiste Richard. The first three were eventually sentenced for the crime of Free Masonry. The lodge was closed, and for a time active Free Masonry disappeared from Portugal.

4. MASONRY IN COUSTOS'S LODGE

4.1. How Do We Know?

Despite the obscurity of certain details, we are relatively well informed about the procedures followed in Masonic lodges of Coustos's time. Particularly valuable for our purposes is a detailed description provided by Coustos himself in 1743. This evidence was published in the *Transactions* of Quatuor Coronati Lodge for 1968. Some excerpts are transcribed below. A few alterations have been made in the wording; they are explained in a note at the end of the introduction. In the interests of easier comprehension, some of the capitalization and punctuation has also been changed.

NOTE: We must emphasize that the following pages are intended to discuss ceremonial matters of the 1730's and 1740's. They are not concerned with present-day Masonic practices, and they take no account of the extensive changes that have been introduced in the past two centuries and a half. New traditions have evolved and old procedures have been discarded. Students will note with interest what details have survived from the time of Coustos.

4.2. Admission to the Lodge

"When any person wishes to join the said Lodge, first of all the Grand Master [i.e., the Worshipful Master] is asked if he will accept him in the said Lodge. And being told that a reply will be sent to him, the Master thereupon sets about communicating the candidate's name to the other members of the Lodge, which to be complete, consists of seven members or Brothers. And all having committed their votes to writing, these are placed in boxes or urns which they have for this purpose, the votes then being examined to see if anyone is opposed to his admission, it being the Law and

Statutes of the said Society not to grant admission whenever there is a contrary vote. And if all the votes are in agreement, a day is selected and assigned to him for his admission, for which a definite place is named, the Master appointing one of the Brothers whom they call a Warden to conduct and guide him in this ceremony. And the person who is to be initiated having arrived at the door of the house which they call a Lodge, and in which all the other Brethren are assembled, and the door being closed, he strikes thereon three times. And upon being opened, one of the said Brothers inside enquires what it is he wants. And upon his replying that he wants to become a Freemason, the door is again shut, and notice of the request is given to all of that Lodge; which again sends to ask of the said person who is at the door what his name and surname be, and whether he comes of his own free will, and with all his heart, to join as a member and Brother of the said Society. And upon his replying, 'Yes,' they blindfold him, and take away from him everything that is of metal, such as gold, silver, brass, or any other, and conduct him within, to where the Master and the other Brethren are. And being presented to all, the Master again asks him if he comes of his own free will to join that Society; and answering affirmatively, they unbind his eyes, withdrawing the handkerchief they had tied on him."

4.3. THE OBLIGATION

"And then the Master tells the Warden who accompanies him to teach him the posture he should place himself in as a Mason, which is to join the right foot to the left by the heel, and place the right hand on the left breast, then taking three paces towards where the Master was. And this being done, he is told to uncover the right knee and place it upon an instrument like a Mason's Square, placing his right hand upon a Bible, which is opened at the Gospel of St. John, and at the same time he is bidden to lay hold of a Compass with the left hand; whereupon, the left breast being uncovered, he places thereon the point of the Compass. And being in this position, the Master, in the name of that Fraternity, and of the Grand Master of England, France, and other Kingdoms, informs him that by the Oath which he is taking he must know that he is thereby obliged to keep inviolable secrecy about everything which takes place in the said Fraternity, and not to do anything which might offend any of the said Brethren, nor against the King, Republic, or his Religion; because if he should do the contrary, his tongue will be torn out, and his heart in the same manner, to be buried by the edge of the sea, and the ashes of his burned body to be cast to the wind, so that there shall be no more memory or further remembrance of him; and that he keep this Oath so faithfully that, in the foreign kingdoms, he will more readily allow himself to be killed than to permit the secrecy to which he has bound himself to be discovered."

4.4. INVESTITURE

"And this being duly accomplished, the Master thereupon takes the newly-joining Brother by the hand; and drawing him nigh, he calls two Wardens of the said Lodge, and bids them do their Office; whereupon they place upon him the appropriate insignia pertaining to that Order to which he now belongs, while the Master tells the Initiate that the Religion [sic] which he now professes is very much more noble than the Order of the Golden Fleece, of the Holy Spirit, of Christ, and of all others in the World, for its being more Noble and more Ancient than all those.

"And thereafter the said two Wardens place an Apron of white leather upon the one newly joining, tied about the waist, and give him two pairs of gloves, one for him to wear, and the other pair for his wife if he is married; and if unmarried, then for him to give to the person for whom he has the greatest affection."

4.5. SIGNS, GRIPS, AND WORDS

"And then the said Master teaches him the signs he should observe so as to be recognised in any part of the World by the other Brethren, and to be able to warn himself against those who are not: which is the putting of the right hand in front of the throat in the manner of seeking to cut it, and then allowing the right arm to fall straight down remaining fully extended; and also gives him the following signs: to take the right hand of another person and place his thumb upon the last joint of the other finger next thereto, there thus being embraced the greater part of the hand, and saying at the same time 'Jaquem;' as also placing the right hand on the left breast, and from thence placing the hand on the last joint of the middle finger, saying at the same time the word 'Boas.'

"And after performing all this the Master tells him that he must keep all these secrets under the Oath which he took in that assembly, and that he observe great care not to talk about these matters if not in a closed Lodge; and that if he should happen to be in the street, or in any other place, talking to any Brother, and another person approaches who is not in that Society, he must immediately say that it is raining; so that his companion may be aware that a person is present in whom they must not confide. . . .

"The above signs appertain to those newly joined who are called Apprentices and Fellows, and . . . those who attain to the title of Master have other different signs which are the following: placing the thumb, the hand being open, upon the heart, and then taking the hand of the other companion and grasping the wrist thereof with his fingers, and saying at the same time the words 'Mag Binach;' and those who are Masters have the Obligation not to disclose these their signs, touchings, and words, to the Fellows and Apprentices, and can only perform them with those who are Masters; which also those who are Fellows observe with the Apprentices. . . ."

4.6. THE BANQUET

"After having carried out the aforementioned, they all, by order of the Master, go to the Table, which is found already laid out with food and drink at the expense of the newly joined Brother. And being all seated according to their rank, they proceed with the dinner until the Master knocks three times on the table with a small hammer, which is the signal established amongst them that they should all rise; which they do, and each taking hold of his glass at the same time as the Master, they raise them aloft with the same uniformity, and thence convey them to their lips to drink, observing in these actions the same formality which soldiers are in the habit of practising in the handling of their muskets. And all drinking the health of the King, and of the Fraternity, they again raise their glasses aloft, and thence convey them three times to their faces, finally sitting down again at the table, and continuing to eat until the Master asks some of those, who he knows can sing, to sing the song of the Apprentices, to another the song of the Fellow Crafts, and to another the song of the Master; all of which ceremonies take place within three hours, more or less, for it is a rule amongst them that they may not exceed the said time, nor keep the Lodge open for more than the aforesaid period of three hours. And during that time they drink various healths, some to the Grand Master of the Fraternity throughout the World, others to the Brothers present, and others to the Apprentices and Fellows.

"Eventually, the Master, for the better instruction of the Apprentices and Fellows, calls upon one of the more instructed to repeat all the ceremonies and actions which have taken place, that thus they may the better be enabled to perform and memorise them.

"And if within the said period any of the said Brethren swears by using the name of God lightly, or calls on the Devil, or utters any evil-sounding word, he is mulcted of a pecuniary fine which they have established according to the gravity of the offence committed; which fine is immediately collected and placed in a box which they have for this purpose, and is used for distributing among the poorer brethren of the said Fraternity.

"And the said Ceremony and Dinner thus being concluded they all go to their homes; and if anyone there wishes to stay a bit longer, he may no longer speak about subjects which pertain to the Fraternity. . . ."

4.7. THE FORM OF THE LODGE

"In the house or room in which the Lodge is formed, and where they admit the person to be initiated, the windows are all shut so that the daylight may not enter. And therein is found a table placed lengthwise with three large wax candles on the top thereof in the form of a triangle, viz., two at the extremes of the said table, and the other in the middle of one of the long sides; the which candles signify the Sun, the Moon, and the Master of the Lodge; for as the Sun gives light by day, and the Moon by night, so the Master should govern and direct his Fellows and Apprentices, that they may fulfil their Obligations. At the head of the table is the principal Master of all, and next along the sides are the other Brothers according to their rank up to the last place, where sit those who are called 'Wardens.' The floor of the said Lodge has a design in white chalk, wherein are formed several borders serving as ornament, together with a blazing star with a 'G' in the middle, signifying the fifth science of Geometry, to which all Fellows and Apprentices should aspire. In the same Lodge there is a Bible or Book of the Gospels placed upon a stool, upon which he who newly joins takes the Oath, and which also signifies the Obligation they have of keeping the utmost secrecy and observing the statutes of that Fraternity.

"There is also a [pair of] Compasses in this Lodge, the significance of which is applied to the Master, giving him to understand that, in the same way as the Compasses, placed with one of its points fixed, cannot fail in the correctness of the circle which the other point describes, thus also the Master should circumscribe his actions so that they be without fault, and by thus complying with his Obligation, set a good example to others. Also in the same place there is a Square, a Level, and a Plumb-line, all signifying the Obligations which the Fellows and Apprentices have of governing their actions in such a way that they may be correct in all things and conform to their respective Obligations. In the same Lodge there are delineated, in the manner described above, three pieces of window glass, in the form of three windows, one being to the East, one to the West, and the other to the South, all of which signify the hours and the Lights, with which the Fellows and Apprentices go to and from their labours. . . ."

4.8. THE PILLARS; THE STAIRCASE

"On the floor of the said Lodge there are fashioned two Columns, one with the letter J and the other with the letter B, which mean 'Joaquem' and 'Boas,' which are the signs of the Apprentices and Fellows, as stated above. And the significance of the two Columns indicates this Fraternity of Freemasons to be more ancient than Solomon's Temple, by coming down already instituted from the first Kings of Asia and the East. Albeit Solomon being one of the principal Masons or Free Masons at the time that he built his Temple, he ordered two Columns of Bronze to be made, one on the right hand side with the name of 'Jaquem,' and the other on the left thereof with the name of 'Boas,' thus distinguishing between the Fellows and Apprentices who took part in the work of building, and so being able to distinguish one from the other for the payment of wages due, using the said Signs for the better recognition of each other; all of which is portrayed . . . in the 1st or 2nd Book of Kings, Chapter 7.

"And in the manner as above described they cause these two Columns to be fashioned in the said Lodge for the use of the Fellows and Apprentices, just as Solomon practised in his works. There is also delineated a Staircase with seven steps, whereon those who rise to be Fellows proceed by one step forward for each stair until they reach the last, remaining in that position to join the right foot to the left by the heel, thus forming the shape of a Square, which they use in their ceremonies. And the significance of the Staircase of Seven is this: that Three govern a Lodge, namely the Master and two Wardens; and Five are necessary to constitute a

Lodge; and Seven is the number that makes a Lodge perfect and complete, that being the Master, two Wardens, two Fellows, and two Apprentices, to make seven. . . .

"They are in the habit of giving the above explanations to all those who newly join, in order that they may know and perceive the significance and meaning which each of the said things has; and in addition thereto they also teach that the complete and perfect Lodge should have three Columns to support it; called in the French language: *Sagesse, Force, Beauté*, but in our language: Wisdom, Strength, and Beauty in Adornment. . . ."

4.9. THE DEATH OF HIRAM

"The first institution and origin from which were derived the significance of the Apron, Gloves, and other ceremonies used by the Fellows and Apprentices, as also the signs of the Masters, come from the time when Solomon built his sumptuous Temple; whereby for the better administration of the work, and distinguishing between Fellows and Apprentices labouring therein, he, Solomon, made the separation of Signs above described, which were initiated by a Master named Hiram, who was next in government to Solomon, and to whom alone was revealed the Sign which pertained to him as Master, in order thus to be differentiated from the other and inferior Fellows who worked in the same undertaking. And some of the Fellows or Apprentices perceiving this, and desiring to learn the secret Sign which he had, three of the said Fellows arranged amongst themselves that, upon the first occasion on which he next came to the Temple to give the customary orders, they would compel him to reveal the said Sign, guarding for this purpose the three doors of the said Temple, which faced the East, the West, and the South. And when the said Master was come, he was first asked by the Fellow Craft at one of the doors for the said Sign: to which he replied that he could not divulge it since he was forbidden to do so; and that they, having already been a long time in the service, would in due course attain and discover that position they desired; whereupon the Fellow Craft struck him upon the head with a wooden cudgel. And the Master seeking to escape by the remaining doors, the others likewise gave him other blows, one with a wooden crowbar, and the other with a hammer, also of wood; so that with the last blow he fell dead. And in order that the said Fellows might conceal what has just been described, they buried him in a distant spot where he might not be discovered."

4.10. THE QUEST AND THE DISCOVERY

"After three days King Solomon, having noticed his absence, enquired for him. And seeing that he did not appear, he appointed fifteen of the said Fellow Crafts to use all possible diligence in discovering what had happened to the said Master.

"And fifteen days having gone by in this search, one of the said Fellows came to that spot, and being much fatigued with the journey he sat down on the grass there. And there inadvertently clutching hold of a small bush in that place, he noted on reflection that he had pulled it very easily out of the ground, the earth appearing to have been disturbed in such a way that it was clear it had been well dug over in that spot a few days before. And becoming more curious to know what was there, he discovered the body of the Master, which had been buried there.

"On giving an account of all this to the King, Solomon caused a command to be given to the Fellows and Apprentices that they divest themselves of everything which was of silver, or any other metal; and that, wearing their Aprons tied to their waists, as their custom now is, and gloves on their hands, they should go to the said place and disinter the body; and that the first thing they should do was to take hold of the hand thereof, by making the very Signs which are still used by the Fellows and Apprentices today."

4.11. THE RAISING OF THE BODY

"And setting forth on their errand they arranged between themselves that if on the body of the Master, or in his pockets, they did not find the means of ascertaining what the Signs were which pertained to him in his capacity as Master, they would follow the course of using the first Word and Sign which they used to each other after they had used those normally employed as Fellows and Apprentices. And all being arranged in this manner, they came to the place where the body lay; and making first the Sign of the Apprentices, which is to lay hold of the joint of the finger next the thumb, it became severed due to its rottenness. And making the second Sign, which is to lay hold of the joint of the middle finger, seeking thus to raise up the body, it also became detached in the same manner; whereby they saw clearly that it was necessary to lay hold of the wrist. And thus raising him upright, the first word which he who raised him uttered was in fact 'Mag Binach,' which means in our language that 'it did stink;' and so it came to pass that from that time onwards the Sign of the Master was this last action of laying hold of the wrist, and the said words; and for this reason they still today observe the same insignia, ceremonies and signs as have already been stated above.

"And they took the body of the Master to the King, who ordered it to be buried, being accompanied by the Fellows and Apprentices with the same insignia as stated earlier; and upon his sepulchre there was ordered to be engraved the following: 'Here lies Hiram, Grand Master Architect of the Free Masons.' . . ."

4.12. OPENING AND CLOSING THE LODGE

"When any Apprentice newly joins, the Master explains to him the meaning of the Closing and Opening of the Lodge, to which end he asks what motive or cause brings him to that place. And the Apprentice saying that he comes to learn the Art of Masonry, the Master thereupon explains that, just as the Sun appears in the East to give light to the day, thus the Master should open his own Lodge with promptness and care to direct his Fellows in their work. And for this reason when they hold their meetings they give the first place at the table, which they call the East, to the one they recognise as Master. And thus as the Sun sets in the West, so ending the light and terminating the day, so the Wardens of the Assembly are found in the lower places at the table, which corresponds to the West, for the closing of the Lodge after the determined period of three hours, each of the Brothers being then free to go and attend to his own affairs."

4.13. THE BIBLE; THE MASTER

"The reason and foundation that the Masters of this Fraternity have for causing those who newly join to take the Oath upon a Bible, or Book of the Gospels, at the place of that of St John, is the following. . . . When the destruction of the famous Temple of Solomon took place, there was found below the First Stone a tablet of bronze, upon which was engraved the following word, JEHOVAH, which means GOD; giving thereby to understand that that fabric and Temple was instituted and erected in the name of the same God to whom it was dedicated, that same Lord being the beginning and end of such a magnificent work. And as in the Gospel of St John there are found the same words and doctrine, they for this reason cause the Oath to be taken at that place, thus to show that the whole institution of this Fraternity is founded on the same doctrine which Solomon observed in his sumptuous work. . . .

"The Master of any Fraternity is honoured amongst the Brothers thereof with the title of Venerable and Worthy."

5. WHERE DID COUSTOS LEARN HIS MASONRY?

5.1. Sources of Information

John Coustos had been initiated in London, had ruled a lodge in Paris, and was now working in Lisbon, a city with a Masonic tradition. We know some details about Craft observances of the time in each of the three cities. For British practice, we have a whole sequence of catechisms and exposures, which record the evolution of the ritual down to Coustos's day (*The Early Masonic Catechisms*, by Douglas Knoop, G.P. Jones, and Douglas Hamer; second edition, by Harry Carr, 1973). The latest and finest was Samuel Prichard's pamphlet, *Masonry Dissected* (1730), which has been reprinted as Volume Eight in the present series, together with a masterful introduction by Harry Carr. Several other documents reflect French working at the very time when Coustos was in Paris, and in the years immediately following. The most useful are *Réception d'un Frey-Maçon* (1737), *Le Secret des Francs-Maçons* (1742), and *Catéchisme des Francs-Maçons* (1744). They have been translated and published by Harry Carr in *The Early French Exposures* (1971). For Lisbon, besides Coustos's lodge, we have information on the earlier lodge which had been active in 1738, in the form of testimony sworn by various witnesses before the Inquisitors.

Note: We must emphasize once again that in these pages we are concerned *not* with present-day Masonic ritual, but with details reported from the eighteenth century.

5.2. Basic Uniformity of Practice

Evidently many of the procedures in lodge were uniform throughout Europe. We need hardly set forth the evidence in full. Suffice it to notice a few features which were universally observed, and to point out certain others which had local variations.

No matter whether in Portugal, England, or France, the system of three degrees was in general use. The candidate for Initiation was deprived of all metal, blindfolded, and his knee was made bare. He sought admission by three knocks at the door. Inside the lodge room, the table was set with three candles, which represented the sun, the moon, and the Master of the lodge. For his obligation, the candidate was made to kneel, with one hand resting on the Bible, and with the other extending the compasses to his naked left breast. Then he swore to keep secrecy, under a multiple penalty.

> *London. Masonry Dissected,* 1730: "All this under no less Penalty than to have my Throat cut, my Tongue taken from the Roof of my Mouth, my Heart pluck'd from under my Left Breast, them to be buried in the Sands of the Sea, the Length of a Cable-Rope from Shore, . . . my Body to be burnt to Ashes, my Ashes to be scatter'd upon the Face of the Earth. . . ."
>
> *Paris. Réception d'un Frey-Maçon,* 1737: "I consent that my tongue may be torn out, my heart lacerated, my body burnt & reduced to ashes, to be thrown to the winds. . . ." *Le Secret des Francs-Maçons,* 1742: "I consent that my Tongue shall be torn out, my heart ripped out, my body burnt and reduced to ashes to be thrown to the winds. . . ."
>
> *Lisbon, 1738. Testimony of Denis Hogan:* ". . . In the oath of secrecy which they took, they subjected themselves to the penalty of having the tongue and the heart torn out, the body quartered and thrown to the four corners of the earth, should they disclose the secret. . . . *Testimony of Charles Carroll:* ". . . Those belonging to the said society . . . would be burned, and would have their tongue torn out, and the ashes of their bodies would be thrown into the sea, if they failed to keep the secrets of the same society. . . ."
>
> *Lisbon, 1743. Testimony of John Coustos:* ". . . If he should do the contrary, his tongue will be torn out, and his heart in the same manner, to be buried by the edge of the sea, and the ashes of his burned body to be cast to the wind. . . ." *Testimony of Jean Thomas Bruslé:* ". . . All this he was obliged to observe by the obligation he had taken, under the penalties of having his tongue torn out, his throat

cut across, his heart torn out, his body cut in pieces and thrown into the sea, the length of the longest ship's cable from the shore. . . ."

In all three countries the lodge room was equipped with the representation of a staircase, of seven steps, and perhaps also with a blazing star, bearing in its centre the letter G. If a brother wanted to give warning that a non-Mason was present, he would say the words, "It rains."

Probably the various lodges were equally uniform in other portions of the ceremonies; but the English catechisms do not describe actions in sufficient detail to enable us to compare them with the French and Portuguese narrative sources.

5.3. Features In Which There Is Not Uniformity

Circumambulation: When the candidate was admitted, Prichard's text suggests that he was led once around the lodge before being presented to the Master. In Paris, on the other hand, he was "made to take three turns in the Chamber." In Lisbon, as one of Coustos's members told the Inquisitors, the guide "made him go three times around the room close to the walls, guiding him for this purpose because his eyes were covered."

Posture during Obligation. In *Masonry Dissected*, and other English sources, the candidate is said to kneel on one knee. In Paris, the posture was more awkward: ". . . The Candidate, though kneeling on his right knee, must have his left foot in the air." The same position was also used in Coustos's lodge, according to the testimony of one of his brethren: ". . . he (the confessor) with his hand on the book in front of which he was kneeling on his right knee with his left in the air, promised so to keep it. . . ."

Where the candidate kneels. In England the candidate is frequently described as kneeling on the ground between the arms of a square. In France, he regularly kneels on a stool. Coustos says that he kneels "upon an instrument like a Mason's square." Two other members of Coustos's lodge, Bruslé and Richard, reported that they had been made to kneel on a piece of white leather which was placed on the floor, and which was later given to them as an apron.

The Apron Charge. Prichard speaks of "that Badge of Honour, which (as they term it) is more ancient and more honourable than is the Star and Garter. . . ." The only French exposure to use such a phrase is *La Réception mystérieuse,* 1738, which is based explicitly on Prichard. In connection with the Investiture, Coustos uses the words, "more noble than the order of the Golden Fleece, of the Holy Spirit, of Christ, and of all others in the World." This sounds as if it might be a local adaptation of the same charge.

Gloves. From 1599 on, it had been a regular custom in British Masonry that each initiate, as part of his admission fee, should furnish a pair of gloves to every member of the lodge. The custom was observed in the Lisbon Lodge in 1738. In the Paris Lodges, on the other hand, the initiate was the *recipient* rather than the *donor* of gloves, and a gesture of gallantry was included. ". . . He is given . . . a pair of men's Gloves for himself, and another [pair of] ladies' Gloves, for her whom he esteems the most." This was the practice in Coustos's lodge in Lisbon.

The Words of the First two Degrees. In Prichard's *Masonry Dissected,* the E.A. had two pillar words, while the F.C. used one of them. At some date about 1739, we are told, Grand Lodge arbitrarily decreed that the word for the First Degree should be the one formerly used for the F.C., and that the other word should be used for the Second Degree. This change is reflected regularly in France, from 1742 on, and in Lisbon, in both the Irish lodge of 1738, and in Coustos's lodge of 1743.

The Legend of the Third Degree. The Principal Architect of the Temple is called "Hiram" by Prichard and the earlier French exposures based on him. From 1744 on, the French texts regularly name him "Adoniram." Coustos uses the earlier form.

When the architect disappeared, he was missed the same day, according to Prichard. From 1738 on, the French ex-

29

posures say that his absence was noted on the seventh day. Coustos says, "after three days."

In Prichard's book, and in the French text derived from it, fifteen loving brethren were sent to search for the architect, but from 1744 on, the French exposures describe the seekers as nine Masters. Coustos says "fifteen Fellow Crafts." According to Prichard, the brethren agreed that they should adopt a substitute Master's Word only if they did not find the former word on the Architect's person. In the French sources, beginning in 1744, they agreed to take a new word as a precaution in case the Architect had been forced to reveal the former one. Coustos is closer to Prichard's version.

The Master's Word. The range of variant forms is large, but it appears that they all go back to two different words which were used in the first half of the eighteenth century. One of them occurs in the earlier English catechisms, and was also used in the Irish Lodge in Lisbon. The other word appears first in Prichard's *Masonry Dissected*, is regularly found in the French sources, and was used in Coustos's lodge in Lisbon.

Masonic Fire. In connection with the banquet Coustos describes the military precision with which the brethren drank toasts, raising their glasses aloft, and conveying them three times to their faces. The early English sources have nothing comparable, but it sounds like the French procedures from 1737 on: "they drink to the health of the Brother, carrying the glass to the mouth in three movements." "There is no Military Academy where the drill is performed with greater exactitude."

Jehovah. Coustos tells us that beneath the corner-stone of Solomon's Temple was a bronze plate inscribed with the word "Jehovah." The word had occurred in two of the earlier English catechisms (1725), but with no indication of its proper place in the ritual. In the *Catéchisme des Francs-Maçons* of 1744 we are told that this was the former word of a Master; and in *Le Sceau Rompu* of 1745 that it was inscribed on a golden triangle set over the tomb of the Builder of the Temple. *La Désolation des Entrepreneurs modernes du Temple de Jérusalem*, 1747, tells a story which sounds a bit like the one mentioned by Coustos. The temple at Jerusalem was being rebuilt in the time of the Emperor Julian. "While working on the foundations, a stone from the first row became dislodged & uncovered the opening to a cavern hewn in the rock. A Workman was lowered, attached to a cord. . . . He explored with his hands in all directions, & upon a column . . . he found a Book wrapped in a very fine linen. . . ." On being drawn up, the book was found to be the Gospel according to St John.

5.4. CONCLUSION

In general, the Masonic ritual of Coustos's lodge in Portugal was perfectly orthodox, and coincides with that known from England and France. The few details which are explicitly traceable to one or the other suggest that Lisbon practice was eclectic. In a few features it followed the English tradition (kneeling on the Square, the Apron Charge, details of the Hiramic legend, the Master's Sign); in more details it followed the French (triple circumambulation, the posture during the obligation, the Words, the presentation of gloves, Masonic Fire); occasionally it struck off on its own (the day when the absence of the Architect was noted). It is puzzling to note that occasionally Coustos's testimony differs from that given by other members of his lodge (for example, where the candidate kneels). In the few instances where we have grounds to judge, it looks as if there was no continuity between the earlier lodge in Lisbon and Coustos's Lodge (the presentation of gloves, the Master's Word).

6. THE PAPAL BULL "IN EMINENTI" OF 1738

6.1. INTRODUCTION

An apostolic decree issued by the Pope over his own seal is called a Papal Bull (from the Late Latin *bulla*, "a lead seal"). In 1738 Pope Clement XII published a Bull entitled *In eminenti apostolatus specula*, or just *In eminenti*; its subject was Free Masonry.

The most familiar English translation, by W. J. Chetwode Crawley, professes to be one "in which elegance has been rigidly subordinated to fidelity, and from which may be gathered some idea of the bewildering intricacy of the ecclesiastical verbiage." The intention is laudable, but misguided. Latin prefers long complex sentences, which seem stiff and obscure when put literally into English. We venture therefore to offer another version, which accurately reflects the original without going beyond the limits of acceptable English.

6.2. TITLE AND SALUTATION

"Condemnation of the Society, or Lodges, commonly known as *Liberi Muratori* or *Francs Maçons*, under the Penalty of Automatic Excommunication; with Absolution Reserved for the Supreme Pontiff, except at the Point of Death.

Clement, Bishop, Servant of the Servants of God, to all the Faithful in Christ, Greeting and Apostolic Benediction."

6.3. PREAMBLE: THE POPE'S RESPONSIBILITY TO THE FAITHFUL

"God in His mercy has set us in the lofty watch-tower of Apostleship, though our merits are not equal to it. We must therefore take precautions for the flock entrusted to our keeping. With unceasing devotion and concern (so far as has been vouchsafed to us from On High) we have been directing our thought to those measures by which we may shut the door on sin and wickedness. Thereby we may preserve in its fullest splendor the integrity of the Orthodox Religion, and protect the whole Catholic world from risk of disturbance in these trying times."

6.4. Free Masonry and its Evil Reputation

"It has come to our attention, particularly through the reports of public rumor, that certain Societies, Meetings, Assemblages, Gatherings, Groups, or Lodges, commonly known by the name of *Liberi Muratori* or *Francs Maçons*, or some other title in accordance with the variations of language, have been gaining ground far and wide, and growing stronger day by day. In these Lodges men who subscribe to any religion or sect at all, and are satisfied with a kind of semblance of uncultivated goodness, are united together in a firm and inviolable covenant, by virtue of the laws and regulations which they have passed. They are bound by a strict oath taken on the Holy Bible, and by the imposition of severe penalties, to veil in impenetrable silence whatever goes on at their meetings.

Such is the nature of sin that it betrays itself, and shouts its character aloud. These Societies or Lodges have sown such strong suspicions in the minds of the Faithful, that membership in them is regarded by wise and good men as the mark of vice and corruption. If the Lodges were not doing wrong, they would not be averse to the light. So far has their reputation spread, that in several regions the Secular Powers have proscribed them, and long since carefully eradicated them, for working against the security of the state."

6.5. The Reasons for Banning Free Masonry

"We have been pondering the serious mischief which such Societies or Lodges do even to the spiritual well-being of souls, not to mention the serenity of the Temporal State; they are consistent with neither civil nor canon law. The

Word of God teaches us that, like a good and faithful servant set to oversee his Master's household, we must keep watch day and night, in order that such men may not like thieves break through and steal, or like foxes try to spoil the vines; that is to say, so that they may not corrupt the hearts of the simple, and shoot their secret arrows at the innocent. They have the potentiality for opening up a broad highway to unpunished sin. So, in order to preclude this, and for other just and reasonable causes known to us: by the advice of several of our Reverend Brother Cardinals of the Holy Church at Rome, and by our own motivation, from our sure knowledge and mature deliberation, in the fulness of our Apostolic Power, we have decided and decreed: that these same Societies, Meetings, Assemblages, Gatherings, Groups, or Lodges, known by the name of *Liberi Muratori* or *Francs Maçons* or by any other name, are to be condemned and prohibited; just as we, by this present proclamation which is to be valid for all time, do condemn and prohibit them."

6.6. Detailed Prohibitions

"Accordingly, by virtue of the Holy Obedience, we strictly enjoin the Faithful in Christ, all and singular, no matter what their station, degree, condition, order, dignity, and eminence, be they laymen or priests, secular or regular, even those who deserve specific and individual mention and expression: that no one, under any pretext or excuse whatsoever, venture or presume to enter into the aforesaid Societies known by the name of *Liberi Muratori* or *Francs Maçons* or by any other name. You shall not promote them, encourage them, or receive or conceal them in your houses, homes, or anywhere else; you shall not be enrolled in them, join them, or attend them; you shall not give them opportunity or occasion to meet anywhere; you shall not furnish them with anything, or otherwise offer them advice, help, or favor, openly or secretly, directly or indirectly, in your own person or through others, in any way whatsoever. You shall not urge, instruct, invite, or persuade others to be enrolled in such Societies, or join, attend, help, or foster them in any way at all. On the contrary you must hold absolutely aloof from these same Societies, Meetings, Assemblages, Gatherings, Groups, or Lodges: under penalty of Excommunication, to be incurred automatically without proclamation, by the mere fact of acting contrary to the aforesaid injunctions; from which Excommunication none can receive the benefit of Absolution from any but us, or the Pontiff at Rome for the time being, except he be at the point of death."

6.7. THE CHARGE TO THE INQUISITORS AND OTHERS IN AUTHORITY

"It is our further wish, and order, that Bishops, Superior Prelates, and other local Ordinaries, as well as those locally named in all places as Commissioners of Inquiry into the Wickedness of Heretics, shall take action against transgressors, no matter what their station, degree, condition, order, dignity, or eminence; investigate them, punish them with appropriate penalties, on strong suspicion of heresy, and suppress them. To all of you, and each of you, we delegate and grant the free power to take action against the aforesaid transgressors, investigate them, suppress them with appropriate penalties, and punish them, invoking if need be even the assistance of the Secular Arm."

6.8. CLOSING FORMULA

"It is our wish also that copies of the present proclamation shall have the same force as would the original if it were exhibited or displayed; provided that they have been certified by the signature of a notary public, and sealed by some person of authority in the Church.

Therefore let no person infringe or rashly contravene the present document, which embodies our declaration, condemnation, charge, prohibition, and interdiction. If anyone be so presumptuous as to try, let him know that he will incur the wrath of God Almighty and the blessed apostles Peter and Paul.

Given at Rome, at the Church of Santa Maria Maggiore,

in the year of the Incarnation of our Lord 1738, the 28th day of April, in the eighth year of our Pontificate."

6.9. REASONS FOR THE BULL

The Pope singled out two features of Free Masonry which were offensive: its religious tolerance, and its oath of secrecy. Either might interfere with the Church's discipline. Masonry was an English institution, and therefore might reasonably be assumed to be Protestant; moreover, it expressly avowed indifference to the religious beliefs of individual members. It therefore provided an opportunity for Catholics to mingle freely with heretics. Again, any society which refuses to declare publicly what it is doing leaves itself open to suspicion of immoral or even illegal activities. Who outside the Craft could say what vile orgies, pagan rites, or subversive plots were being hatched within the tyled recesses of the lodge? The secrecy might well obstruct the freedom of the confessional.

But beyond the two explicit reasons, we are told, the ban was imposed "for other just and reasonable causes known to us." Is this expression just a tic of the Vatican chancery style? Or did the Pope's advisors in fact have other reasons which they chose not to make public? We simply do not know. We can only say that the situation that triggered the ban was specifically Italian, and was associated with the lodge in Florence, which had been working as early as August 4, 1732. The whole subject wants further discussion, but would take us too far from John Coustos.

6.10. SIGNIFICANCE OF THE BULL

The Bull *In Eminenti* was the opening salvo in a prolonged Papal assault on Masonry, an assault which continued right down into this century. The Vatican's condemnation was reiterated again and again. Catholic leaders came to suspect Masons practically from force of habit. In accordance with the *Code of Canon Law* of 1917, No. 2335, automatic excommunication continued to be the lot of any member of the Church who joined Freemasonry. This policy, in Harry

Carr's words, "kept thousands of Roman Catholics from the Craft and, in many countries, imbued them with a wholly unfounded mistrust and even hatred of the Order."

The Second Vatican Council (1962-1965) ushered in a new era of Ecumenism for Catholics, and the Church began to re-examine its traditional position with regard to Free Masonry. Finally, in 1974, the Vatican sent the following letter to every Catholic bishop in the world.

The Sacred Congregation for the Doctrine of the Faith . . . has ruled that Canon 2335 no longer automatically bars a Catholic from membership of masonic groups. . . . And so a Catholic who joins the Freemasons is excommunicated only if the policy and actions of the Freemasons in his area are known to be hostile to the Church. . . .

For Masons in English-speaking countries, this letter writes "Finis" to two hundred and thirty-six years of hostility.

7. THE INQUISITION

7.1. INTRODUCTION

Pope Clement gave orders for his decree to be enforced by, among others, "those locally named in all places as Commissioners of Inquiry into the Wickedness of Heretics" (*haereticae pravitatis ubique locorum deputati Inquisitores*). These are the infamous Inquisitors, the officers of the Inquisition, the Church's court of enquiry.

They have passed into folklore, and many of our ideas about them come not from history but from imaginative literature. Edgar Allan Poe's horror story "The Pit and the Pendulum" (published in 1843) portrays for us the black-robed judges in the Spanish city of Toledo, condemning a victim to death by torture. Longfellow's poem "Torquemada" (1863) tells of a Spaniard who denounced his own daughters to the Holy Office, and kindled the very fire to burn them at the stake. In Ponchielli's opera *La Gioconda* (first produced in 1876) the villains are the chief of the State Inquisition for Venice, and one of his spies; the stage-setting includes a drop-box in the form of a lion's mouth, "For secret denunciations to The Inquisition against any person." Gilbert and Sullivan's operetta *The Gondoliers, or The King of Barataria* (1889) introduces Don Alhambra del Bolero, the Grand Inquisitor of Spain, who observes blithely, of a reluctant witness, "the persuasive influence of the torture chamber will jog her memory." None of these sources gives any clear idea of why the institution existed or how it operated. Coustos's book provides many of the facts, and spares us the necessity of going over the same ground in detail.

The Inquisition was instituted in Southern France at some date close to 1200, in order to locate, punish, and suppress heresy, that is, any deviation from religious orthodoxy. It later spread to Italy, Spain, Portugal, the Netherlands, and the Spanish and Portuguese colonies beyond the seas. The Spanish Inquisition was reorganized in 1478, under Ferdinand and Isabella, and soon became notorious for its severity. It was not abolished until 1834, although its authority had been curtailed some years earlier. The Portuguese Inquisition followed roughly the same course.

7.2. PROCEDURE

In Portugal in Coustos's day the Inquisition was empowered to proceed against suspects for any one of six charges: heresy, suspicion of heresy, favouring heretics, magic, blasphemy, and opposing the Inquisition. If the Inquisitor suspected anyone of these crimes, or if an individual was denounced, the Holy Office would set about collecting evidence. All sorts of witnesses could be examined: felons, members of the suspect's family, and other persons whose testimony would not be accepted today. They were permitted, or even encouraged, to repeat statements on hearsay. Then, when the evidence was complete, the suspect was arrested.

He had to take an oath to tell the full truth, and thereby to testify (if need be) against himself. The identity of his accusers was kept secret, and he could not confront them face to face, or challenge them, or examine them. The prisoner was presumed to be guilty, for otherwise he would not have been on trial. The Inquisitor served at once as prosecutor and judge.

After the hearings were complete, the judicial decision was pronounced at a public religious ceremony known as an *auto da fé* ("act of faith"). Normally capital sentences were carried out immediately.

Conviction could be won on the testimony of witnesses, but it was easier and neater if the prisoner confessed. The Inquisitor therefore spared no pains to obtain a confession, and to this end he exerted all the persuasive power at his disposal, both psychological and physical: threats, promises, cajoling, maltreatment, deprivation, and even torture.

It need hardly be said that the system was very effective, both in extorting confessions and in winning convictions.

7.3. TORTURE

The Inquisitors did not act according to the whim of the moment, but were guided by rules of procedure. Here is an excerpt from the Portuguese Inquisitorial Code of 1640.

> Ordinarily the torture shall be that of the pulley; and when the doctor and surgeon judge that, by reason of weakness or indisposition, men are not able to stand [the torture] of the pulley, it will be given to them on the rack, to which he [the prisoner] shall then be taken. But it will never be given to women on the rack, because of the extent to which that must violate their honor; and in the case in which they cannot endure any torture of the pulley, and there is no occasion to dispense with it [torture], the Inquisitors shall report to the Council, so that it may be determined there what course justice shall take. Since it is necessary to give the *trato esperto* [on the pulley] fifteen days before the *auto da fé*, so that prisoners will not go to it showing signs of torture, [in the last two weeks] it will be given to them on the rack; and in the session that takes place in the torture chamber the Inquisitors will always cause to be declared the reason that there was for putting them on the rack and not on the pulley. And at all sessions the hour will be announced at which the torture begins, and ends.

It seems that only two forms of torture were permitted. In "the pulley" (usually called "the strappado" in English), a rope was passed over a pulley set in the ceiling, one end being fastened to the prisoner's arms, which were bound behind him. He was hoisted from the floor and then lowered to just above it, either fairly gently (*trato corrido*), or with a sudden jerk (*trato esperto*). In the latter event, dislocation of the shoulders was likely. "The rack" is usually thought of as an instrument to stretch and unhinge the limbs; on the Portuguese rack however it seems that the arms and legs were each bound in two places, and then the thongs were progressively tightened.

There were gradations of severity, and every step was clearly specified in the regulations. We have, for instance, a tabular summary which informs us what degree of the torture on the rack corresponds to each successive stage on the pulley.

Pulley	Rack
1. *Ad faciem* ["before the eyes"].	1. Placing on the rack.
2. Begin binding.	2. Binding in eight places without tightening.
3. First strap.	3. Putting staves in four places without going to the wheel.
4. Second strap.	4. Putting staves in eight places.
5. Perfectly bound.	5. Begin to tighten in four places.
6. Begin to lift [another source tells us that this means "as far as the first floor"].	6. Begin to tighten in eight places.
7. Lift as far as the Place of the Book ["as far as the second floor"].	7. One quarter turn in four places.
8. Lift as far as the pulley ["as far as the top, and start gently lowering by hand"].	8. One quarter turn in eight places.
9. One *trato corrido*.	9. Half turn in eight places.
10. One *trato esperto*.	10. Full turn in eight places.

The table continues, up as far as "three *tratos espertos*" on the pulley, and "three complete turns in all eight places" for the rack.

7.4. COMMENTS

Beyond any question the Inquisition was responsible for much wanton cruelty. There is no way to mitigate its excesses. At the same time we must recall that human life and human rights were valued much more lightly two or three hundred years ago than they are today. Measured against the standards of that day, the Inquisition appears less randomly savage. There are two main points to bear in mind.

(1) Religious tolerance is a relatively recent aberration.

The first amendment to the Constitution of the United States (1791) guaranteed freedom of religion. But the standard doctrine of an earlier age was *cujus regio ejus religio*, which means, the religion of the ruler dictates that of his subjects. Little room was given to nonconformists; there was an essential unity of Church and State. This was true not only in Catholic countries; in England, Catholics laboured under many disabilities, and could not hold public office, or even vote, until 1829.

(2) The penal code was much more severe. In the 1760's the noted jurist Sir William Blackstone listed 160 offences which were capital in England. Some of these would seem trivial to us. From 1603 to 1661 and again from 1693 to 1775, the very bearing of the name MacGregor was proscribed. Until 1833, a theft of any amount more than two pounds Sterling could be punished by death. In 1772 a boy named Peter M'Cloud was hanged in London for an attempt at housebreaking which failed, so that he was caught. In 1777 Dr William Dodd, Past Grand Chaplain of the Grand Lodge of England, was hanged for forgery. In 1789 a woman named Christian Murphy was burnt at the stake in London for counterfeiting.

The Eighth Amendment to the Constitution of the United States (1791) prohibits "cruel and unusual punishment." But in earlier times judicial torture was common enough. During the Salem witch trials in 1692, Giles Cory was pressed to death by placing heavy weights upon his chest. In France in 1757 Robert François Damiens, who had tried unsuccessfully to kill the King, had his hand burnt, his body pinched with red hot pinchers; boiling oil, melting wax and rosin, and melted lead were poured into all his wounds, and then he was torn asunder by four horses. In London in 1750, for forgery, Timothy Penredd was condemned to be put in the pillory on two successive market days; on each occasion one of his ears was to be nailed to the pillory. When we take such practices into account, a turn or two on the rack seems mild enough in comparison!

7.5. The Inquisition and Free Masonry

Masonry had been condemned on suspicion of heresy, and the Inquisition had been founded to combat heresy. Wherever the two institutions co-existed, a confrontation was practically inevitable. In 1739, Dr. Tommaso Crudeli, the Secretary of the lodge in Florence, Italy, was arrested and interrogated at length. In 1744, a Spanish priest, Don Francisco Aurion de Roscobet, was brought before the Holy Office of Toledo, and convicted of Masonry. In 1754, a French doctor, Bro. Nicolas Bresson, was tried in Venice. Another Frenchman named Pierre Tournon is said to have been examined in Madrid in 1757. In 1770, Ayres de Ornellas Frazão, head of the Freemasons on the island of Madeira, was imprisoned. The notorious Count Cagliostro was arrested in Rome in 1789, and died in prison in 1795. In 1811 a book was published in London, under the title *A Narrative of the Persecution of Hippolyto Joseph da Costa Pereira Furtado de Mendonça . . . imprisoned and tried in Lisbon, by the Inquisition, for the pretended crime of Free-masonry*.

This puts the sufferings of John Coustos in perspective. He was not the only victim; but he is one of the few to have written about his treatment.

8. COUSTOS'S BOOK

8.1. THE FRENCH EDITION

Soon after he got back to London Coustos put together an account of his sufferings. He probably wrote it in French, his first language. In fact it seems almost certain that a book published not too long afterwards was his original version. It had a title page which is translated herewith.

At this period all books printed in France had to be licensed by the Government. Those published without official sanction generally had a fictitious imprint, and so we don't know just when or where this book appeared. It was advertised for sale in London, England, on January 31, 1746. Presumably it was published very early in 1746, or even in 1745.

The Foreword of the French edition is addressed "To the Very Worshipful, Worshipful, and Honorable Brethren, dispersed over the face of the earth." It closes with the words, "That Heaven may preserve every true Mason from this tyrannical tribunal is the sincere wish, Very Worshipful, Worshipful, and Honorable Brethren, of your very affectionate Brother, L.T.V.I.L.R.D.M." We don't know the identity of this Masonic editor.

The book is, as the title page says, divided into three parts.

(1) "A true and exact account of the prison and trial of W. Bro. Coustos."

(2) "The origin of the Inquisition." ("Taken from a book which gives its truthful and sincere history—a book which, thanks to the care taken by the Inquisition and its familiars to buy up and burn all copies, is no longer available").

(3) "Authentic verified facts which serve as proofs for the two earlier parts."

It sold in London for two shillings and sixpence.

EXTRAORDINARY PROCEDURES OF THE INQUISITION IN PORTUGAL AGAINST THE FREE-MASONS

To discover their SECRET; with the Examinations
and the Answers, the Cruelties practised
by this Court; the Description of the Inside
of the Holy Office, its Origin,
and its Excesses.

DIVIDED INTO THREE PARTS,

By a brother Mason who has come out of the Inquisition.

Reviewed and published by L.T.V.I.
L.R.D.M.

IN THE VALLEY OF JEHOSHAPHAT

In the year of the Foundation of SOLOMON'S
Temple
2803

8.2. THE FIRST ENGLISH EDITION

Some time in 1745, Coustos showed a copy of his manuscript to an Englishman; we don't know who he was, but he tells us that he had lived in France for a time, and that he was not a Free Mason. "A Person of Eminence," he says, had asked him to edit Coustos's papers and to publish them as soon as possible. He had improved the style, made the narrative flow more smoothly, and had added further historical details.

It also seems likely that he was the man who translated the work into English. At any rate we can be certain that it was not Coustos himself, nor in fact any Mason, who was responsible for the English text. From an early date British Freemasonry has had what we now call "the Loyal Toast," and its wording has been unchanged since Anderson's *Constitutions* of 1723 (see Volume Two in the present series, page 35): "(God bless) The King (*or* The Queen) and the Craft." In the French edition of Coustos's book this appears, quite correctly, as "Dieu bénisse le Roi & le Métier." In the English version, however, it has been put back into English by someone who was ignorant of the proper form, "God preserve the King and the Brotherhood."

The book was published, as we have seen, on December 23, 1745, and it bore on its title page the date 1746. The printer was William Strahan, who lived from 1715 to 1785, a Scotsman by birth. He subsequently became quite prosperous, and from 1769 he bore the title "King's Printer." He has another connection with Masonry, for from 1760 on he was the employer of William Preston (1742-1818), the author of *Illustrations of Masonry* (Volume Four in the present series).

8.3. CONTENTS: PRELIMINARIES

Dedication. Coustos dedicates his book to the Earl of Harrington, "One of his Majesty's Principal Secretaries of State." He enlarges on his debt of gratitude to Harrington, to the Duke of Newcastle, and to the King himself, for having set him free from the Galleys. The King's kindness leads him to reflect on the "unnatural Rebellion now carrying on against His Majesty." We may note in passing that both Harrington and Newcastle were Freemasons.

The List of Subscribers includes the names of 328 people who had placed advance orders for a total of 368 copies. It is headed by "the Brethren of the Union Lodge," that is, Coustos's Masonic associates in Union French Lodge, London. In the October advertisement, the subscription rate had been set at five shillings, "half to be paid at subscribing, and the Remainder on the Delivery of a complete Book in Sheets." Two subscribers voluntarily contributed more. The brethren of Union Lodge paid "for One Copy, a Guinea;" and "Her Grace the Dutchess Dowager of Manchester, 5 Guineas for one Book." The total amount subscribed was then ninety-seven pounds sixteen shillings.

Editor's Preface. The Editor explains how he came to be involved in the production, and what was the nature of his contribution. He notes that the book is particularly timely because of the Jacobite invasion. There is great need, he says, to keep England Protestant. The rebellion is sponsored, he says, by the French, but it will end up a blessing in disguise, for it will inspire loyal Britons everywhere.

8.4. CONTENTS: THE BOOK PROPER

The book is divided into five parts.

(1) "The History of the Sufferings of John Coustos, in the Inquisition at Lisbon;"

(2) "Origin of the Inquisition, and its Establishment in various Countries;" this seems to be drawn chiefly from Philippus van Limborch's *History of the Inquisition* (translated by S. Chandler; London, 1731);

(3) "A Distinct Account of the Inquisition, and of the several Things appertaining to it;" this is a full description, apparently reliable, of the working of the Portuguese Inquisition; it concludes with four eye-witness accounts of various *Autos da Fé*, culminating in Coustos's own;

(4) "Examples of the Injustice and Cruelty of the Inquisi-

47

tion;" this is a chamber of horrors, a collection of anecdotes culled from various sources, to illustrate the savagery of the Holy Office;

(5) "Practice of the primitive Church, in bringing over Hereticks, compar'd with that of the Inquisition;" this is an attempt to show that the methods employed by the Holy Office are an innovation in the body of the Church.

Generally speaking, the historical portions are carefully documented. Given the nature of the sources available, Coustos and his editor seem to have verified the facts as best they could. How far the autobiographical portions are to be believed is a separate question which we shall consider subsequently.

The book as a whole is relentlessly anti-Catholic and anti-Inquisition. It is a violent and effective piece of propaganda. No one can deny that Coustos had grounds for feeling the way he did; but his book came at an opportune time, when anti-Catholic sentiments were being fanned.

8.5. OTHER EDITIONS

Coustos's book found a real audience. It was calculated to appeal to two types of reader: Freemasons would find a glorious example in the hero's unshaken fidelity; anti-Catholics would find much ammunition with which to assail the reputation of the Church of Rome. It was regularly reprinted, sometimes curtailed in length, sometimes augmented by other material. The following editions are known. (The titles vary considerably; we shall simply list them by date and publisher.)

1. 1745 or 1746; French edition (see above).
2. 1746, London: W. Strahan (the text presented here).
3. 1746, Dublin: W. Powell.
4. 1755 or 1756; German edition.
5. 1756, Hamburg: German edition.
6. Probably 1790, Birmingham: M. Swinney, for J. Sketchley.
7. 1790, Birmingham: M. Swinney, for J. Sketchley.
8. 1793-1794, *Freemasons' Magazine*, London.
9. 1797, New York: Jacob S. Mott, for Charles Smith.
10. 1798, Norwich, Connecticut: J. Trumbull.

11. 1798, Putney, Vermont: C. Sturtevant, for Justin Hinds.
12. 1800, Brookfield, Massachusetts: E. Merriam.
13. 1803, Boston: Nathaniel Coverly.
14. 1805, *Magazin für Freimaurer*, Leipzig.
15. 1810, Hull: Robert Peck, for Adolphus Neil.
16. 1817, Boston: "printed for the purchasers."
17. 1817, Sunderland: G. Summers.
18. 1820, Hartford: W. S. Marsh.
19. 1820, Hartford: R. Storrs.
20. 1821, Enfield, Connecticut: P. Reynolds and H. Thompson.
21. 1847, George Oliver's *Golden Remains*, London.
22. 1856, *Universal Masonic Library*, New York.
23. 1858, *Freemasons' Magazine and Masonic Mirror*, London.
24. About 1930, *British Masonic Miscellany*, Dundee.
25. 1964, Worcester, Massachusetts: microprint of Nos. 9, 10, 11.
26. 1965, Worcester, Massachusetts: microprint of No. 13.
27. 1979, Bloomington, Illinois: The Masonic Book Club (the present text).

9. COUSTOS'S INTERROGATION

9.1. The Inquisitorial Archives

Coustos's book tells one side of the story. The other is found in the Archives of the Inquisition in Lisbon, for the records of this very case have been preserved. They include the evidence which was collected against him, the official warrant for his arrest and the notice of his admission to prison, and a transcription of his interrogation by the Holy Office, together with the deliberations and decisions of the Council. They enable us to reconstruct the sequence of events in the case.

March 5, 1743 Warrant for his arrest.
March 14, 1743 Admission to prison.
March 21, 1743 First session of interrogation by the Inquisitors.
March 26, 1743 Second session with the Inquisitors.
March 30, 1743 Third session with the Inquisitors.
April 1, 1743 Fourth session with the Inquisitors.
November 14, 1743 Fifth session with the Inquisitors.
November 18, 1743 Sixth session with the Inquisitors.
December 11, 1743 The charges are read to him.
April 25, 1744 Session in the torture chamber.
June 21, 1744 *Auto da fé*.

Of particular interest to us are the transcripts of Coustos's own evidence.

9.2. The First Two Sessions with the Inquisitors

On March 21, 1743, a week after his arrest, Coustos was brought before the Inquisitor. After being sworn, he gave a full description of the lodge and its activities. Most of his testimony has been quoted above, under the title "Masonry in Coustos's Lodge" (Sections 4.2-4.12). He closed his statement with a mention of the *Book of Constitution*, a notice of the various meeting places of his lodge, and a list of its members.

Five days later, on March 26, he returned, and continued his account. This session was much shorter; he had not left himself much to add. We have already quoted what he said on "'The Bible; the Master" (Section 4.13). Then, after a few words on the purpose of secrecy, he went on to explain the Charity Fund.

> ... Their only aim is to help one another; for which purpose there are in England and other Kingdoms special boxes, in which are kept the fees which the members pay every month and upon the occasion of their Initiation, withdrawing therefrom only that portion which is necessary for the dinners they give. And with what is left over, they help their poorer Brethren who are in need of such assistance. ... All the Lodges and lesser fraternities which are to be found dispersed among the different Kingdoms unite to send to the principal Lodges in England and France all the fees which they receive and collect from the members who newly join, so that thus there may be a better and more equal distribution amongst the poorer Brethren needing such help.

This completed his statement. Coustos was escorted back to his cell.

9.3. THIRD SESSION

Four days later, on March 30, Coustos was brought back again. This time he was examined on various details of his confession. The session proceeded as follows. (The Inquisitorial documents report the dialogue in the third person. In what follows, we have tried to recreate, in essence, the actual exchange of words.)

Inquisitor: You will place your hand on the Holy Gospels. Do you promise and swear, under a penalty appropriate to those who perjure themselves upon the Holy Gospels, that you will tell the truth, and keep secret all that you see and hear while in prison?

Coustos: I do.

I.: Have you carefully pondered your offences, as we

charged you? Do you at last wish to confess them, in order to clear your conscience and bring your case to a speedy conclusion?

C.: I have, and can remember nothing more.

I.: How long have you lived in this city? Why did you come here? What is your religion? How do you make your living?

C.: I came here two years ago, more or less, to earn my living by cutting precious stones. I am an Anglican Protestant, as I already told you.

I.: Were you brought up a Protestant from the years of discretion? Or were you once a Roman Catholic, and then you changed to this sect voluntarily for some reason or other?

C.: I was raised as a Protestant. My parents and relatives are all Protestants.

I.: You told us that you belonged to the new sect and brotherhood of Free Masons, that you were the Master, and presided at certain meetings in this city, and that in those meetings you did all those things you told us about. Do you remember saying this? Is it true?

C.: I do, and it is.

I.: Who was the Master that instructed you? What book taught you the rules and doctrines that you have confessed? How long have you been a member and preceptor? Where did you join?

C.: I learned it all in England. Various Masters taught me, but I can't remember who they were. It was fourteen or fifteen years ago that I joined, in the city of London when I lived there.

I.: In lodges in foreign countries, do they do anything more than you told us?

C.: They do just what I told you, and nothing more.

I.: If they are not doing anything more, then why do they have all those ceremonies, solemn Oaths, and preparations?

C.: Only to maintain secrecy.

I.: Only to maintain secrecy! But what is the purpose of

this secrecy? The serious and unusual Penalties of your Obligation, and the nature of your other rites and ceremonies, all clearly suggest some more weighty motive.

C.: The ultimate aim is secrecy; so that Brethren dispersed throughout the World may recognize each other by Signs which are not communicated to persons outside the Fraternity. The advantage we derive is that we can help one another, no matter where we happen to be.

I.: How can what you are saying be true? It is completely irrational that men should consent to such extraordinary Penalties for such ridiculous motives. There must be some greater influence to mould their minds and make them submit to such severity.

C.: The Penalties have no other explanation than what I have told you. We use them, not with the intention of carrying them out, but just to instill fear and respect in new members. I can see that it is a mistake to impose such severe Oaths for such trivial matters.

I.: You allege that the only reason for these Oaths and Penalties is to maintain the secrecy of your Signs. What connection is there between these Oaths and Penalties, and the ceremony of the three lighted Candles, or the peculiar nature of all your practices, or the false and superstitious explanations you give for them all? These things are all separate and distinct from the Oaths and Signs.

C.: I can see that the ceremonies and practices are not appropriate for the purpose that we use them for. But I have always been taught that we observe them because they come from the Temple of Solomon, whom we recognize as one of the principal Free Masons; and because the founders of the Fraternity adopted them. That is why we keep them.

I.: Why are you trying to exonerate yourself by offering such frivolous reasons and explanations? Your aim is very different from what you have told us. Obviously there is no necessary connection between being able to help one another, and giving Signs; nor with the explanations and doctrines you find in Solomon's Temple, nor with the other ceremonies and secrets that you are so extraordinarily cautious about!

C.: I can see that some of these things don't have any connection with others. I don't know, I can't tell you, why we perform these ceremonies. I've already told you why! Only somebody more clever than I, like Mr Dogood, could explain things better, and discuss all the implications.

I.: If your Lodges have no laws and ceremonies beyond what you have told us, how can you say that the Order of Free Masons is more noble than any other in the World?

C.: Because it comes from the time of King Solomon, when there was no other Order in existence; and because it has been followed and embraced by all the Princes and Exalted Persons in the World. That is why it is more noble and more illustrious than any other.

I.: Where did you hear that the Fraternity comes from the time of Solomon? Who told you the other reasons you have given for honouring it beyond others, as the most ancient and most noble?

C.: I have always heard this. Besides, some Masters of the Fraternity have told me that the answers to these questions are to be found in some old books which I do not know.

I.: In your confession you mentioned the Order of Christ, and the Order of St James, and others. Do you know that they have been instituted and approved by the Rulers of the Church?

C.: Yes, I do.

I.: Then how dare you tell us that the Order of the Free Masons is the noblest of all? You know very well, as you have admitted, that it has been condemned by a Supreme Apostolic Edict.

C.: I have already told you why I said it was nobler. Even if I did know of the Pope's prohibition, I saw nothing wrong being done in the Lodges; and besides, I was told that the prohibition didn't apply to foreigners. So I continued to practise Masonry, and to think it was a good thing.

I.: Do you know that you ought not to bring new sects

and abuses into this country? And that you should not cause scandal to good Roman Catholics?

C.: I know my duty very well, and in the future I shall do it. I introduced the Fraternity here because I was persuaded to do it, and I didn't think that I was doing wrong.

Inquisitor: Why do you pretend to offer these wicked excuses? This new sect is hateful; it has been condemned by the Supreme Legislator whose province it is. You know very well that you don't have to look for any other reason.

Coustos: I admit that various people told me about the prohibition. I persuaded myself that it was nothing but talk, and that it didn't apply to foreigners. Other people told me the same thing.

"And the time being used up, he was asked no further questions, nor was the matter continued beyond this; but his record having been read, heard, and understood by him, the prisoner stated that it was truly written; and he signed it together with the said Lord Inquisitor."

9.4. FOURTH SESSION

Two days later, on April 1, Coustos came back to the Audience Chamber, and the interrogation continued. (Once again, we have put the report back into direct speech.)

Inquisitor: Have you thought carefully about your offences, as we admonished you? Are you willing to confess them fully, so that your case may be concluded quickly, and that mercy may be shown to you?

Coustos: I have thought about this, and I have no more offences to confess.

I.: Do you remember telling us that the Free Masons have regulations and fines for those Brethren who use bad language, or speak of the Devil, or say anything against the State? Is this true?

C.: I remember saying that.

I.: Does the Fraternity have any other rules, statutes, or doctrines that pertain to Religion? What are they? Who wrote them? Are they in fact kept by all the Brethren?

C.: The Fraternity has no laws about Religion.

I.: You have confessed all the other rules that you Masons keep about the way of life of your Brethren. How is it possible that there are no laws and statutes about Religion?

C.: I have already told you that we have no laws or statutes about Religion. Besides, foreign Kings don't let us deal with matters of Religion in our Lodges.

I.: Can each of your members follow any Religion he wishes? Or must they all follow some particular one? If so, which one?

C.: Our Members may follow any Religion they please. Furthermore, in his Obligation each candidate promises to follow his own Religion.

I.: How do you hope to persuade us that your Lodges are doing nothing culpable, nothing that deserves punishment? You confess, you admit, that you allow Liberty of Conscience in them. By this means, you provide motive and opportunity for all your members to follow this horrible, scandalous, and abominable licence!

C.: We do this in order that we may admit all classes of men, who follow different Religions. (By saying this, I do not mean to censure or defend either of the two ways of doing things.) But our way, for better or worse, leaves discretion free to work. For this reason, every topic of religious discussion is forbidden in our Lodges.

I.: Why are you trying to excuse yourself like this? If people of different religions join, they will inevitably practise the doctrines that belong to the Lodges. This is natural, and appropriate, when the errors and sects to which they subscribe are so similar.

C.: In Lodge we are not allowed to speak of Religious matters. This is for our own protection. If Kings and Parliaments learned that we did, they would no doubt close the Lodges.

I.: What book, or statute, or rule, authorizes the Masters of your Lodges to administer the Oath to all Initiates, and to admit persons of any Religion at all?

C.: Every year the Masters of the main Lodges in England elect a Duke, or some other person of rank, as Grand Master. In order to administer the Lodges, they issue the regulations, which are taken from a book they have for this purpose. The regulations are scrupulously kept by all the Masters of all the Lodges in the Kingdom.

I.: Who wrote this book? Where was it published? Who in this City sends for it? Who has copies of it?

C.: The book goes back to the time of Queen Elizabeth of England. She wanted to know the constitution of the Society of Free Masons, and sent the Archbishop of Canterbury to investigate. He brought her a book that contained all the regulations of the Society. It has been kept and augmented through the course of time up to the present. The rules and regulations which I mentioned still come from it. I don't know who the Master was who began the book, but I seem to remember hearing that it was one of the Kings of England.

I.: Do you know everything in the Book? What does it deal with? What are they trying to do? Does it have anything more than what you have told us?

C.: No, I don't know everything in the Book. I have always heard that everything in it is connected with Free Masons. It also tells about the trouble they had in ancient times in getting the King's permission for Lodges to meet; and it lists the important things that each Master has done.

I.: You confess that they had trouble getting the King's permission! How can you deny that the Lodges are dealing with important matters?

C.: The Kings mistrusted the Lodges because they didn't know what they consisted of. On investigation, they found that they were harmless. Actually the King of England himself, and his son the Prince of Wales, are Free Masons. The King was initiated when he was a Prince; he could not be initiated after his coronation, because in the course of the ceremony he would have to kneel, and to submit. In fact, I was present at the Initiation of the Prince of Wales.

I.: How can this be true? What you say about Kings should be just as valid for Princes. It would be improper for persons of their rank to submit to these ceremonies, as if they were subjects.

C.: Princes are initiated just exactly as I described. They are not considered to be Absolute Monarchs as the Kings are; so they submit to the ceremonies, and take the Obligation, except for the Penalties, which are omitted, in deference to their rank.

I.: If the Lodges don't do anything except what you have said, what reason do Princes have for joining?

C.: None, except to learn the Secrets of the Lodge. That is why they join.

I.: Why do you keep excusing yourself with these frivolous and pointless answers? You know very well that, if a Prince wants to know what happens in the Lodge, there's no need for him to submit to actions so unworthy of his rank. He has the authority and power to make his subjects reveal what goes on in the meetings, down to the smallest detail.

C.: England is a free country. The King could not force his subjects to tell him the Secrets of the Lodge unless he was convinced that criminal acts were being done. He has no information to that effect. The Princes simply want to know what goes on in Lodge, and so they submit to the ceremonies of Initiation.

I.: Do you remember telling us that the Lodge met in places and houses chosen for this purpose? Do you recall any others than the ones you mentioned?

C.: No, I don't know any more than the ones I told you about.

I.: Do they have a place set aside where they store the equipment they use in Lodge? When you were arrested, where were your things?

C.: Each member looks after his own material. Mine is in the house of an Englishwoman named Richard, who lives in Rua Nova in the City.

I.: Do people of all sexes and quality join the Lodge? Have any Portuguese joined the Lodges which you founded here? If so, who are they?

C.: People of all estates join the Lodges. There is no way that we can admit women, because they cannot keep a secret.

I don't know of any Portuguese who have joined up till now, though the Lodge has no prohibition.

Inquisitor: Did you "help one another" in the Lodges in this city? Have you a cash fund for this purpose?

Coustos: We have no fund that I know of in Portugal. Things have not progressed as far as they have in foreign countries, so we spend the Initiation Fees on dinners. I only remember giving a charitable donation of money to a foreign lady of nobility who was ill.

The Inquisitor admonished Coustos to examine his conscience further to see if he had any more offences to confess, and then sent him back to his prison.

9.5. LATER SESSIONS

More than seven months elapsed before the next session of which we have any record. On November 14, 1743, Coustos was examined about his ancestry, family, religion, and education. Four days later came his final interrogation (on November 18). When the defendant declared right at the beginning that he had nothing further to confess, the Inquisitor summarized the offences he had already admitted, and concluded ominously, "All the evidence makes it clear that these extraordinary deeds were directed to many other diverse ends which the said prisoner has not stated." He warned him that there would be no further opportunity for a full confession until after the Judicial Charge had been drawn up, and remanded him to his cell.

On December 11, 1743, Coustos was brought before the Tribunal, and the full charges against him were read. He was asked whether he wanted an attorney to help him in his defence, but he said not. The charges concluded with another foreshadowing of evil to come.

And in that the prisoner was on many occasions with much charity admonished . . . and asked to confess ALL his offences, and the true and heretical purpose which he had in seeking to introduce into this kingdom the new and damnable sect . . .; he, the prisoner, not being willing to do this, and maintaining the same heretical attitude of one who has caused disturbance and scandal, is not deserving of the least clemency, but rather that he should be punished with the gravest penalties.

Apparently on the same occasion Coustos was shown a summary of the evidence against him, and once again he declined the help of an attorney. The Inquisitor asked him, "What are your convictions in the matter of religion? Do you wish to be admitted to our Holy Roman Faith? Or are you determined to persevere indefinitely in the errors of those Protestant sects in which your feet are now set?" The prisoner responded, "I wish to continue in the Protestant religion in which I have lived till now, and in which I was raised and instructed by my parents."

Then he was shown a copy of the Judicial Proof against him. "When he saw the same, he asked if he might have an attorney to deal with the said matter; but he was told that he could not . . ., since the proof was certain."

9.6. THE END OF THE CASE

The Inquisitors met on February 20, 1744, and resolved that the prisoner "should be put to the torture without any further delay, so that the real truth may be discovered; . . . that he should be given one *trato corrido* [on the pulley], being able so to suffer in the judgement of the doctors and surgeon. . . ."

Nine weeks later, on April 25, he was brought to the Torture Chamber.

He was at once told that, from the nature of the chamber in which he found himself, and the instruments present therein, he would readily understand how arduous and thorough would be his examination, which he could avoid by truly and faithfully confessing his sins. And on declaring he had nothing more to say, he was sent below. . . . The torture prescribed for the accused was then ordered to be executed. And stripped of those clothes which might impede the proper execution of the torture, he was placed on the rack, and the binding up commenced; and he was then informed by me, the notary, that if he died during the operation, or if a limb was broken, or if he lost any of his senses, the fault would be his. . . . And being perfectly bound, he was given the full torture prescribed, which lasted more than a quarter of an hour.

This was, it seems, the last attempt to wring more information from the wretched man. The case was declared closed on May 19, 1744. The Council reached its decision, and on June 21, at an *Auto da fé* celebrated in the Convent Church of Santo Domingos, Coustos was sentenced to four years in the galleys.

9.7. The Torture Employed Against Coustos and His Brethren

There is some ambiguity in the Inquisitorial records about the nature of the torture actually suffered by Coustos. Most of the documents (Inquisitorial decision; the Order for torture; Conclusion of the sentence) speak of one *trato corrido* on the pulley; this is stage No. 9 in the table of progressive severity given above in Section 7.3. The official report of the session in the torture chamber, on the other hand, seems to speak of the rack, and of being "perfectly bound" (stage No. 5 of the pulley). The discrepancy is at first sight hard to explain, and we might be tempted to conclude that Coustos underwent several different tortures.

When we come to look at the records of the other Masons, we find a similar situation. It was ordered that Bros. Bruslé and Mouton both be tortured to the degree of being "perfectly bound" (stage No. 5 of the pulley); and that Bro. Richard be taken as far as "binding with the first strap" (stage No. 3). Yet the reports of the torture session for all three use practically the same contradictory terms as we saw used of Coustos—the rack, "perfectly bound;" it looks as if a fixed formula was used in the report, regardless of the form of torture actually employed.

It is the ultimate irony that, after these four Masons had told in great fullness what Masonry was, and what it did, the Inquisitors did not believe them. They were put to the torture in order to make them disclose what *really* went on at their lodge meetings.

10. COMPARISON BETWEEN COUSTOS'S BOOK AND THE INQUISITORIAL RECORDS

10.1. THE DENUNCIATIONS

Coustos tells us that he was incriminated by "the barbarous Zeal of a Lady, who declar'd, at Confession," that he was a Free Mason. The story is further embellished in the French version, which says that there was another jeweller, Monsieur LeRude by name, resident in the city. His wife resolved to rid her husband of his business rivals and conspired with a friend, Donna Rose, to give information on Coustos and Mouton (both diamond-cutters) to the Inquisition. Coustos says that Mouton was betrayed and arrested in the business establishment of another goldsmith and jeweller.

All this may be gossip, or surmise, or jealousy. The records of the Inquisition preserve the actual denunciations which furnished grounds to arrest Coustos. The informants were as follows:

1. Henrique Machado de Moura, from Madeira, attorney; appeared before the Inquisition on October 6, 1742, and again on February 12, 1743;

2. Cornelius Leruitte, Frenchman, from Liège, goldsmith; appeared before the Inquisition on February 11, 1743;

3. John Elliot, Frenchman, book-keeper; appeared before the Inquisition on February 13, 1743;

4. Pedro Bersan, Armenian, merchant; appeared before the Inquisition on February 14, 1743;

5. Joseph Gregorio, Frenchman, from Paris, merchant; appeared before the Inquisition on February 16, 1743;

6. Maria Rosa Clavé, Frenchwoman, from Paris; wife of Jeronimo Gabriel Clavé; appeared before the Inquisition on February 18, 1743;

7. René Roger, Frenchman, from Paris, goldsmith; appeared before the Inquisition on February 23, 1743.

We note that two of the informants were Monsieur Leruitte, goldsmith, and Maria *Rosa* Clavé. Furthermore two of the witnesses (Machado de Moura and Mme Clavé) professed to have little direct acquaintance with the Masons, but to have got their reports from Monsieur and Madame "Larrut" or "Larrutt." Thus far Coustos's assertion is corroborated.

There may have been other currents of hostility at work. The first witness, Henrique Machado, had spontaneously requested audience with the Holy Office and "sought to make a statement . . . regarding certain matters affecting him." No hint of any coercion! He also admitted having tried to persuade John Elliot to give evidence, but Elliot had replied, "I shall do no such thing, for I shall not hurt friends who have done no harm." He came forward only when ordered. In fact Machado conceded that he had said what he did "not for any spite which he may have towards the accused—except that he wishes harm only to Lambert Boulanger, who ordered him to be stabbed for appearing as procurator against him, and also Alexandre Jacques Mouton, for the same reason." He sounds like a sordid vengeful little informer.

10.2. Chronology of Coustos's Sojourn in Prison

In the English version of his book, Coustos says that he was arrested on March 5, 1743. This is incorrect. The original French edition correctly places the event on March 14, the same as the Inquisitorial records. The translator was aware that there was a difference of several days between the Gregorian Calendar, which was used in Catholic countries, and the Julian Calendar, which Britain did not abandon until 1752. Unfortunately he erred in his computations. The Julian date which corresponds to March 14 (Gregorian) is March 2.

The English version is, as we have seen, slightly farther

from the truth than is the French. Here is the sequence of events as it is given in the French text. We shall note details where the English text differs.

March 14, 1743	Admission to prison.
(On the fifth day)	First session of interrogation by the Inquisitors.

[The number of days is not given in the English.]

(Three days later)	Second session with the Inquisitors.
(Fifteen days later)	Third session with the Inquisitors.

[The number of days is not given in the English. This session took place during the seven weeks when Coustos was confined to another miserable "deep Dungeon." In this part of the English version he is taken before the Inquisitors "three Times" (page 32); of these the French original knows only one.]

"A few Days after," Coustos fell sick, and was moved to another Dungeon, "which admitted some glimmerings of Day-light." His illness, "happily, was not of long Continuance."

(After his recovery)	Fourth session with the Inquisitors.

[At this stage the English text, pages 40-42, introduces another session with the Inquisitors, which is not in the original.]

(Some days later)	Fifth session with the Inquisitors.
(Four days later)	Sixth session with the Inquisitors.
(A few days later)	The charges are read to him.
(Six weeks later)	Coustos dictates his defence.
(A few days later)	Decision of the Tribunal.
(Some days later)	First session in the torture chamber.

(Six weeks later)	Second session in the torture chamber.
(Two months later)	Third session in the torture chamber.
(After an unknown interval)	*Auto da fé.*

Because of the uncertainties it is impossible to give absolute dates, except for the first four events in the sequence. Even so, the schedule clearly does not coincide with that derived from the Inquisitorial Archives (see above, Section 9.1). The six sessions with the Inquisitors occur in both lists. Some of the intervals between them are the same. Other details diverge. Most striking is the fact that the Book has three sessions of torture, whereas the Archives report only one.

Some discrepancies may be blamed on faulty memory. Coustos was not able to keep any written records. Right after his admission to prison he was searched, and all papers were taken from him. Later, when he wanted to compose his defence, he was told "that the Holy Office did not allow Prisoners the use of Pen, Ink and Paper."

10.3. SIMILARITIES IN THE TWO ACCOUNTS

Let us call the two sources "A" (for Archives) and "B" (for Book). In many details "A" serves to confirm the account in "B". We may list some of the coincidences.

1. He was arrested March 14, 1743 (A; B, French version).
2. He underwent six sessions with the Inquisitors (A, B).
3. At the first session, he took an oath on the gospels, and was required to give his name, his birthplace, his profession, and his religion (A, B).
4. He was asked, on being brought before the Inquisitors again, whether he had reflected on his sins, as directed by the Tribunal, and whether he wished to clear his conscience by confessing anything further (A, a regular formula; B, second session).
5. He told them that Masonry included members of dif-

ferent religions, and that therefore religious controversy within the lodge was forbidden (A, fourth session; B, second session).
6. He pointed out that Kings and Princes are Masons (A, fourth session; B, second session).
7. He spoke of the Book of Constitutions, and then told the story of Queen Elizabeth and the Archbishop of Canterbury (A, fourth session; B, second session).
8. He insisted that Masons are loyal to the King and to the State (A, first session; B, second session).
9. At the beginning of a subsequent session, he renewed his oath to keep the secrets of the Inquisition, and to tell the truth (A, regular formula; B, third session).
10. He explained that Masonic secrecy serves to identify strangers as Masons; and in this context he mentioned charity (A, third session; B, third session).
11. He explained further that women were not admitted because of the risk they pose to secrecy (A, fourth session; B, third session).
12. He said that no Portuguese had joined his lodge (A, fourth session; B, fourth session).
13. He was told that he should not have enticed or scandalized Roman Catholics (A, third session; B, fourth session).
14. He referred to an Englishman, Mr Dogood, who would be able to give better explanations of Masonry than he can (A, third session; B, English version only, page 42).
15. He recollected that he had exercized charity on behalf of a woman (A, fourth session; B, fifth session).
16. He said that fines were levied on brethren for bad language (A, first session; B, fifth session).
17. He noted that the money derived from fines was to be used for charitable purposes (A, first session; B, fifth session).
18. He was invited to become Catholic, but refused to do so (A, after the reading of the Charges; B, sixth session).
19. He was offered counsel, but refused it (A, after he saw the evidence; B, before the reading of the Charges).

20. In the torture chamber, he was told that if he died under torture, it would be his own fault (A, B).
21. He was tortured (A, B).
22. He was given a bill of the expenses the Inquisitors had undergone on his behalf (A, the account is preserved; B, p. 228).
23. The Auto da Fé took place on June 21, 1744, and eight people (whose names are given) were executed (A, the official list is preserved; B, pages 216, 224-225).

10.4. Discrepancies

In fact the places in which the Archives differ from the Book are much fewer than the points of agreement between them. In at least some, we can even see reasons for the discrepancy.

When he was asked whether any Portuguese citizens joined the lodge, Coustos went on for quite some time in the Book about a Monsieur de Calliaris who was anxious to join, but whom he discouraged from so doing. The name does not occur in the Inquisitorial Archives. Likewise, when he was asked about the recipients of charity, Coustos told in the Book about contributions to a Catholic woman, a Franciscan monastery, and the Catholic father of a family. In the transcript of his interrogation, he spoke only of a donation to "a foreign lady of nobility who was ill." In both instances the enquiry bore upon his relationships with the Portuguese people. In the Archives these connections are made to be much less important than they are in the Book.

Then too in matters which reflect on his own firmness in adversity, Coustos is less frank than we might have expected. In the Book, he says that he turned down legal counsel when it was offered to him. In the Archives on the other hand, it appears that, though at first he rejected counsel, when he heard the Charges he asked for one but was turned down. Again, in the Book he says that he refused to sign the statement of charges against him when it was read. The document survives, and he did sign it. But most shocking is the way he dealt with attempts to learn the secrets of the Craft.

In the Book he insists that, though repeatedly asked, he steadfastly refused. Actually, in the very first session, he gave one of the fullest accounts we have of Masonry in the 1740's—and with very little prompting.

In the matter of torture we meet another difficulty. The Book describes how Coustos endured three different tortures, a total of nine times: four times on the rack; three times by having his arms winched backwards; and twice by having a chain wrapped around his body and alternately loosened and tightened. The Archives say that the only tortures permitted were the rack and the pulley, and that Coustos was put to the pulley only once. The two accounts cannot be reconciled. If Coustos *did* embroider his tale, we must recall that he had after all been roughly used, and his only means to avenge himself on his tormentors was to blacken their reputations with his pen.

The autobiographical part of Coustos's book is not, cannot be, historically accurate in every detail. It must be a generalized picture, a composite impression, a synthesis of how prisoners were treated. It relies primarily on his own recollections, somewhat edited. No doubt it incorporates, as if they were his own, the experiences of other men. It also includes purely fictional material, things that Coustos *wishes* he'd said, but didn't actually say. The net result is to make the Inquisition look a little worse, and Coustos a little better, than they really were. The technique, we may note, is still used when politicians write their memoirs.

11. SIGNIFICANCE OF JOHN COUSTOS

For many years Coustos was regarded as a Masonic hero, a fit example for every Mason to emulate. In his Preface to the 1790 edition, for example, James Sketchley writes as follows.

The sufferings of Mr. John Coustos, in the horrid Inquisition in Portugal, where he underwent the most cruel tortures, sooner than divulge the secrets of the ROYAL ART, was thought by many of his brothers (whom the Editor consulted,) a proper present for every candidate for the honour of the Misteries of the Craft, as well as a very acceptable companion to those already of the Fraternity.

The summation in Mackey's *Encyclopaedia of Freemasonry* perhaps reflects the traditional viewpoint as well as any.

John Coustos has not, by his literary researches, added anything to the learning or science of our Order; yet, by his fortitude and fidelity under the severest sufferings, inflicted to extort from him a knowledge he was bound to conceal, he has shown that Freemasonry makes no idle boast in declaring that its secrets "are locked up in the depository of faithful breasts."

It is a curious chance that in the past generation we have learned so much more about him, from the minute book at Paris and from the Archives at Lisbon. Particularly in the light of the latter, one might argue that we can no longer look upon him as a hero.

What then are we to think of him? Contempt is the easy first reaction towards a man who so violates the sacred trust reposed in him. Yet the Inquisitors had ways (as the saying goes) to loosen tongues. They had great powers, they knew how to use them, and they saw that people realized the extent of those powers. Arrest by the Holy Office was practically as good as a conviction; rare was the prisoner who did not confess whatever was wanted of him. The officials would take him to the torture chamber, and show him all the instruments so that "he would readily understand how arduous and thorough would be his examination." Again and again they would give him time by himself, to ponder his situation. He could brood about whether he would rather talk now or later. For talk he certainly would. In this century we have seen how effective psychological pressure can be when exerted by a powerful institution against an isolated individual. "Brain-washing" has been reduced to a fine art; its methods, we see now, are not new.

Seen in this light, Coustos's capitulation is quite intelligible; there is no need to spurn him for his confession, given the extremity to which he was reduced. Who of us would be brave enough to endure the *strappado*, or the rack, or even the threat of them, without cracking?

But there may be even more to say. Silence before the Tribunal was unthinkable, and overt disobedience out of the question. Coustos's lodge brother, Jean Baptiste Richard, escaped sentencing by turning Catholic. Coustos himself was made of sterner stuff. "I wish," he told them, "to continue in the Protestant religion in which I have lived till now, and in which I was raised and instructed by my parents."

When they wanted information, he was not in a position to keep silent. Yet did he tell all? Every witness was asked what Masons he knew. Mouton catalogued twenty-five. Bruslé named eighteen. Boulanger listed fourteen, and Richard thirteen. Coustos contented himself with twelve, of whom two were from other lodges. Was the Master of the lodge so rattled that he forgot the names of half his members, including even his two Wardens?

Coustos outlined the Masonic ceremonies of the lodge for the Inquisition. He told how the candidate knelt on a Mason's square (a practice followed in England in 1730); yet two of his members agreed that he knelt on an apron. Did the Master not know how things were done in his own lodge?

Where was he born? He told the Holy Office that he was

"Swiss by Nationality and born in the canton of Basel." In his book however, he says "I am a native of *Berne* in *Switzerland*." Did the man not know? His friend Richard confirms for us that Coustos was "a native of the canton of Bern."

These are puzzling little points, but there may be an explanation. Is it possible that Coustos was not in fact completely crushed by the Inquisition? That he did, after all, keep something back from his tormentors? That he salvaged a vestige of self respect by these petty deceptions? Perhaps so. In Coustos we see a man who had ruled Masonic lodges in three countries; a man who had won the admiration of the lords and barons of Paris; a man who under duress had the presence of mind to protect his brethren; a man who, though not an accomplished writer, determined to win his revenge by telling the world of his sufferings. And he did so with such simplicity, with such wealth of circumstantial detail, that his book seemed more like fiction than autobiography. Many could not or would not believe. In the late nineteenth century, even his Masonic brethren dismissed the work as the product of a fertile imagination. But in these last few years, new sources have sustained him. The very records of the Inquisition serve to establish the main truth of Coustos's narrative.

His early death at the age of forty-three, within two years of deliverance, was undoubtedly hastened by his torture and imprisonment. He is worthy to be enshrined among those who give up their lives for a principle. Yes, John Coustos was a true Masonic hero.

12. BIBLIOGRAPHY AND ACKNOWLEDGEMENTS

12.1. Abbreviations

A.Q.C. Ars Quatuor Coronatorum, Transactions of Quatuor Coronati Lodge, No. 2076, London.

M.I.I. José A. Ferrer Benimeli, *Masoneria, Iglesia e Ilustracion* (Madrid, 4 volumes, 1976-1977).

12.2. Chief Works on Coustos

(Anonymous), "Le premier Livre d'architecture de la Maçonnerie française: Le Registre Coustos-Villeroy (1736-1737)," *Bulletin du Centre de Documentation du Grand Orient de France*, No. 51 (May-June 1965), pp. 33-68.

Dashwood, J. R., "The Trial of John Coustos by the Inquisition," *A.Q.C.* 66 (1952-1953), pp. 107-123.

Ferrer Benimeli, José A., "El Tribunal de la Inquisición de Lisboa y la Masoneria; Proceso de Alexandre Jacques Motton; Proceso de Joao Thomas Bruslé; Proceso de Joao Bauptista Richart; Proceso de John Coustos y Lamberto Bolanger," *M.I.I.* 2, pp. 133-194, together with Appendices 41-46, pp. 349-474.

McLeod, W., "John Coustos: His Lodges and His Book," to appear in *A.Q.C.* 92 (1979).

Mellor, Alec, "Un procès de l'Inquisition sur le 'secret maçonnique,' le procès Coustos, 1742," *Revue Internationale de Criminologie et de Police Technique*, 15 (1961). (Not seen.)

Vatcher, S., "John Coustos and the Portuguese Inquisition," *A.Q.C.* 81 (1968), pp. 9-77.

12.3. Additional References

Section 2.1: For the improvements introduced into other

countries by the Huguenots, see Charles Weiss, *History of the French Protestant Refugees from the Revocation of the Edict of Nantes to the Present Time* (translated by Frederick Hardman; Edinburgh and London, 1854).

Section 2.5: The quotations from the Boston newspapers come from Melvin M. Johnson, *The Beginnings of Freemasonry in America* (New York, 1924), pp. 274, 294; that from a Paris paper, from *M.I.I.* 2, p. 468.

Section 3.1: The quotation from the *St. James' Evening Post* is given by H. C. de Lafontaine, *A.Q.C.* 42 (1929), pp. 294-295.

Section 3.2: See S. Vatcher, "A Lodge of Irishmen at Lisbon, 1738," *A.Q.C.* 84 (1971), pp. 75-102.

Sections 4.2-4.13: These sections are based on N. Cryer's translation, published by S. Vatcher, *A.Q.C.* 81 (1968), pp. 47-51, 52, with the following changes: the word rendered as "officer(s)" by Cryer is instead translated "Fellow" (twenty-six times) or "Fellow Craft(s)" (four times); "attendant(s)" is changed to "Warden(s)" (eight times); "principal finger" is changed to "middle finger" (twice); four or five other small alterations and corrections have been introduced as well.

Section 6.1: The Latin text of the Bull is given in *M.I.I.* 1, pp. 290-291; W. J. Chetwode Crawley's translation is found in *A.Q.C.* 24 (1911), pp. 62-63, and again in H. L. Haywood, *Freemasonry and Roman Catholicism* (Chicago, 1943), pp. 17-21.

Section 6.10: On recent developments in the relationship between Catholicism and Masonry, see Harry Carr, *The Freemason at Work* (London, 1976), pp. 277-281; Alec Mellor, "The Roman Catholic Church and the Craft," *A.Q.C.* 89 (1976), pp. 60-69.

Section 7.3: The details on torture in the Portuguese Inquisition come from António Baião, *Episódios Dramáticos da Inquisição Portuguesa*, 2 (3rd edition, Lisbon, 1973), pp. 241-251.

Section 7.4: The information about torture and capital punishment in other countries comes from George Ryley

Scott, *The History of Capital Punishment* (London, 1950), and L. A. Parry, *History of Torture in England* (1934; reprinted Montclair, N.J., 1975.

Sections 9.2-9.4: These sections are based on N. Cryer's translation, published by S. Vatcher, *A.Q.C.* 81 (1968), pp. 47-58.

12.4. Acknowledgements

Some debts the writer can never repay, but he can at least acknowledge them. He is grateful to Louis L. Williams for help and encouragement; to Harry Carr, for criticising an earlier draft of the sections on the origins of Coustos's Masonry; to Dr S. Vatcher, for providing copies of the unpublished translations of documents from the Inquisitorial Archives, and for giving permission to use them; to E. E. Cromack for the same courtesies; to C. N. Batham, for permission to make extensive use of material which has been published in *A.Q.C.*, and for other kindnesses; to J. M. Hamill and T. O. Haunch, both of London; to Alphonse Cerza of Riverside, Illinois, and to Professor José A. Ferrer Benimeli of the Colegio de Salvador, Zarogoza, Spain, for patiently answering questions; to Professor H. S. F. Collins of Victoria College in the University of Toronto, for help in translating Portuguese texts; to the Libraries of the University of Toronto, and the Public Archives of Canada, and their staffs, for providing copies of works not otherwise available; to Mme Florence de Lussy, of the Bibliothèque Nationale in Paris, for furnishing microfilm of the minute-book of the Coustos-Villeroy lodge; and to Donna-Grace Burns for deciphering and typing a very messy manuscript.

The Facsimile

THE
SUFFERINGS
OF
JOHN COUSTOS,
FOR
FREE-MASONRY,
AND FOR

His refusing to turn ROMAN CATHOLIC,

IN THE

INQUISITION at *Lisbon;*

Where he was sentenc'd, during Four Years, to the GALLEY; and afterwards releas'd from thence by the gracious Interposition of his present Majesty King GEORGE II.

To which is annex'd,

The ORIGIN of the INQUISITION, with its Establishment in various Countries. A distinct Account of that Tribunal, with many Examples of its Injustice and Cruelty; and the Practice of the PRIMITIVE CHURCH, in bringing over Hereticks, compared with that of the INQUISITION.

Extracted from a great Variety of the most approved AUTHORS.

Enrich'd with SCULPTURES, design'd by Mr. BOITARD.

Quid hoc majus poterat intendere accusator sacerdos? fuit enim, fuit & hoc'delatorum genus, qui nominibus antistites, revera autem satellites, atque adeo carnifices, non contenti miseros evolvisse patrimoniis, calumniabantur in sanguinem, & vitas premebant reorum jam pauperum.
  Latinus Pacatus, in Panegyrico Theodosio dicto, Cap. xxix. p. m. 509.

LONDON:
Printed by W. STRAHAN, for the AUTHOR, 1746.

To the RIGHT HONOURABLE

THE

EARL of *HARRINGTON*,

One of his MAJESTY's Principal SECRETARIES of STATE.

My LORD,

PLEASE to permit me, with an Heart overflowing with Gratitude, to give this public Testimony of my Obligations

tions to Your Lordſhip; Obligations which the ableſt Pen cou'd never ſet in their full Light, much leſs mine.

To Your Lordſhip's Goodneſs, and the Favour of his Grace the Duke of *Newcaſtle*, I not only owe the Felicity I now enjoy, of again treading this bliſsful Land of Liberty; but, very probably, that I breathe and have my preſent Exiſtence. For the grievous Torments I ſuffer'd, by Command of the mercileſs Inquiſitors, had ſo weakned my Body; and the diſmal Reflections, on my wretched Condition, ſo diſtracted my Mind; that it would have been almoſt almoft impoffible for me not to have funk under the dire Toils of the *Portugueze* Galley, to which I afterwards was fentenc'd during four Years; and for no other Reafon, than becaufe I cou'd not be prevail'd upon, by Menaces or Tortures, to abjure the excellent Religion in which I was born and educated, and profefs the idolatrous Principles of the Church of *Rome*.

Your Lordfhip had then the great Humanity, on an humble Appplication made to You, to appear as my Guardian Angel; and by the gracious Interpofition

tion of his Majesty King GEORGE II. to snatch me, like another *Shadrach*, out of the Flames.

 I must be the most ungrateful among Mankind, and quite unworthy of enjoying the Light of Heaven, or any other Benefit from Thence; did not His Majesty's exceeding Goodness, in condescending to interpose, so very seasonably, for One of the humblest and most unfortunate of His Subjects, rouze all the Faculties of my Soul; and powerfully increase the Veneration, the Duty and Zeal, with which I ever was inflamed for His Service.

Hence

DEDICATION.

Hence I cannot reflect, without Horror, on the unnatural Rebellion now carrying on against His Majesty, whose Lenity ought to have secured Him the Hearts of all but the most abandoned; a Rebellion which, but for that Lenity, cou'd not have broke out; and thence, in what Point of Sight so ever view'd, must necessarily appear odious and detestable to all Persons of Honour and Virtue.

I only wish that those mistaken *Britons*, whose Hearts may be alienated from His Majesty, and His Illustrious House, or ever so little wavering in their Allegiance, had seen the *Inquisition*

sition and its tremendous Attendants; certain I am, that a bare Glimpse wou'd strike the most Intrepid among them with Dread; and not only fire them with an extreme Hatred to the Cause they before might wish well to; but instantly reconcile them to the only just and wise One, that of their Country, and of their righful Sovereign; wou'd engage them, not only to enlist chearfully under his Banners; but if requisite, to shed the last Drop of their Blood for His Defence, for that of their Altars, and of every Thing worth preserving.

May your Lordship's Zeal for the Prosperity of your Country,

DEDICATION.

try, and His Majesty's Service, be imitated by all His Subjects. Here wou'd be the Place, did it become me, to expatiate on Your Lordship's Talents as a Minister; on Your Love for the Polite Arts; and on every other Part of Your Lordship's exalted Character, which have justly won You universal Esteem: But it were superfluous, (supposing me qualified for the Task) to inform the Public, of what is so well known to It already.

Your Lordship will be so good as to pardon this Intrusion; and to give me Leave, with the greatest Deference, to make this

DEDICATION.

this Public Declaration; that I shall pray, with my latest Breath, for every Blessing from the Almighty on your Lordship; no One being, with more profound Respect,

My LORD,

Your Lordship's

Most obliged,

Most obedient,

and most devoted

Humble Servant.

John Coustos.

A LIST

OF THE

SUBSCRIBERS NAMES.

From the BRETHREN of the UNION LODGE, for One Copy, a Guinea.

A

HIS Grace the Duke of ATHOL, 2 Books,
Mr. A. Atkins
Mr. Giles Alsop
Mr. Angier
Mr. Anderson
Mr. Christopher Anderson.
Mr. William Armstrong

Mr. Francis Ainell
Mr. James Afhley
Mr. Afhrfield
Mr. Heven St. André, 2 Books
Mr. David Audré
Mr. Archambo

B

Mr. John Berry
Mr. William Beammand
William Blair, Efq;
Savage Barrel, Efq; 2 Books
Mr. John Blakefley
Mr. P. Bouillard
Mr. James Bernardeau
The Rev'd Mr. John Peter Bernard
Mr. Nicholas Biron
Mr. Thomas Brooke
Mr. R. Bridgewater
Mr. Matthew Brown
Mr. Arthur Brown
William Briftowe, Efq;
Captain Barbutt
Mr. Bouville, 2 Books
Mr. Bifhop
Mr. Barbie, Junior
Mr. Blondo, 15 Books
Mr. David Buchanan
Mr. James Bennet, 2 Books
------Blunt, Efq; 2 Books
Mr. Jeremiah Barret
Mr. Daniel Baylie

Captain Bradstreet
Mr. Claude Bennet
Capt. Barnage
Mr. Blagny
Capt. Bancons
Mr. John Peter Blaquier
Mrs. Balchen
Mr. Vidal Thomas Barber

C

The Right Hon. Lord COKE
The Right Hon. Lord Conway
Sir James Carnegy
Walter Cary, Esq;
Mr. David Curry
Mr. Collin Camphell
Mr. Robert Cheek
Mr. Francis Creuze, Junior
Mr. Walter Cameron
Mr. William Cherry
Mr. Cockburn
Capt. Chapeau
Mr. John Cobb
Mr. James Coleman, 2 Books
Mr. Robert Coats
Mr. Gilbert Caldecot
Mr. John Catanah
Mr. Collins, 2 Books
Mr. Crespin
Mr. John Covert
Mr. Carpentier
Mr. Peter La Coste

Mr. John Combcrose
Mr. Cambrowne
The Rev'd Mr. Carnaby
Mr. la Chaux
Mr. Combrune
Mr. Richard Comber
The Right Hon. Lord Carteret
Mr. Honour Carpenter
Mr. Collins
Mr. Chamberat
Mrs. Cato
Mr. William Campbell
Mr. Thomas Chafe
Mr. Crifwell
Mr. de Couzcette

D

Mr. Doxy
The Rev'd Mr. Henry Dan
Mr. Thomas Davenport
Mr. Charles Dodd
Mr. William Dickens
Mr. Peter Dupont
Mr. Gabriel Defgoutes
Mr. Francis Deftrade
Mr. Dappe
Mr. George Defnoyers
Mr. Robert Dawfon
Mr. Mofes Depaiba
Mr. Humphry Dunfulf
Mr. Dewitz
Mr. Charles Dubuy

Mr. Peter Deschamps
Capt. Dezieres
Major Dumas
Dr. Duval
Mr. Dutens
Mr. Dickens, 5 Books

E

The Right Hon. the Earl of EGLINTON.
Mr. Evans
Mr. Jonathan Fade
Mr. Elderton
Mr. John Elhers
Herneft Eller, Esq;
Mr. Henry Eclmead
The Rev. Mr. John Ever

F

The Right Hon. Viscount FANE.
The Right Hon. Viscountess Fitz-Williams
Sir Everard Fawkener
Mr. William Fead
Mr. Edward Feline
Mr. Foit
Mrs. Fosdike
Mr. Fordham
Mr. Flot, 2 Books

G

Mr. James Gibſon
Mr. Thomas Gleniſter
Mr. Henry Gretton, Junior
Mr. Robert Glide, Junior.
Mr. George Goney
Mr. William Goudge
Mr. John Gilbert
Mr. William Goff
Mr. Gignoux
Mr. Paul Girardot
Mr. William James Gambia
Mr. John Gardens

H

Mr. William Humphrys
Mr. Bartholomew Hammond
Mr. John Harding
Mr. Hiſter
Mr. David Humphrys
Mr. Thomas Harrache
Mr. Philip Hardel
Mr. George Hornſby
Mr. Harling
Mr. Richard Hutt
Mr. Peter Hemet
Mr. Hare
Mr. Herdman
Dr. Hoddy
Mr. Hollwell

The Hon. Alexander Hume
Capt. Hanway
Mr. Roger Hog
Mr. Charles Hamilton

I

Mr. Inchinwood
Mr. Ifiat, Meſſenger

J

Mrs. James
Mr. Laplant Jurquet
Mr. Jos. Jones
Mr. Benjamin James, Eſq;
Mr. William Johnſon
Mr. John Jarquet
Mr. Thomas Jefferys
Mr. Richard Jefferys
Robert Jenner, Eſq;
The Rev. Dr. Jenner
Mr. John Johnſon
Mr. Thomas Johnſon
Mr. Johnſon
Mr. Cloud Johnſon
Mr. Jellé

K

Mr. John Keith
Mr. Alexander Kirkpatrick

xviii SUBSCRIBERS NAMES.

Mr. Kirkstall
John Kervill, Esq;
Mr. Richard King

L

The Right Hon. the Earl of LEICESTER
Mr. Frankbon Limborch
Capt. Sam. Lofting
Thomas Lediard Esq;
Mr. Le Blon
Mr. Ronjat Lehook
Mr. Jacob Lopez dias
Mr. Larpent.
Mr. Leroy
Mr. Layard
Mr. Lejay
Mr. Longmore
Mr. Legois
Mr. Legleise, 10 Books
Mrs. Leveus
Mr. Lacam

M

The Right Hon. Lord Montfort.
Her Grace the Dutchess Dowager of Manchester, 5 Guineas for one Book.
Mr. Mac Intosh
Mr. La Motte
Miss Mary Morisco

SUBSCRIBERS NAMES.

Mr. Peter Mulman
Mr. Matthie
Mr. Millar
Mr. Manners
Mr. Charles Molloy
Mr. Moses Macchorro
Mr. Jo. F. Milliquet
Mrs. Mendes da Costa
Miss Mendes da Costa
Mrs. Catherine Mendes da Costa
Mr. Moses Mendes da Costa, junior
Mr. Isaac Mendes
Mr. George Mason
Mr. Thomas Moore
Mr. Maddock
Mr. Murray.
Mr. Richard Meares
Mr. Le Maitre, senior
Mr. Mess, one of his Majesty's Messengers
The Rev'd Dr. Morgan, four Books.
Mr. John Martin
Mr. Moren

N

Mr. Newhouse
Mr. Neale
Mr. Solomon Nathan.
Mr. Norton Nicholls
Mr. Nicholls

O

Mr. John Owen

P

The Right Hon. the Earl of PEMBROKE.
Mr. Peccarrere
Mr. John Payne
Mr. Edward Payne
Mrs. Payne.
Mr. George Paterson
Mr. Palmer,
Mr. James Pharoh
Mr. Jof. Pickford
Mr. Samuel Parker
Mrs. Porter at Windsor
Mr. William Potterer
Mr. Perry, Steward to Lord Conway
Mr. Joseph Pouchose

R

The Right Hon. Alex. Lord RUTHERFORD
Samuel Rush, Esq;
Mr. Andrew Robbins
Mr. J. B. Remy
Mr. Walter Robertson
Mr. James Rigby
Mr. Alexander Ross

Mrs. Round
Mr. Frederick Remy
Mr. Moses Roberts
Mr. Peter Russel
Mr. John Rayner
Mr. Recter
Mr. Riou
Mr. John Rice
Mr. Ravenel
Mr. Rustat, Brewerstreet
Mr. Stephen Rimbault
Mr. Rosamberg
Mr. Philip Rigail

S

The Right Hon. Charles Stanhope
Sir William Stanhope, Bart.
John Stone, Esq;
Mr. George Sympson
Mr. Robert Shirley
Mr. William Shirley
Mrs. Stiers
Mr. Sacam
Mrs. Savice.
Mr. F. U. Schicke
Mr. Matthew Strickland
Mr. George Spencer
Mr. Thomas Saunders

Mr. John Sauret
Mr. Christopher Seton
Mr. Richard Scrafton
Mr. John Sommer
Mr. John Sorro
Mr. Sailly
----Sollicoffer, Esq;
Mr. Robert Shepherd at Richmond
Mr. John Smith
Mr. Shebbins
Mr. Shebbins
Mr. Storer, Postmaster at Guilford
The Hon. Mr. Selwyn, junior
William Scawens, Esq;
Gerard Stael, Esq;
Mr. John Smith
Mr. Charles Scott
Mr. Walter Stirling
Mr. Edward Spink

T

Hubert Taffel, Esq;
Capt. William Thompson
Mr. Trible
Dr. Tolot
Mr. Godfrey Thornton
Mr. Thomson
Mr. Robert Turner
Mr. Andrew Taylor

Subscribers Names.

Mr. Thomas Taylor
Mr. John Turner
Mr. William Townshend

V

Colonel Vanderduffen
William Vaughan, Esq;
Mr. William Vol
Mr. James Vigne

W

Mr. Thomas Williamson
Mr. Thomas Woodward
Mr. William Wharry
Mr. Wardon
Mrs. Winterbottom
Mr. Henry Webster
Mr. Gervas Weston
Mr. Richard Winter
Hayford Wainwright, Gent.
Mr. Walton
Mr. Ward, Master Cook to the Side Kitchen
Mrs. Wiat
Mr. John Wenham

xxiv Subscribers Names.

Mr. John Whitemore
Mrs. West
Mr. Wayte

Names omitted in their proper Places.

Mr. J. Cam
Mr. Florio Senior
Mr. Barker Junior
Mr. Barbu, junior
Mrs. de Boyville, 2 Books
Mr. Nash
William Hamilton, Esq;

The Right Hon. Lord Cranston, Grand Master of the ancient and noble Society of Free and Accepted Free-Masons.

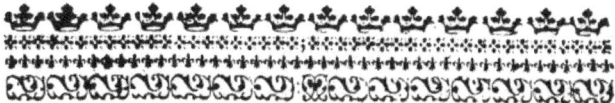

A

PREFATORY DISCOURSE,

On Occaſion of the Preſent Rebellion,

By the EDITOR.

THE rough Draught (as to the Style) of the following Sheets was put into my Hands by the unhappy Man who is the Subject of them, Mr. *John Couſtos*, in order for me to prepare them for the Preſs; a little after which I was deſired, by a Perſon of Eminence, to give my Attention to, and publiſh them as ſoon as might be convenient.

I had both read and heard ſo much concerning the iniquitous and horrid Tribunal of the Inquiſition, that I engag'd with Pleaſure in the Taſk, (tho' ſo gloomy in its Nature) from a Perſuaſion

suasion that every new Treatise of this kind, is an Addition of Strength to the Protestant Cause; as such open still more and more the Eyes of Mankind with Regard to their natural Rights, and true Interest; by exhibiting to them fresh Examples of the shocking Barbarities of a Tribunal which, under the most dangerous of all Masks, that of Religion; and a pretended Zeal for the Welfare, both temporal and eternal, of Mankind, commits Cruelties unknown to the most savage Heathens; Cruelties highly injurious to the Almighty, and a Disgrace to human Nature.

In working upon Mr. *Coustos'* Papers, I can affirm that I have not altered the smallest Circumstance in them; all I did was to make now and then some little Transposition in the Narrative, and to improve the Style; in every other Respect, the Relation is exactly as I received it from him, without any Addition or Diminution.

As

PREFACE.

As to the Articles of Free-Masonry, Mr. *Coustos* is the best Judge with regard to them, I myself not being of the Brotherhood. 'Twas enough to engage me to take these Papers in hand, that the Author of them had met with cruel Treatment, (I myself having seen the sad Marks thereof still remaining on his Body) by those Infernal Spirits, in human Shape, the Inquisitors; only for his belonging to a Society, which, I am persuaded, if of no Benefit to the Community, is not prejudicial to it; whereas the Tribunal he suffer'd under, must be the heaviest Curse to every Country where it is established.

Some Time after Mr. *Coustos* had given me the Papers relating to himself; he communicated to me others concerning the Rise and Progress of the Inquisition; the Usage Hereticks met with in the early Ages; with many Instances of Persons who had been miserable Victims to the Tribunal in Question.

Turning them over, I found them to be a Compilation from various Authors, moftly of Reputation, and particularly *Limborch*. Thefe I afterwards re-digefted, (fo far as my Time wou'd permit) expunging or adding, as I judg'd neceffary. The prefent Crifis of Things made me prefume, that fome Strokes of this Sort, tho' before given by the fineft Pens, wou'd, fo far from being improper, be exceedingly neceffary.

For this Reafon I likewife interwove many Examples of Perfons who had fuffer'd in the Inquifition; as well as Reflections on its abominable Proceedings, drawn from Writers of the greateft Character, particularly Mr. *Bayle*, and Mr. *la Croze*, whofe Authorities I have every where quoted, and all which were never before introduced in any Treatife of this Kind.

The Reader will be fo good as to excufe fome Repetitions in the Work. As the whole was undertaken in an honeft View, I hope my Endeavours will

will be candidly receiv'd by all sincere Lovers of their Country.

'Tis my humble Opinion that, in the present Situation of Affairs, it is highly incumbent on every One who merits the Name of *Englishman*; that 'tis his Duty to exert every Endeavour in Favour of our Religion, our Sovereign, our Lives, our Liberties, and our Fortunes. All shou'd contribute to this glorious End; their Tongues, their Pens, their Purses, their Persons, accordingly as these can be most advantageously employ'd. Were our Island threatned with an universal Inundation, surely every thinking Man wou'd lend a helping Hand to oppose the raging Ocean. The like Efforts ought to be us'd, to stem the Flood of Popery and Tyranny now driving in; a Flood, which, was it to reach us, wou'd be more fatal than that of the Sea, since this wou'd soon put a Period to our Lives; whereas the other might preserve us, only to add one dire Calamity

mity to another; and, after dragging us through a Scene of Misery, very probably close it with a cruel Death.

That this is not merely a Flourish of the Pen, but strict Truth, is evident to every Person who has liv'd in *Romish* Countries, or is conversant in the History of Popery in all Countries, and consequently in *England*. Let our Annals speak how inhumanly the Protestants have been treated by *Romish* Governors! and then let every *Englishman* seriously ask himself, whether it wou'd not be the Extremes of Stupidity and Madness in Us; whether we shall not become a laughing Stock to the whole World, and our Memories be detested by latest Posterity, shou'd we look on supinely at this critical Juncture, and ignominiously expose ourselves again to the like Horrors?

Nor wou'd the Calamity, very probably, stop with us. Persons acquainted with the Division (as to Religion) of *Europe*, into *Protestant* and *Romish*,
know

PREFACE. xxxi

know that *England* is the Bulwark of the Former; and confequently, that fhould Popery be again eftablifhed in thefe Realms, Proteftantifm in general would fuffer confiderably, and perhaps be totally extirpated. The Reformation, the Purchafe and Security of which coft Millions of Lives, greatly damp'd the Spirit of Folly, Ignorance, Error, Fraud, Cruelty, and every Thing finifter, all which, till then, had rioted over the nobleft Part of the Globe; and introduc'd, inftead of them, Wifdom, Knowledge, Truth, Juftice, Humanity, and the round of amiable Virtues: Shall not the *Britons*, then, One and All, ftrive to repel an Evil whofe dire Influence would be fo extenfive? Alas! fhould we continue unactive at this Time, how will our Name appear in Hiftory? a defpicable Contraft to that of thofe *Greeks* and *Romans*, whofe Virtue, in bravely facrificing Life to fave their bleeding Countries, ftill crowns them with Glo-

ry,

PREFACE.

ry, and will do fo to the End of Time.

However, I no Ways doubt, but that Things will take a moſt auſpicious Turn, from the pleaſing View of them, at this Time, on the loyal Side. That a glorious Spirit is abroad, appears from the Aſſociations now forming in all the great Cities, and in the ſeveral Counties throughout the Kingdom; from the many eloquent and pathetic Diſcourſes deliver'd by Divines; from the Dramas exhibited on our Theatres; from the Writings inſerted daily in our News Papers; and even from the Frame of Mind and Temper of the common People, who, ſo far from wiſhing for a Revolution, ſeem to ſhudder at the bare Thoughts of it; and reſolutely determin'd to oppoſe the wicked Attempt with all their Might.

Having, myſelf, liv'd in *Romiſh* Countries, tho' not in Thoſe where the Inquiſition ſpreads its baleful In-fluence, I have been an Eye-Witneſs

to

PREFACE.

to the Tyranny, both civil and religious, under which they groan. I am certain that, in *France*, all Things pay an implicit Obedience to military and prieſtly Government. I have ſeen the Reſtraint laid there on the Preſs (that mighty Bulwark againſt Slavery) which is ſo ſevere, that not even the ſmalleſt Hand-Bill can be printed, till the Cenſor's Permiſſion, and afterwards that of the *Lieutenant de Police*, are obtain'd for this Purpoſe; both which muſt be ſpecified at the Bottom of it †.

I know that Soldiers are diſperſed every where in that Kingdom. That, at *Paris*, no Perſon, coming from the Country, can ſtep out of a Boat on the River *Seine*, without being imperiouſly aſk'd, by Fellows with Muſkets on their Shoulders, concerning contraband

---

† What Idea ought we to entertain of a Government, which ſuppreſs'd one of the nobleſt and moſt beautiful political Works ever writ (*The Adventures of Telemachus*) and baniſh'd its excellent Author?

Goods. That no Coach can enter the Metropolis in queſtion, without being firſt ſtopt and examin'd, in like manner, at the various Barriers; and that Paſſengers in Stage-Coaches, &c. are forc'd to alight, and are often ſearch'd: That Guards come to the ſeveral Scenes of public Diverſion; and there, like proud Taſk-maſters, command, about ten at Night, each Aſſembly to break up. That no Man dares to deliver himſelf, with becoming Freedom, on the only two Topicks which beſt deſerve enquiring into, (Religion and Government) without firſt turning about, and obſerving who may ſtand near him; upon pain of running the Hazard of having his whole Poſſeſſions ſeiz'd; of himſelf being dragg'd to Priſon, quite loſt to, and conceal'd from his Family and Friends; and there lead a diſmal Life, poſſibly during a long Courſe of Years, without his being ever brought to a Trial: And this at the ſole Will and Pleaſure of the Monarch, whoſe

Lettres

PREFACE.

Lettres de Cachets are dreadful as the Bolts from Heaven, and ftrike as fure.

Should I proceed in the Defcription of this arbitrary Government, how affecting wou'd be the Picture! Was an *Englifhman* of Humanity to be in *Paris*, whilft an endlefs Train of Galley-Slaves, with Iron Collars about their Necks, and faftened together by one common Chain, were paffing along the Streets (as is the Cuftom annually;) when, afking the Crime of One of them, fhould be told, that 'twas only for fhooting a Pigeon, how fincerely would he pity his Fate! But was he afterwards to furvey the Tyrannies of the Baftile, and the Horrors of the Torture; fhould he fee and hear a Criminal broke upon the Wheel, how greatly would his Eye and Ear be fhock'd! How ftrongly would he deteft the Severity of this Government, and with what Rapture blefs the Lenity of his Own!---Such is the dire State of Countries where Parliaments and Juries are un-

unknown; the want of which in *France*, some of its Natives, Men of great Honour and Learning, have secretly bewail'd to me; making, at the same Time, the highest Panegyric (from what they had read and heard) on the Freedom and Independence enjoy'd in *Great Britain*.

Should we now turn to that whimsical Pageant, the *Romish* Religion, how spacious a Field must this open for Satyr! a Religion which, besides its being exercis'd in an unknown Tongue, is a profane Spectacle; a Counterpart to the simple and decent Majesty of true Religion: A Worship which, so far from lifting the Mind to Things celestial, fills it with sublunary Ideas of Vanity and sensual Delights.---
To reflect, on one Hand, that Multitudes of young inconsiderate Women, are, in direct Opposition to the Dictates of Nature, and the Design of their Parents and Friends, seduc'd and inveigled, by artful Nuns, into Convents, where

PREFACE. xxxvii

where they are fentenc'd to languifh away Life, entirely cut off from the reft of Society; and with this only Confolation, of talking now and then through Iron Grates, like fo many Criminals, to Such as may be permitted to vifit them. To furvey the numberlefs fine Eftates engrofs'd by a Sett of ignorant (and often leud Drones) by thofe Locufts, the Monks; the fole Employment of many of whom is to riot in Dainties; and feemingly pray for the Profperity of the Laity, whilft they are fucking their Vitals. To confider that fuch Pefts, who thruft themfelves into all Companies, are triumphant in the Government; This protecting their Perfons and Houfes from any Infults, which might juftly be offer'd Them by the impoverifh'd, abus'd Laity, over whofe Minds they gain the moft powerful Afcendant, by means of Confeffion and Penance.----On the other hand, what fenfible *Englifhman* could forbear fmiling at the grofs Su-

PREFACE.

perftition which overfpreads *France*? To fee his Driver, as they are travelling on the Road, pull off his Hat very devoutly to a coarfe, rotten Piece of Wood, in form of a Crofs; or rufh, Madman like, into the Dirt, at the Approach of a Wafer carried in Proceffion: To obferve fome People kiffing a gilded old Shoe, whilft others are adoring a Tooth: Would not this naturally recall to his Mind Heathen *Egypt*, where Things, even below the moft groveling Reptile, were the Objects of public Worfhip? Tho' some few, of the *French* Priefts and Friars, may be weak enough to believe in all this idle Mummery; yet moft of them are as fenfible as we can be, of the fcandalous Impofition. Never did I behold a more glaring Picture of Hypocrify and Juggling, than in the leering Eye and rofy Countenance of the fat Benedictine, who fhow'd me the Treafures of St. *Denys*, near *Paris*; whilft he, Dr. *Fauftus* like, ftood pointing,

PREFACE.

ing, with his Wand, to the various splendid Trumpery, depofited in that immenfely rich Abbey.---This, however, is a Subject fit chiefly for Laughter. But were we to reflect on the cruel Spirit of this idolatrous Religion; could we view its Prifons, its Chains, its Daggers, its Halters, its Axes, its Flames!--- Alas! the Imagery is too dreadful for us to dwell upon.

I am not here inveighing againft *France* itfelf, or its Inhabitants: On the contrary, I know them to be a very complaifant People; Lovers of the polite Arts; and have been a Spectator of the many Bleffings indulg'd by Providence to their Country. My feveral Reflexions are levell'd only at their Religion and Government, both which their defpotic Mafter never fails to introduce wherever his Arms prevail; and all Perfons acquainted with Hiftory are fenfible, that a bad Religion and Government, can greatly impair the Face of the moft beautiful Country;

PREFACE.

can introduce Poverty in Places on which Plenty had, before, diffus'd her whole Store, and quite alter a People; as is finely exemplified by one of our most nervous Poets, with regard to the *Italians* and *Italy*, where he introduces the Goddess of LIBERTY thus speaking:

> ---- *The People mark*
> *Matchless, whilst fir'd by* ME, *to public Good;*
> *Inexorably firm, just, generous, brave,*
> *Afraid of nothing but unworthy Life;*
> *Elate with Glory, an heroic Soul*
> *Known to the vulgar Breast :— Behold them now*
> *A thin, despairing Number, all subdued;*
> *The Slaves to Slaves, by Superstition fool'd;*
> *By Vice unmann'd and a licentious Rule;*
> *In Guile ingenious, and in Murther brave.—*
> *Such in one Land, beneath the same fair Clime,*
> *Thy Sons,* OPPRESSION, *are; and such were*
>   *Mine.*
>   LIBERTY, (Part I.) a Poem by Mr. THOMSON.

'Tis certain that the natural Advantages of *France* would, under proper Regulations, be sufficient to make its Inhabitants very happy. But, unfortunately for them, a great Part of the extorted

extorted Treasures, which ought to be wholly employed for this excellent Purpose, are wafted to foreign Realms, merely to corrupt certain Politicians; and thus, instead of promoting the Welfare of Those from whom they are torn, serve only to increase the Weight of their Shackles, and aid the Views of their ambitious Statesmen. The Intrigues of these in the Divan; the Flame lighted up by them in *Germany*, and at present in *Scotland*, are but too flagrant Instances, among a Multitude which might be quoted, of this Truth.

There is no wise Man, if left to his own Choice, that wou'd prefer a pompous, but fluctuating Condition; to one decently-plain, yet permanent. He wou'd, on such an Occasion, consider the Dignity of his own Nature; and congratulate himself for being Owner of Possessions, which, tho' small, shou'd be secure from the Caprice, the rapacious Hand of arbitrary Power. Such a Man, tho' he might have been prevailed

vailed upon, by wily Arguments, to change his humble calm State, for a glittering but tumultuous One; yet a little Experience and Reflection wou'd soon convince him of his Error; wou'd make him pant for his former Way of Life; and say, with the rural Mouse in *Horace*,

haud mihi vitâ
Est opus hac, ait; & valeas: me silva, cavusque
Tutus ab insidiis tenui solabitur ervo.
Satir. VI. Lib. II.

Give me again, ye Gods, my Cave and Wood;
With Peace, let Tares and Acorns be my Food.
Cowley.

Those who have liv'd among the *French* (as I observ'd elsewhere) know that the Pride of their Politicians causes them to think meanly of most other Nations; that a false, tinsel Glory is the darling Object of their Politicks; and that the Felicity of the People is perpetually sacrific'd to its Pursuit. Very luckily for the Monarch, his deluded Subjects, even when rul'd with a Rod
of

PREFACE. xliii

of Iron, are yet fir'd with the warmeft Enthufiafm in his Favour; a glaring Inftance whereof, among others, is found in the late *Lewis* XIV. who, tho' he brought fo many Calamities upon his Kingdom, his Memory is ftill worfhipp'd; he ftill is called the *Grand Monarque*; and even Altars are embellifh'd with his Cypher, in *Mofaic*; as tho' Tyranny were an Attribute of the Deity.

But the Syftem of the genuine *Britifh* Politicks is built upon a much nobler Bafis. Their firft Aim is directed to the well-being of the feveral Individuals who live under their Influence. Their great Endeavour is to procure the People, by Induftry and Commerce, the various Bleffings which kind Nature has fpread over different Parts of the Globe. To enable them to pafs away Life, in full Eafe and Independance, as becomes rational Creatures; to fpeak and act with unlimited Freedom, except when this may be injurious to the

Caufe

Cause of Virtue, or endanger the Preservation of the Whole. These several Things being once firmly secured, their next View is to aggrandize the Monarch, by such Steps as are truly glorious, and to spread the *British* Name. Heroism (in the Ear of true *British* Politicks) is, at best, only an empty Sound, an *Ignis Fatuus*, except where solid Benefits may arise from it. Happily circumscrib'd by the Ocean, the *Britons* don't meditate Atchievements on the Continent; except the Possession of these, by their natural Enemies, may interfere with their Welfare. But when this is endanger'd, either by Foreign or Domestic Foes, they chearfully follow their King into the Field; are proud to share with him in Danger; ready to die in his Defence; or, in case of Victory, to hail him with the most joyful, the sincerest Acclamations. 'Tis then their Reverence rises almost to Adoration, when they image him as the Defender of their Lives and For-

Fortunes; as the Guardian of their Liberties; in a Word, as their mighty Friend.---To confider the *Englifh* and *French* in thefe oppofite Lights; the Former feem as a Community of Freemen, the Latter of Slaves.

The Political State of the *French* Nation, with regard both to Spirituals and Temporals, being fuch as I have tranfiently defcrib'd them in the foregoing Pages, I heartily rejoice in my being born an *Englifhman*; and almoft worfhip the Memory of thofe among our Anceftors, who hazarded their All; who waded thro' Seas of Blood, to free themfelves, and their Pofterity, from the dire Papal Yoke, with its infeparable Attendant, arbitrary Sway.

How fenfelefs then, how unnatural muft it be, for any *Englifhmen*, any Proteftant, to affift in forging Chains to load himfelf! For fuch wou'd inevitably be our Doom, fhou'd the Rebels triumph.

xlvi   *PREFACE.*

Our Histories evidently show, the eager Desire the *French* have entertained, from Time immemorial, to conquer our happy Island; and the many secret Machinations carried on by them, as well as the open Attempts made, for that horrid Purpose. *Great-Britain* is so delicious a Morsel, and its Power so formidable a Check to the iniquitous Views of the *French* Politicians; that 'tis no Wonder the Court of *Versailles* shou'd set every Engine at Work, in order to compass them. 'Tis well known that *France* has foster'd, in her Bosom, the Pretender to these Realms, together with his Sons, and their principal Adherents now fighting under his Standard in *Scotland*. What then may we naturally expect, shou'd the Rebels succeed, but *French* Government and Popery? To be treated even worse than the Natives of *France* themselves, since *Great-Britain* wou'd, in that Case, be a conquer'd
Pro-

PREFACE.

Province?----So extreme is my Abhorrence (from what I myself have seen in *Romish* Kingdoms) to the two Articles just mentioned, that I had infinitely rather (from the bottom of my Soul I speak it!) sink into the Grave, than live to be a Spectator of the dread Slavery, of the Desolation of my late envied, but then bleeding Country, was it possible for our own present excellent Constitution to be subverted.

But his Majesty, and the Fathers of the Nation, are now assembled; from the Wisdom and Unanimity of whose Councils, the most blissful Effects are justly expected; such an Unanimity, as will not only crush the present wicked Enterprize of our cruel and bigotted Enemies, by marching an invincible Force against them; but dishearten them from ever attempting the Like again. May the noble Spirit which now animates our Senate, diffuse itself far and wide, till the meanest *Plebeian* catch the salutary Enthusiasm! As the Enemy

Enemy is at our Gates, as our all is at Stake, nothing but Harmony among ourselves, and an entire Reliance on his Majesty's Generosity and Goodness can preserve us. There is no Room to doubt but that our Sovereign, strongly touch'd with the uncommon Zeal, and true Heroism of free-born Subjects, will, in return, continue a most tender Parent; will even anticipate their fondest Wishes; and indulge them in all Things which may have ever so little Tendency to promote their common Welfare; till he himself be ador'd like a second *Titus*, and his faithful, his happy *Britons* (as a Nation of Patriots) become the Envy and Wonder of every other People.

Struck with the inchanting Prospect at Hand, I humbly venerate the mysterious Ways of Providence, in frequently producing Good out of Evil; and thence please myself with imagining, that Heaven permitted this unnatural Rebellion to break out, like some peccant

cant Humour in the Body, with no other Design than to perfect the national Health and Vigour. Our bitter Enemies, the *French* and *Spaniards*, wildly suppos'd our Disaffection was become so universal, that not only *Scotland*, but all *England* and *Ireland*, wou'd, at the least Glimpse of the Pretender's Standard, instantly croud to fight under it. How happily (for us) they have been mistaken in their Conjectures, is apparent from the glorious Stand now making against the Rebels. Common and imminent Danger shall unite even Enemies; endear such one to another; and exasperate them against the Authors of it; whence I doubt not but that all our Countrymen, fir'd with due Indignation, both against the intestine Hydra, and those who breath'd Life into it; will, after subduing the Rebels, exert themselves with so much Bravery, both in the Field and on the Ocean, as shall make our foreign Enemies dearly repent their detestable, secret

PREFACE.

cret Machinations againſt us; and ſo completely diſcourage them from any future Enterprize of the like wicked kind, as may force them, not only to ſue for Peace; but to leave us in the undiſturbed Enjoyment of that greateſt of Bleſſings, during a long Courſe of Years.

> *Cantemus Auguſti tropæa*
> – – – – – – – –
> *Intraque præſcriptum Gelonos*
> *Exiguis equitare campis.*
> Horat. Ode IX. Lib. II.

October 20. 1745.

Directions to the Book-binder for placing the Cuts.

<blockquote>
The Portrait to face the Title.
The 1ſt Torture facing Page 62.
The 2d Torture facing Page 64.
The 3d Torture facing Page 66.
</blockquote>

IN Order to give the Reader all the Proof *possible*, in the Nature of the Thing, that I have really undergone the Tortures mention'd in the following Account of my Sufferings, I shew'd the Marks still remaining on my Arms and Legs, to Dr. Hoadly, Mr. Hawkins, and Mr. Cary, *Surgeons:* And I think myself particularly obliged to these Gentlemen, for the Leave they have given me to assure the Public, they were quite satisfied that the Marks must have been the Effect of very great Violence; and that, in their Situation, they correspond exactly to the Description of the Torture.

THE
HISTORY
OF THE
SUFFERINGS
OF
JOHN COUSTOS,
IN THE
INQUISITION at *Lisbon.*

INTRODUCTION.

I Can justly affirm, that 'twas not Vanity that induc'd me to publish the following accurate and faithful Relation of my Sufferings in the Inquisition of *Lisbon.* A strong Desire to justify myself with regard to the false Accusations

cufations brought by that Tribunal against me; as well as againſt the Brotherhood of Free-Maſons, of which I have the Honour to be a Member, were the chief Motives for my taking up the Pen. To this I will add, that I was very willing the whole World ſhould receive all the Lights and Informations I was capable of giving it, concerning the ſhocking Injuſtice, and the horrid Cruelties exerciſed in the pretended holy Office. Perſons who live in Countries where this Tribunal is had in Abomination, will, from the Peruſal of the following Sheets, have freſh Cauſe to bleſs Providence, for not fixing their Abode among the *Spaniards*, the *Portugueze*, or the *Italians*.

Such of my Readers as may happen to go and reſide in Countries where this barbarous Tribunal is eſtabliſh'd, will here find very ſalutary Inſtructions for their Conduct; and conſequently be leſs liable to fall into the Hands of the unrelenting Inquiſitors.

Thofe who, fpite of all the Precautions taken by them, may yet have the fad Misfortune to become their innocent Victims, will here be taught to avoid the Snares laid, in order to aggravate the Charge brought againft them. Thefe Snares ought the more to be guarded againft, as they are but too often fpread by the Inquifitors, merely to give a fpecious Air of Juftice and Equity to their iniquitous Profecutions.

For this Reafon, I fhall firft give an impartial Relation of my own Profecution and Sufferings, on account of my being a Free-Mafon. I fhall add, for the Satisfaction of the Curious, a fuccinct Hiftory of the pretended Holy-Office; its Origin; its Eftablifhment in *France*, *Italy*, *Spain* and *Portugal*; the Manner how it grafp'd, by infenfible Degrees, the fupreme Authority now exercifed by it, not only againft thofe confidered by it as Hereticks, but even againft *Roman* Catholicks: How Prifoners soners are proceeded againſt; the Tortures inflicted on them, in order to extort a Confeſſion; the Execution of Perſons ſentenced to die; with an accurate Deſcription of the *Auto da Fé*, or Goal-Delivery, as we may term it; together with the Sufferings of many Perſons who fell Victims to this Tribunal. I likewiſe will add a Plan of the Houſe of the Inquiſition at *Liſbon*, in which I was confin'd ſixteen Months, and whence I was remov'd to the Galley, as 'tis call'd, in that City. I will deſcribe this *Portugueze* Galley; and the Manner how Priſoners are lodged and treated in both thoſe Places.

I ſhall conclude with a Compariſon between the Methods employed by the Primitive Church, in order to ſuppreſs Hereſy, and convert Hereticks; and thoſe now made uſe of by the Inquiſitors (under the Cloak of Religion) indiſcriminately towards all Mankind, for the ſame Purpoſe, as they pretend. I ſhall relate what I myſelf was Eyewitneſs

witness of; and will annex the Remarks of many ill-fated *Roman* Catholicks, who, as well as myself, were the innocent Victims to this dreadful Tribunal.

I shall think it a Happiness, if the Relation which I now offer should be found of Use to the Publick; and shall consider it as a still greater, in case it may help to open the Eyes of those, who, hurried on by an indiscreet, or rather blind Zeal, think it a meritorious Work, in the Sight of Heaven, to persecute all Persons whose religious Principles differ from theirs.

PART I.

I Am a Native of *Berne* in *Switzerland*, and a Lapidary by Profession. In 1716, my Father came, with his whole Family to *London*; and as he proposed to settle in *England*, he got himself naturalized there.

After living twenty two Years in that City, I went, at the Sollicitation of a Friend, to *Paris*, in order to work in the Galleries of the *Louvre*. Five Years after I left this Capital, and removed to *Lisbon*, in Hopes of finding an Opportunity of going to *Brasil*, where I flatter'd myself that I should make my Fortune. But the King of *Portugal*, whom I address'd in order to obtain Permission for this Purpose, being informed of my Profession, and the Skill I might have in Diamonds, &c. his Majesty, by the Advice of his Council, refused

refused my Petition, upon the Supposition that it would be no ways proper to send a Foreigner, who was a Lapidary, into a Country abounding with immense Treasures, whose Value the Government endeavours, by all means possible, to conceal, even from the Inhabitants.

Whilst I was waiting for an Answer, from Court, to my Petition, I got acquainted with several substantial Jewellers, and other Persons of Credit, in *Lisbon*; who made me the kindest and most generous Offers, in case I would reside among them, which I accepted, after having lost all Hopes of going to *Brasil*. I now was settled in the abovemention'd City, equally to the Satisfaction of my Friends, my Employers, and myself; having a Prospect of gaining wherewithal, not only to support my Family with Decency, but also to lay up a Competency for old Age, could I but have escaped the cruel Hands of the Inquisitors.

I muft obferve, by the way, that the Inquifitors have ufurp'd fo formidable a Power in *Spain* and *Portugal*, that the Monarchs of thofe Kingdoms are no more, if I may be allowed the Expreffion, than as their chief Subjects. Thofe Tyrants don't fcruple to incroach fo far on the Privilege of Kings, as to ftop, by their own Authority, at the Poft-Office, the Letters of all whom they take it into their Heads to fufpect. In this manner I myfelf was ferv'd, a Year before the Inquifitors had order'd me to be feiz'd; the Defign of which, I fuppofe, was to fee, whether among the Letters of my Correfpondents, fome Mention would not be made of Free-Mafonry; I paffing for one of the moft zealous Members of that Art, which they refolved to perfecute, upon Pretence that enormous Crimes were committed by its Profeffors. However, tho' the Inquifitors did not find, by one of my intercepted Letters, that Free-Mafonry either ftruck

at

at the *Romish* Religion, or tended to disturb the Government; still they were not satisfied, but resolved to set every Engine at Work, in order to discover the Mysteries and Secrets of Masonry. For this Purpose, they concluded that it would be proper to seize one of the chief Free-Masons in *Lisbon*; and accordingly I was pitch'd upon, as being the Master of a Lodge; they likewise cast their Eye on a Warden, an intimate Friend of mine, Mr. *Alexander James Mouton*, a Diamond-Cutter, born in *Paris*, and a *Romanist*. He had been settled six Years, before his Seizure, at *Lisbon*, in which City he was a House-keeper; and where his Integrity, Skill and Behaviour were such, as gain'd him the Approbation of all to whom he was known. Mr. *Mouton* will soon settle in *London*.

The Reader is to be informed, that our Lodges, in *Lisbon*, were not kept at Taverns, &c. but alternately at the private Houses of chosen Friends. In these

these we used to dine together, and practice the Secrets of Free-Masonry.

As we did not know that our Art was forbid in *Portugal*, we were soon discovered by the barbarous Zeal of a Lady, who declar'd, at Confession, that we were Free-Masons; that is, in her Opinion, Monsters in Nature, who perpetrated the most shocking Crimes. This Discovery immediately put the vigilant Officers of the Inquisition upon the Scent after us; on which Occasion my Friend Mr. *Mouton* fell the first Victim, he being seized in manner following.

A Jeweller and Goldsmith, who was a Familiar of the Holy Office, sent a Friend, (a Free-Mason also) to Mr. *Mouton*; upon Pretence that he wanted to speak with him, about mending a Diamond weighing four Carrats. They agreed upon the Price; but as this was merely an Artifice, in order for our Familiar to know the Person of the said *Mouton*, he put him off for two

two Days; upon Pretence that he muſt firſt enquire of the Owner of the Diamond, whether he approved of the Price ſettled between them.

I happened to be at that Time with Mr. *Mouton*; a Circumſtance which gave the higheſt Joy to the Jeweller; finding that he had got a Sight, at one and the ſame time, of the very two Free-Maſons whom the Inquiſitors were determined to ſeize.

At our taking Leave, he deſired us to come together, at the Time appointed, to which we both agreed. The Jeweller then made his Report to the Inquiſitors, who ordered him to ſeize us, when we ſhould return about the Diamond in queſtion.

Two Days being elapſed, and my Buſineſs not permitting me to accompany Mr. *Mouton*, he went alone to the Jeweller, to fetch the Diamond, which was computed to be worth an hundred Moidores. The firſt Queſtion the Jeweller aſk'd, after the uſual Compliments, was,

was, "Where is your Friend *Couſtos?*" ---As this Jeweller had before ſhown me ſome precious Stones, which he pretended I ſhould go to work upon; Mr. *Mouton*, imagining he was deſirous of putting them inſtantly into my Hands, replied: "That I was upon "Change; and that, if he thought "proper, he would go and fetch me." However, as this Familiar, and five Subaltern Officers of the Inquiſition, who were along with him, were afraid of loſing half their Prey; they inveigled Mr. *Mouton* into the Back-Shop, upon Pretence of aſking his Opinion concerning certain rough Diamonds. After ſeveral Signs and Words had paſſed between them, the oldeſt of the Company riſing up, ſaid, he had ſomething particular to communicate to Mr. *Mouton*; upon which he took him behind a Curtain; when, enquiring his Name and Sirname, he told him that he was his Priſoner, in the King's Name.

Being

Being sensible that he had not committed any Crime for which he could justly incur his *Portugueze* Majesty's Displeasure, he gave up his Sword the Moment it was demanded of him. Immediately several trusty Officers of the Inquisition, called Familiars, fell upon him, to prevent his escaping: They then commanded him not to make the least Noise, and began to search him. This being done, and finding he had no Weapons, they asked whether he was desirous of knowing in whose Name he had been seiz'd? Mr. *Mouton* answering in the Affirmative: "We seize "you (said they) in the Name of the "Inquisition; and, in its Name, we "forbid you to speak, or murmur ever "so little." Saying these Words, a Door at the Bottom of the Jeweller's Shop, and which look'd into a narrow By-Lane, being open'd; the Prisoner, accompanied by a Commissary of the Holy Office, was thrown into a small Chaise, where he was so closely shut up, (it being Noon-day) that no one could fee him. This Precaution was ufed to prevent his Friends from getting the leaft Information concerning his Imprifonment; and confequently from ufing their Endeavours to procure his Liberty.

Being come to the Prifon of the Inquifition, they threw him into a Dungeon, and there left him alone; without indulging him the Satisfaction they had promifed, which was, to let him fpeak, immediately upon his Arrival, to the Prefident of the Holy Office; to know, from him, the Reafon of his Detainder. On the contrary, they were fo cruel to Mr. *Mouton*'s Reputation, as to fpread a Report he was gone off with the Diamond abovementioned. But how greatly were every one of his Friends furpriz'd and fhock'd at this Slander! As we all entertain'd the higheft Idea of his Probity, none of us would give Credit to this vile Report; whence we unanimoufly agreed, after duly weighing this Matter, to go in a

Body

Body to the Jeweller, who was the Owner of the Diamond, and offer him the full Payment of it; firmly perſuaded, that nothing but the moſt fatal and unexpected Accident could have made him diſappear thus ſuddenly, without giving ſome of his Friends Notice of it. However, the Jeweller refus'd our Offer in the politeſt Manner; aſſuring us at the ſame time, that the Owner of the Diamond was ſo wealthy a Man, that the Loſs of it would be but a Trifle to him.

But as Truth frequently breaks through all the Veils with which Falſhood endeavours to cloud her; this Generoſity in Perſons to whom we were, in a great meaſure, Strangers, made us ſuſpect ſome iniquitous, dark Act. Our Conjecture appear'd but too well grounded, from the ſevere Perſecution that was immediately rais'd againſt the Free-Maſons; I myſelf being ſeiz'd four Days after.

I perhaps should have escap'd their merciless Paws, had I not been betray'd, in the most barbarous Manner, by a *Portugueze* Friend of mine, as I falsely suppos'd him to be; and whom the Holy Office had order'd to watch me narrowly. This Man seeing me in a Coffee-house, the 5th of *March* 1742-3, between nine and ten at Night; went and gave Notice thereof to nine Officers of the Inquisition, who were lying in wait for me, with a Chaise, near that Place.

I was in the utmost Confusion, when, at my going out of the Coffee-house with two Friends, the above Officers seiz'd me only. Their Pretence for this was, that I had pass'd my Word for the Diamond which Mr. *Mouton* had run away with: That I must certainly be his Accomplice, since I had engag'd my Friends to offer to pay for the Diamond; all which (added they) I must have done in no other View than to conceal my Villainy. 'Twas to no
Purpose

Purpose that I alledged a thousand Things in my own Justification. Immediately the Wretches took away my Sword; hand-cuff'd me; forc'd me into a Chaise, drawn by two Mules; and in this Condition, I was hurried away to the Prison of the Inquisition.

But, spite of these Severities, and their commanding me not to open my Lips, I yet called aloud to one of my Friends (Mr. *Richard*) who had been at the Coffee-house with me, and was a Free-Mason; conjuring him to give Notice to all the rest of our Brethren and Friends, of my being seiz'd by Command of the Holy Office, in order that they might avoid the Misfortune which had befallen me, by going voluntarily to the Inquisitors, and accusing themselves.

I must take Notice, that the Inquisitors very seldom cause a Person to be seized in broad-day Light, except they are almost sure that he'll make no

Noise nor Resistance. This is a Circumstance they observe very strictly, as is evident from the Manner in which they took Mr. *Mouton*. Farther, they frequently make Use of the King's Name and Authority on these Occasions, to seize and disarm the pretended Criminal, who is afraid to disobey the Orders he hears pronounced. But as Darkness befriends Deeds of Villainy, the Inquisitors, for this Reason, usually cause their Victims to be secured in the Night.

The *Portugueze*, and many Foreigners, are so apprehensive of the sinister Accidents which often happen at *Lisbon* in the Night-time, especially to a Person who ventures out alone, that few are found in the Streets of this City at a late Hour.

I imagin'd myself so secure in the Company of my Friends, that I should not have been afraid of resisting the Officers in question, had the former lent me their Assistance. But unhappily

pily for me, they were ftruck with fuch a fudden Pannic, that every one of them fled; leaving me to the Mercy of nine Wretches, who fell upon me in an inftant.

They then forced me to the Prifon of the Inquifition, where I was deliver'd up to one of the Officers of this pretended Holy Place. This Officer prefently calling four Subalterns or Guards, thefe took me to an Apartment, till fuch Time as Notice fhould be given to the Prefident of my being catch'd in their Snare.

A little after, the abovemention'd Officer coming again, bid the Guards fearch me; and take away all the Gold, Silver, Papers, Knives, Sciffars, Buckles, &c. I might have about me. They then led me to a lonely Dungeon, exprefly forbidding me to fpeak loud, or knock at the Walls; but that, in cafe I wanted any Thing, to beat againft the Door, with a Padlock, that hung on the outward Door; and which

I could reach, by thrusting my Arm through the Iron Grates. 'Twas then that, struck with all the Horrors of a Place, of which I had heard and read such baleful Descriptions, I plunged at once into the blackest Melancholy; especially when I reflected on the dire Consequences with which my Confinement might very possibly be attended.

I pass'd a whole Day and two Nights in these Terrors, which are the more difficult to describe, as they were heightned at every little Interval, by the Complaints, the dismal Cries, and hollow Groans (ecchoing through this dreadful Mansion) of several other Prisoners, my Neighbours; and which the solemn Silence of the Night made infinitely more shocking. 'Twas now that Time seem'd to have lost all Motion, and these threescore Hours appear'd to me like so many Years.

However, afterwards calling to mind, that Grief would only aggravate my Calamity, I endeavoured to arm my
Soul

Soul with Patience; and to habituate myself, as well as I could, to Woe. Accordingly I rouz'd my Spirits; and banishing for a few Moments, these dreadfully-mournful Ideas, I began to reflect seriously, on the Methods how to extricate myself from this Labyrinth of Horrors. My Concioufness that I had not committed any Crime which could justly merit Death, would now and then soften my Pangs; but immediately after, dreadful Thoughts overspread my Mind, when I imag'd to myself the crying Injustice of which the Tribunal, that was to judge me, is accus'd. I consider'd that, being a Protestant, I should inevitably feel, in its utmost Rigours, all that Rage and barbarous Zeal could infuse in the Breast of Monks; who cruelly gloried, in committing to the Flames, great Numbers of ill-fated Victims, whose only Crime was their differing from them in religious Opinions; or rather who were obnoxious to those Tygers, merely because they thought worthily of human Nature; and had, in the utmost Detestation, these *Romish* Barbarities, which are not to be parallel'd in any other Religion.

These Apprehensions, together with the Reflections which Reason suggested to me, *viz.* that it would be highly incumbent on me to calm the Tumult of my Spirits, in order to prevent my falling into the Snares which my Judges would not fail to spread round me; either by giving them an Opportunity of pronouncing me guilty, or by forcing me to apostatize from the Religion in which I was born; these Things, I say, work'd so strongly on my Mind, that, from this Moment, I devoted my whole Thoughts to the Means of my Justification. This I made so familiar to myself, that I was persuaded neither the Partiality of my Judges; nor the dreadful Ideas I had entertained of their Cruelty, could intimidate me, when I should be brought before them; which

which I accordingly was, in a few Days, after having been shaved, and had my Hair cut by their Order.

I now was led, bareheaded, to the President and four Inquisitors, who, upon my coming in, bid me kneel down, lay my Right-hand on the Bible; and swear, in the Presence of Almighty God, that I would speak truly with regard to all the Questions they should ask me. These Questions were; my Christian and Sirnames, those of my Parents; the Place of my Birth, my Profession, Religion; and how long I had resided in *Lisbon*. This being done, they addressed me as follows:—' Son, you have
' offended and spoke injuriously of the
' Holy-Office, as we know from very
' good Hands; for which Reason we
' exhort you to make a Confession of,
' and to accuse yourself of the several
' Crimes you may have committed,
' from the Time you was capable of
' judging between Good and Evil, to
' the present Moment. In doing this,
' you

'you will excite the Compassion of
'this Tribunal, which is ever merciful
'and kind to those who speak the
'Truth.'

'Twas then they thought proper to inform me, that the Diamond mention'd in the former Pages, was only a Pretence they had employed, in order to get an Opportunity of seizing me. I now besought them, 'To let me
'know the true Cause of my Imprison-
'ment; that, having been born and
'educated in the Protestant Religion,
'I had been taught, from my Infancy,
'not to confess myself to Men, but to
'God, who, as he only can see into
'the inmost Recesses of the human
'Heart, knows the Sincerity or In-
'sincerity of the Sinner's Repentance,
'who confess'd to him; and being his
'Creator, 'twas he only could ab-
'solve him.'

The Reader will naturally suppose, that they were noways satisfied with my Answer;—'They declaring, that
'it

' it would be indispensably necessary for
' me to confess myself, what Religion
' soever I might be of; otherwise, that
' a Confession would be forced from
' me, by the Expedients the Holy Of-
' fice employed for that Purpose.'

To this I replied, ' That I had ne-
' ver spoke in my Life against the *Ro-*
' *mish* Religion; that I had behaved in
' such a Manner, ever since my living
' at *Lisbon*, that I could not be justly
' accus'd of saying or doing any Thing
' contrary to the Laws of the King-
' dom, either as to Spirituals or Tem-
' porals; that I had always imagin'd
' the Holy Office took Cognizance of
' none but those Persons who were
' guilty of Sacrilege, Blasphemy, and
' such like Crimes, whose Delight
' is to depreciate and ridicule the
' Mysteries receiv'd in the *Romish*
' Church, but of which I was noways
' guilty.' They then remanded me
back to my Dungeon, after exhorting
me to examine my Conscience.

Three

Three Days after, they sent for me, to interrogate me a second Time. The first Question they asked was; 'Whe- ther I had carefully look'd into my Conscience, pursuant to their Injunc- tion.' I replied, 'That after care- fully reviewing all the past Transacti- ons of my Life, I did not remember my having said or done any Thing that could justly give Offence to the Holy Office; that from my most tender Youth, my Parents, who had been forced to quit *France* for their Religion; and who knew, by sad Experience, how highly it concerns every one that values his Ease, never to converse on religious Subjects, in certain Countries; that my Parents, (I say) had advised me never to engage in Disputes of this kind, since they usually embitter'd the Minds of the contending Parties, rather than recon- cil'd them; farther, that I belong'd to a Society, compos'd of Persons of different Religions; one of the Laws of

'of which Society expresly forbid its
'Members ever to dispute on those
'Subjects upon a considerable Penalty.'
As the Inquisitors confounded the Word
Society with that of *Religion*; I assur'd
them, 'that this Society could be con-
'sider'd as a Religious one, no other-
'wise than as it obliged its several
'Members to live together in Charity
'and Brotherly Love, how widely so-
'ever they might differ in religious
'Principles.-----They then enquired,
'how this Society was called?'---I replied,--' That if they had order'd me
'to be seiz'd, because I was one of its
'Members, I would readily tell them
'its Name: I thinking myself not a
'little honoured in belonging to a So-
'ciety, which boasted several Christian
'Kings, Princes, and Persons of the
'highest Quality among its Members;
'and that I had been frequently in Com-
'pany with some of the latter, as one of
'their Brethren.'

Then one of the Inquisitors ask'd
me,

me, ' Whether the Name of this Soci-
' ety was a Secret ?' I anſwer'd, ' that
' it was not ; that I could tell it them
' in *French* or *Engliſh*, but was not able
' to tranſlate it into *Portugueze*.' Then
all of them fixing, on a ſudden, their
Eyes attentively on me, repeated, alternately, the Words *Free-Maſon*, or *Franc-
Maçon*. From this Inſtant I was firmly
perſuaded, that I had been impriſoned
ſolely on Account of Maſonry.

    They afterwards aſk'd, ' What were
' the Conſtitutions of this Society.' I
then ſet before them, as well as I could,
' the antient Traditions relating to this
' noble Art, of which (I told them)
' *James* VI. King of *Scotland**, had de-
' clared himſelf the Protector, and en-
' couraged his Subjects to enter among
' the Free-Maſons : That it appeared,
' from authentic Manuſcripts, that the
' Kings of *Scotland* had ſo great a Re-
' gard for this honourable Society, on

---

* *The Conſtitutions of the Free-Maſons*, &c. *for the Uſe of the Lodges*, by Dr. *Anderſon*, Page 38, *London*, 1723. Some other Paſſages here, are taken from the ſame Work.

' Account

' Account of the strong Proofs its
' Members had ever given of their Fi-
' delity and Attachment; that those
' Monarchs established the Custom a-
' mong the Brethren, of saying, when-
' ever they drank, *God preserve the
' King and the Brotherhood*: That this
' Example was soon followed by the
' *Scotch* Nobility and the Clergy, who
' had so high an Esteem for the Bro-
' therhood, that most of them entred
' into the Society.

' That it appeared from other Tra-
' ditions, that the Kings of *Scotland* had
' frequently been Grand-Masters of the
' Free-Masons; and that, when the
' Kings were not such, the Society were
' impower'd to elect, as Grand-Master,
' one of the Nobles of the Country,
' who had a Pension from the Sove-
' reign; and received, at his Election,
' a Gift from every Free-Mason in *Scot-*
' *land.*'

I likewise told them; ' That Queen
' *Elizabeth*, ascending the Throne of
' *England,*

'*England*, at a time that the King-
' dom was greatly divided by Factions
' and clashing Interests; and taking
' Umbrage at the various Assemblies of
' great Numbers of her Subjects, as not
' knowing the Designs of those Meet-
' ings; she resolved to suppress the As-
' semblies of the Free-Masons: How-
' ever, that, before her Majesty pro-
' ceeded to this Extremity, she com-
' manded some of her Subjects to enter
' into this Society, among whom was
' the Archbishop of *Canterbury*, Pri-
' mate of her Kingdom: That these,
' obeying the Queen's Orders, gave her
' so very advantageous a Character, of
' the Fidelity of the Free-Masons, as
' removed, at once, all her Majesty's
' Suspicions and political Fears: So that
' the Society have, ever since that time,
' enjoyed in *Great Britain*, and the
' Places subject to it, all the Liberty
' they could wish for, and which they
' have never once abus'd.'

They

They afterwards enquir'd, What
' was the Tendency of this So-
' ciety?'---I replied: 'Every Free-
' Mason is oblig'd, at his Admission,
' to take an Oath, on the Holy Gospel,
' that he will be faithful to the King;
' and never enter into any Plot or Con-
' spiracy against his sacred Person, or
' against the Country where he resides:
' And that he will pay Obedience to
' the Magistrates appointed by the
' Monarch.'

 I next declared, ' That Charity
' was the Foundation, and the Soul,
' as it were, of this Society; as it link'd
' together the several Individuals of it,
' by the Tye of fraternal Love; and
' made it an indispensable Duty to assist,
' in the most charitable Manner, with-
' out Distinction of Religion, all such
' necessitous Persons as were found true
' Objects of Compassion.'---'Twas then
they called me Liar; declaring ' that
' 'twas impossible this Society should
' profess the Practice of such good
Maxims,

'Maxims, and yet be so very jealous of its Secrets as to exclude Women from it.' The judicious Reader will perceive, at once, the Weakness of this Inference, which perhaps would be found but too true, were it applied to the inviolable Secrecy observed by this pretended Holy Office, in all its Actions.

They presently gave Orders for my being conveyed into another deep Dungeon; the Design of which, I suppose, was to terrify me compleatly; and here I continued seven Weeks. 'Twill be naturally suppos'd, that I now was overwhelmed with Grief. I will confess, that I then gave myself up entirely for lost; and had no Resource left but in the Almighty, whose Aid I implor'd continually with the utmost Fervency.

During my Stay in this miserable Dungeon, I was taken three Times before the Inquisitors. The first Thing they made me do was, to swear on the Bible, that I would not reveal the

Secrets of the Inquisition; but declare the Truth with regard to all such Questions as they should put to me: They added, ' That it was their firm Opi-
' nion that Masonry could not be found-
' ed on such good Principles as I, in
' my former Interrogatories, had affirm-
' ed; and that, if this Society of Free-
' Masons was so virtuous as I pretended,
' there was no Occasion of their con-
' cealing, so very industriously, the Se-
' crets of it.'

I told them, ' That as Secrecy na-
' turally excited Curiosity, this prompt-
' ed great Numbers of Persons to enter
' into this Society; That all the Mo-
' nies given by Members, at their Ad-
' mission therein, were employed in
' Works of Charity: That by the Se-
' crets which the several Members prac-
' tic'd, a true Mason instantly knew
' whether a Stranger, who would in-
' troduce himself into a Lodge, was re-
' ally a Free-Mason; that, was it not
' for such Precautions, this Society
' would

' would form confus'd Assemblies of
' all Sorts of People, who, as they were
' not obliged to pay Obedience to the
' Orders of the Master of the Lodge;
' it consequently would be impossible to
' keep them within the Bounds of that
' Decorum and good Manners, which
' are exactly observ'd, upon certain Pe-
' nalties, by all Free-Masons.

' That the Reason why Women were
' excluded this Society, was, to take
' away all Occasion for Calumny and
' Reproach, which would have been
' unavoidable, had they been admitted
' into it. Farther, that since Women
' had, in general, been always consi-
' der'd, as not very well qualified to
' keep a Secret; the Founders of the
' Society of Free-Masons, by their Ex-
' clusion of the other Sex, thereby
' gave a signal Proof of their Prudence
' and Wisdom.'

They then insisted, upon my reveal-
ing to them the Secrets of this Art.---
' The Oath (says I) taken by me at my
Admission,

'Admission, never to divulge them, directly or indirectly, will not permit me to do it; Conscience forbids me; and I therefore hope your Lordships are too equitable to use Compulsion.' They declar'd, 'That my Oath was as nothing in their Presence, and that they would absolve me from it.'--- 'Your Lordships (continued I) are very gracious; but as I am firmly persuaded, that it is not in the Power of any Being upon Earth to free me from my Oath, I am firmly determin'd never to violate it.' This was more than enough to make them remand me back to my Dungeon, where, a few Days after, I fell sick.

A Physician was then sent, who finding me exceedingly ill, made a Report thereof to the Inquisitors. These, upon their being informed of it, immediately gave Orders for my being removed from this frightful Dungeon, into another, which admitted some Glimmerings of Day-light. They appointed, ed, at the same time, another Prisoner to look after me during my Sickness, which, very happily, was not of long Continuance.

Being recovered, I was again taken before the Inquisitors, who asked me several new Questions with regard to the Secrets of Masonry; 'and whether, 'since my Abode in *Lisbon*, I had re-'ceived any *Portugueze* into the Socie-'ty?'---I replied, 'that I had not: 'That it was true, indeed, that Don '*Emanuel de Sousa*, Lord of *Calliaris*, 'and Captain of the *German* Guards, 'hearing that the Person was at *Lisbon*, 'who had made Duke *de Villeroy* a Free-'Mason by Order of the *French* King '*Lewis* XV. Don *Emanuel* had desir'd 'Mr. *de Chavigny*, at that Time Minister 'of *France* at the *Portugueze* Court, to 'enquire for me: But that, upon my 'being told that the King of *Portugal* 'would not permit any of his Subjects 'to be Free-Masons, I had desir'd two 'of the Brethren to wait on Mr. *de Cal-*
'*liaris*

' *liaris* abovemention'd, and acquaint
' him with my Fears; and to assure
' him, at the same time, that, in case
' he could obtain the King's Leave, I
' was ready to receive him into the
' Brotherhood; I being resolved not to
' do any thing which might draw up-
' on me the Indignation of his *Portu-*
' *gueze* Majesty: That Mr. *de Callia-*
' *ris* having a very strong Desire to en-
' ter into our Society, declared, that
' there was nothing in what I had ob-
' served with regard to his Majesty's
' Prohibition; it being (added this
' Nobleman) unworthy of the Regal
' Dignity, to concern itself with such
' Trifles. However, being certain that
' I spoke from very good Authority;
' and knowing that Mr. *de Calliaris*
' was a Nobleman of great Oecono-
' my; I found no other Expedient, to
' disengage myself from him, than by
' asking fifty Moidores for his Recep-
' tion; a Demand which, I was per-
' suaded, would soon lessen, or rather

'suppress at once, the violent Desire
'he might have to enter into the So-
'ciety of Free-Masons.'

To this one of the Inquisitors said:
'--- That 'twas not only true that his
'*Portugueze* Majesty had forbid any
'of his Subjects to be made Free-
'Masons; but that there had been
'fixed up, five Years before, upon the
'Doors of all the Churches in *Lisbon*,
'an Order from his Holiness, strictly
'enjoining the *Portugueze* in general,
'not to enter into this Society; and
'even excommunicated all such as
'were then, or should afterwards be-
'come Members of it.'----Here I besought them to consider, 'that if I
'had committed any Offence in prac-
'tising Masonry at *Lisbon*, 'twas mere-
'ly thro' Ignorance; I having resided
'but two Years in *Portugal*:---That,
'farther, the Circumstance just now
'mentioned by them, entirely de-
'stroyed the Charge brought against
'me, *viz.* of my being the Person
'who

'who had introduced Free-Masonry in
'*Portugal*.'---They answered, 'That
'as I was one of the most zealous Par-
'tizans of this Society, I could not
'but have heard, during my Abode
'in *Lisbon*, the Orders issued by the
'Holy Father.'--- I silenced them, by
'the Comparison I made between my-
'self and a Traveller, (a Foreigner)
'who, going to their Capital City, and
'spying two Roads leading to it, one
'of which was expresly forbid (upon
'Pain of the severest Punishment) to
'Strangers, tho' without any Indica-
'tion or Tokens being set up for this
'Purpose; that this Stranger, I say,
'should thereby strike accidentally,
'merely thro' Ignorance, into the for-
'bidden Road.'

They afterwards charged me with
'drawing away Roman Catholics, of
'other Nations, residing in *Lisbon*.---
I represented to them, 'That Roman
'Catholics must sooner be informed of
'the Pope's Injunction than I, who

'was a Protestant: That I was firmly of Opinion, that the severe Orders issued by the *Roman* Pontiff, had not a little prompted many to enter among the Free-Masons: That a Man, who was looked upon as a Heretic, was no ways qualified to win over Persons who considered him as such: That a Free-Mason, who professed the *Romish* Religion, was, I presumed, the only Man fit to seduce and draw away others of the same Persuasion with himself; to get into their Confidence; and remove successfully such Scruples as might arise in their Minds, both with regard to the injurious Reports spread concerning Masonry, and to the Pope's Excommunication; of which a vile Heretic entertained an Idea far different from that of the *Romanists*.'
----They then sent me back to my Dungeon.

Being again ordered to be brought before the Inquisitors, they insisted upon

upon my letting them into the Secrets of Masonry; threatning me, in case I did not comply.----I persisted, as before, ' in refusing to break my Oath;
' and besought them, either to write,
' or give Orders for writing, to his
' *Portugueze* Majesty's Ministers both
' at *London* and *Paris*; to know from
' them, whether any thing was ever
' done, in the Assemblies of the Free-
' Masons, repugnant to Decency and
' Morality; to the Dictates of the
' *Romish* Faith; or to the Obedi-
' ence which every good Christian
' owes to the Injunctions of the Mo-
' narch, in whose Dominions he lives.'
I observed farther, ' That the King of
' *France*, who is the eldest Son of the
' Church, and despotic in his Domi-
' nions, would not have bid his Favou-
' rite enter into a Society proscribed by
' Mother-Church; had he not been
' firmly persuaded that nothing was
' transacted in their Meetings, contrary
' to the State, to Religion, and to the
' Church.'

' Church.'---I afterwards referred them to Mr. *Dogood*, an *Englishman*, who was both a *Roman* Catholic and a Free-Mason.---This Gentleman had travelled with, and was greatly beloved by Don *Pedro Antonio*, the King's Favourite; and who (I observed farther) having ' settled a Lodge in *Lisbon* fifteen ' Years before, could acquaint them, ' in case he thought proper, with the ' Nature and Secrets of Masonry.---' The Inquisitors commanded me to be taken back to my dismal Abode.

Appearing again before them, they did not once mention the Secrets of Masonry; but took notice that I, in one of my Examinations, had said, *That it was a Duty incumbent on Free-Masons to assist the Needy*; upon which they asked, *Whether I had ever relieved a poor Object?*---I named to them a Lying-in Woman, a *Romanist*, who being reduced to the Extremes of Misery, and hearing that the Free-Masons were very liberal of their Alms, she addressed herself

to

to me, and I gave her a Moidore.---
I added, 'That the Convent of the
' *Franciscans* having been burnt down,
' the Fathers made a Gathering; and
' I gave them, upon the Exchange,
' three Quarters of a Moidore."--- I
declared farther, ' That a poor *Roman*
' Catholick, who had a large Family,
' and could get no Work; being in the
' utmost Distress, had been recom-
' mended to me, by some Free-Ma-
' sons; with a Request that we would
' make a Purse, among ourselves, in
' order to set him up again, and there-
' by enable him to support his Family:
' That accordingly we raised among
' seven of us who were Free-Masons,
' ten Moidores; which Money I my-
' self put into his Hands.'

They then asked me, *Whether I
' had given my own Money in Alms?*--
I replied, That these arose from the
' Forfeits of such Free-Masons as had
' not behaved properly in the Meetings
' of the Brotherhood.'---*What are the
Faults*

Faults (said they) *committed by your Brother-Masons, which occasion their being fined?* --- 'Those (said I) who
' take the Name of God in vain, pay
' the Quarter of a Moidore; such as
' utter any other Oath, or pronounce
' obscene Words, forfeit a new Cru-
' sade †; all who are turbulent, or
' refuse to obey the Orders of the Ma-
' ster of the Lodge, are likewise fined.
They remanded me back to my Dungeon, having first enquired the Name and Habitation of the several Persons hinted at a little higher; on which occasion I assured them, ' that the
' last-mentioned was not a Free-Ma-
' son; and that the Brethren assisted,
' indiscriminately, all Sorts of People,
' provided they were real Objects of
' Charity.'

   I naturally concluded, from the Behaviour of the Inquisitors, at my being brought before them four Days after, that they had enquired into the Truth

---

† A new Crusade is 2 *s*. 6 *d*. Sterling.

Truth of the several Particulars related above. They now did not say a Word concerning Masonry, but began to work with different Engines.

They then employed all the Powers of their Rhetoric to prove, ‘ That it
‘ became me to consider my Imprison-
‘ ment, by Order of the Holy Office,
‘ as an Effect of the Goodness of God;
‘ who (added they) intended to bring
‘ me to a serious Way of Thinking;
‘ and, by this means, lead me into
‘ the Paths of Truth, in order that I
‘ might labour efficaciously at the Sal-
‘ vation of my Soul. That I ought
‘ to know that Jesus Christ had said
‘ to St. *Peter*; *Thou art Peter, and*
‘ *upon this Rock I will build my Church,*
‘ *and the Gates of Hell shall not pre-*
‘ *vail against it* †; whence it was my
‘ Duty to obey the Injunctions of his
‘ Holiness, he being St. *Peter*'s Suc-
‘ cessor.’ --- I replied, with Spirit and Resolution, ‘ That I did not acknow-

† St. *Matthew*.

‘ ledge

'ledge the *Roman* Pontiff, either as
'Succeffor to St. *Peter*, or as infal-
'lible: That I relied entirely, with
'regard to Doctrine, on the Holy
'Scriptures, thefe being the fole Guide
'of our Faith: I befought them to
'let me enjoy, undifturbed, the Privi-
'leges allowed the *Englifh* in *Portugal*:
'That I was refolved to live and die in
'the Communion of the Church of
'*England*; and therefore that all the
'Pains they might take to make a Con-
'vert of me, would be ineffectual.'

Notwithftanding the repeated Declarations made by me, that I would never change my Religion, the Inquifitors were as urgent as ever. Encouraged by the Apoftacy of one of my Brother-Mafons, they flattered themfelves with the Hopes of prevailing upon me to imitate him; and, for this purpofe, offered to fend fome *Englifh* Friars to me, who (they faid) would inftruct me; and fo fully open my Eyes, that I fhould have a diftinct

View

View of my wretched Condition, which (they declared) was the more deplorable, as I was wholly infenfible of its Danger.

Finding me ftill immoveable, and that there was no Poffibility of their making the leaft Impreffion on me; the Indulgence which they feemed to fhow at the Beginning of my Examination, was fuddenly changed to Fury; they venting the moft injurious Expreffions; ' calling me Heretic, and ' faying that I was damn'd.'---Here I could not forbear replying, ' That I ' was no Heretic; but would prove, ' on the contrary, that they themfelves ' were in an Error.'---And now, raifing their Voice;---' *Take care* (cried they, ' with a Tone of Authority) *what you* ' *fay*.'--' I advance nothing, (replied I) ' but what I am able to prove.--Do you ' believe, (continues I) that the Words ' of our Lord Jefus Chrift, as found in ' the New Teftament, are true ?--They anfwer'd in the Affirmative.-- ' But ' what

'what Inference (said they) do you draw 'from thence? Be so good (adds I) as to 'let me have a Bible, and I will inform 'you concerning this.' I then laid before them the Passage where our Saviour says thus: *Search the Scriptures, for in them ye think ye have eternal Life, and they are they which testify of me* †. Likewise the following: *We also have a more sure Word of Prophesy; whereunto ye do well that you take heed* ‡ : 'And yet (says I) both the 'Pope and your Lordships forbid the 'Perusal of them; and thereby act 'in direct Opposition to the express 'Command of the Saviour of the 'World.--To this the Inquisitors replied, 'That I ought to call to mind, 'That our Saviour says to St. *Peter*, '(and in his Name, to all the Popes his 'Successors) *I will give unto thee the 'Keys of the Kingdom of Heaven; and 'whatsoever thou shalt bind on Earth,*

† St. *John*'s Gospel, v. 39.
2 Epist. St. *Peter*, i. 19.

shall

'shall be bound in Heaven: And what-soever thou shalt loose on Earth shall be loosed in Heaven †. That none but a Heretic, like myself, would dare to dispute the Authority and Infallibility of the Pope, who is Christ's Vicar here below: That the Reason of not allowing the Perusal of this Book was, to prevent the common People from explaining the obscure Passages contained therein, contrary to their true Sense; as was daily the Practice of Schismatics and Heretics like myself.'---I shall omit the other controversial Points that afterwards occurr'd, all which I answer'd to the best of my slender Abilities.

One Thing I can assure my Reader is, that the Inquisitors were not able to alter, in any manner, the firm Resolution I had taken, to live and die a Protestant: On the contrary, I can affirm, that their Remonstrances, and even Menaces, served only to strengthen

† St. Matthew, xvi. 19.

my Resistance; and furnish me abundant Proofs to refute, with Vigour, all the Arguments offer'd by them.

I acknowledge, that I owe this wholly to the divine Goodness, which graciously condescended to support me under these violent Trials, and enabled me to persevere to the End: For this I return unfeigned Thanks to the Almighty; and hope to give, during the Remainder of my Life, convincing Testimonies of the strong Impression which those Trials made on my Mind, by devoting myself sincerely to the Duties of Religion.

I was ordered back, by the Inquisitors, to my dismal Abode; after they had declar'd to me, 'That if I turn'd 'Roman Catholic, it would be of great 'Advantage to my Cause; otherwise, 'that I perhaps might repent of my 'Obstinacy when it was too late.'---I replied, in a respectful Manner, that I could not accept of their Offers.

A few Days after, I was again brought before the Prefident of the Holy Office, who faid, 'That the 'Proctor would read, in Prefence of 'the Court, the Heads of the Indict-'ment or Charge brought againft me.' --The Inquifitors now offer'd me a Counfellor, in cafe I defir'd one, to plead my Caufe.

Being fenfible that the Perfon whom they would fend me for this Purpofe, was himfelf an Inquifitor, I chofe rather to make my own Defence, in the beft Manner I could.---' I therefore de-'fir'd that Leave might be granted me, 'to deliver my Defence in Writing;' 'but this they refus'd, faying, 'That 'the Holy Office did not allow Prifon-'ers the Ufe of Pen, Ink and Paper.' I then begg'd they would permit me to dictate my Juftification, in their Prefence, to any Perfon whom they fhould appoint; which Favour was granted me.

The Heads of the Charge or Indictment brought against me, were; *That I had infring'd the Pope's Orders, by my belonging to the Sect of the Free-Masons;* this Sect being a horrid Compound of *Sacrilege, Sodomy,* and many other abominable *Crimes;* of which the inviolable *Secrecy* observ'd therein, and the *Exclusion of Women,* were but too manifest *Indications;* a *Circumstance* that gave the highest *Offence to the whole Kingdom:* And the said Coustos having refused to discover, to the *Inquisitors,* the true *Tendency* and *Design* of the *Meetings of Free-Masons;* and persisting, on the contrary, in asserting, that *Free-Masonry was good in itself:* Wherefore the *Proctor* of the *Inquisition* requires, that the said *Prisoner* may be prosecuted with the utmost *Rigour;* and, for this *Purpose,* desires the Court would exert its whole *Authority,* and even proceed to *Tortures,* to extort from him a *Confession,* viz. that the several *Articles* of which he stands accus'd, are true.

The

The Inquisitors then gave me the above Heads, ordering me to sign them, which I absolutely refused. They thereupon commanded me to be taken back to my Dungeon, without permitting me to say a single Word in my Justification.

I now had but too much Leisure to reflect on their Menaces; and to cast about for Answers to the several Articles concerning Masonry, whereof I stood accus'd; all which Articles I remembred but too well.

Six Weeks after, I appeared in Presence of two Inquisitors, and the Person whom they had appointed to take down my Defence; which was little more than a Recapitulation of what I before had asserted with regard to Masonry.

' Your Prisoner (says I to them) is
' deeply afflicted, and touch'd to the
' Soul, to find himself accus'd (by the
' Ignorance or Malice of his Enemies)
' in an infernal Charge or Indictment,
' before

' before the Lords of the Holy Office,
' for having practic'd the Art of Free-
' Masonry, which has been, and is still,
' rever'd, not only by a considerable
' Number of Persons of the highest
' Quality in Christendom; but like-
' wise by several Sovereign Princes and
' Crown'd Heads, who, so far from
' disdaining to become Members of this
' Society; submitted, engag'd, and
' oblig'd themselves, at their Admissi-
' on, to observe religiously the Consti-
' tutions of this noble Art; noble, not
' only on account of the almost infi-
' nite Number of illustrious Personages
' who profess it; but still more so,
' from the Sentiments of Humanity
' with which it equally inspires the
' Rich and Poor, the Nobleman and
' Artificer, the Prince and Subject:
' For these, when met together, are
' upon a Level as to Rank; are all
' Brethren, and conspicuous only from
' their Superiority in Virtue: In fine,
' this Art is noble, from the Charity
' which

' which the Society of Free-Masons
' profeſſedly exerciſes; and from the
' fraternal Love with which it ſtrongly
' binds and cements together the ſeveral
' Individuals who compoſe it, without
' any Diſtinction as to Religion or
' Birth.

' Your Priſoner thinks it very hard,
' to find himſelf thus become the Victim
' of this Tribunal, merely becauſe he
' belongs to ſo venerable a Society.
' The Rank and exalted Dignity of
' many, who have been, and ſtill are,
' Members thereof; ſhould be conſi-
' der'd as faithful and ſpeaking Wit-
' neſſes, now pleading in his Defence,
' as well as in that of the Brotherhood,
' ſo unjuſtly accus'd.

' Farther; could any one ſuppoſe,
' without ſhowing the greateſt Raſh-
' neſs, or being guilty of the higheſt
' Injuſtice; that Chriſtian Princes, who
' are God's Vicegerents upon Earth,
' would not only tolerate, in their Do-
' minions, a Sect that ſhould favour the

' abo-

'abominable Crimes of which this Tri-
'bunal accuses it; but even be Ac-
'complices therein, by their entring
'into the Society in question.

'What I have said above, should be
'more than sufficient to convince your
'Lordships, that you are quite mis-
'inform'd as to Masonry; and oblige
'you to stop all Prosecution against
'me. However, I will here add some
'Remarks, in order to corroborate my
'former Assertions; and destroy the
'bad Impressions that may have been
'made on your Lordship's Minds con-
'cerning Free-Masonry.

'The very strict Enquiry made into
'the past Life and Conduct of all Per-
'sons that desire to be received among
'the Brotherhood; and who are ne-
'ver admitted, except the strongest
'and most indisputable Testimonies
'are given, of their having liv'd irre-
'proachably; are farther Indications,
'that this Society is noways guilty of
'the Crimes with which it is charged
'by

'by your Tribunal; the utmost Pre-
'cautions being taken, to expel from
'this Society, not only wicked Wretches,
'but even disorderly Persons.

'The Works of Charity, which the
'Brotherhood think it incumbent on
'themselves to exercise, towards such
'as are real Objects of Compassion,
'and whereof I have given your Lord-
'ships some few Instances; show like-
'wise, that 'tis morally impossible for
'a Society, so execrable as you have
'describ'd that of the Free-Masons to
'be, to practice a Virtue so generally
'neglected; and so opposite to the
'Love of Riches, at this Time the
'predominant Vice, the Root of all
'Evil.

'Besides, wicked Wretches set all
'Laws at Defiance; despise Kings,
'and the Magistrates established by
'them for the due Administration of
'Justice. Abandon'd Men, such as
'those hinted at here, foment Insur-
'rections and Rebellions; whereas
Free-

'Free-Masons pay an awful Regard to
'the Prince in whose Dominions they
'live; yield implicit Obedience to his
'Laws; and revere, in the Magistrates,
'the sacred Person of the King, by
'whom they were nominated; root-
'ing up, to the utmost of their Power,
'every Seed of Sedition and Rebellion;
'and being ready, at all Times, to ven-
'ture their Lives, for the Security both
'of the Prince, and of his Govern-
'ment.

'Wicked Wretches, when got to-
'gether, not only take perpetually the
'Name of God in vain; but blas-
'pheme and deny him: Whereas the
'Free-Masons punish very severely,
'not only Swearers, but likewise such
'as utter obscene Words; and expel
'from their Society, all Persons har-
'den'd in those Vices.

'Wicked Wretches contemn Religi-
'gions of every kind; turn them into
'Ridicule; and speak in Terms un-
'worthy of the Deity worshipp'd in
'them.

' them. But the Free-Masons, on the
' contrary, observing a respectful Si-
' lence on this Occasion, never quar-
' rel with the religious Principles of a-
' ny Person; but live together in frater-
' nal Love, which a Difference in O-
' pinion can noways lessen.'--- I clos'd
my Defence with the four Verses following, compos'd by a Free-Mason.

Thro' trackless Paths each Brother strays,
  And naught sinister can entice:
Now Temples, We, to Virtue raise;
  Now Dungeons sink, fit Place for
    Vice.

To which I added (in my own Mind.)

But here, the contrary is found;
  Injustice reigns, and killing Dread:
In rankling Chains bright Virtue's bound;
  And Vice, with Triumph, lifts its
    Head.

' Such,

'Such, my Lords (continued I) are our
'true and genuine Secrets. I now wait,
'with all possible Resignation, for
'whatever you shall think proper to
'decree; but still hope, from your
'Equity and Justice, that you will not
'pass Sentence upon me, as tho' I was
'guilty of the Crimes mention'd in the
'Indictment ; upon the vain Pretence,
'that inviolable Secrecy can be observ'd
'in such Things only as are of a cri-
'minal Nature.'

I was remanded back to my usual Scene of Woe, without being able to guess what Impression my Defence might have made on my Judges. A few Days after I was brought before his Eminence Cardinal *da Cunha*, Inquisitor and Director General of all the Inquisitions dependent on the *Portugueze* Monarchy.

The President, directing himself to me, declar'd, 'That the Holy Tribu-
'nal was assembled, purposely to hear
'and determine my Cause: That I
'there-

'therefore should examine my own 'Mind; and see whether I had no 'other Arguments to offer in my Ju- 'stification.'—I replied, 'That I had 'none; but relied wholly on their 'Rectitude and Equity.'—Having spoke these Words, they sent me back to my sad Abode, and judged me among themselves.

Some time after, the President sent for me again; when, being brought before him, he order'd a Paper, containing Part of my Sentence, to be read. I thereby was doom'd to suffer the Tortures employ'd by the Holy Office, for refusing to tell the Truth, (as they falsely affirm'd;) for my not discovering the Secrets of Masonry, with the true Tendency and Purpose of the Meetings of the Brethren.

I hereupon was instantly convey'd to the Torture-Room, built in Form of a square Tower, where no Light appear'd, but what two Candles gave: And, to prevent the dreadful Cries and shocking

shocking Groans of the unhappy Victims, from reaching the Ears of the other Prisoners, the Doors are lin'd with a sort of Quilt.

The Reader will naturally suppose that I must be seiz'd with Horror, when, at my entring this infernal Place, I saw myself, on a sudden, surrounded by six Wretches, who, after preparing the Tortures, strip'd me naked (all to Linen Drawers); when, laying me on my Back, they began to lay hold of every Part of my Body. First, they put round my Neck an Iron Collar, which was fastned to the Scaffold; they then fix'd a Ring to each Foot; and this being done, they stretched my Limbs with all their Might. They next wound two Ropes round each Arm, and two round each Thigh, which Ropes pass'd under the Scaffold, through Holes made for that Purpose; and were all drawn tight, at the same time, by four Men, upon a Signal made for this Purpose.

The

The Reader will believe that my Pains muſt be intolerable, when I ſolemnly declare, that theſe Ropes, which were of the Size of one's little Finger, pierc'd through my Fleſh quite to the Bone; making the Blood guſh out at the eight different Places that were thus bound. As I perſiſted in refuſing to diſcover any more than what has been ſeen in the Interrogatories above; the Ropes were thus drawn together four different Times. At my Side ſtood a Phyſician and Surgeon, who often felt my Temples, to judge of the Danger I might be in; by which Means my Tortures were ſuſpended, at Intervals, that I might have an Opportunity of recovering myſelf a little.

Whilſt I was thus ſuffering, they were ſo barbarouſly unjuſt as to declare, that, were I to die under the Torture, I ſhould be guilty, by my Obſtinacy, of Self-Murder. In fine, the laſt Time the Ropes were drawn tight, I grew ſo exceedingly weak, occaſioned

casioned by the Blood's Circulation being stopp'd, and the Pains I endur'd, that I fainted quite away; insomuch that I was carried back to my Dungeon, without my once perceiving it.

These Barbarians finding that the Tortures above describ'd could not extort any farther Discovery from me; but that, the more they made me suffer, the more fervently I address'd my Supplications, for Patience, to Heaven; They were so inhuman, six Weeks after, as to expose me to another kind of Torture, more grievous, if possible, than the former. They made me stretch my Arms in such a Manner, that the Palms of my Hands were turn'd outward; when, by the Help of a Rope that fastned them together at the Wrist, and which they turn'd by an Engine; they drew them gently nearer to one another behind, in such a Manner that the Back of each Hand touch'd, and stood exactly parallel one to the other; whereby both my Shoulders

ders were diflocated, and a confiderable Quantity of Blood iffued from my Mouth. This Torture was repeated thrice; after which I was again taken to my Dungeon, and put into the Hands of Phyficians and Surgeons, who, in fetting my Bones, put me to exquifite Pain.

Two Months after, being a little recover'd, I was again conveyed to the Torture-Room; and there made to undergo another Kind of Punifhment twice. The Reader may judge of its Horror, from the following Defcription thereof.

The Torturers turn'd twice round my Body, a thick Iron Chain, which, croffing upon my Stomach, terminated afterwards at my Wrifts. They next fet my Back againft a thick Board, at each Extremity whereof was a Pulley, through which there run a Rope, that catch'd the Ends of the Chains at my Wrifts. The Tormentors then ftretching thefe Ropes, by Means of a Roller, press'd or bruis'd my Stomach, in proportion as the Ropes were drawn tighter. They tortur'd me, on this Occasion, to such a Degree, that my Wrists and Shoulders, were put out of Joint.

The Surgeons, however, set them presently after; but the Barbarians not having yet satiated their Cruelty, made me undergo this Torture a second time, which I did with fresh Pains, tho' with equal Constancy and Resolution. I then was remanded back to my Dungeon, attended by the Surgeons who dress'd my Bruises; and here I continued till their *Auto da Fé*, or Goal Delivery.

The Reader may judge, from the faint Description, of the dreadful Anguish I must have labour'd under, the nine different Times they put me to the Torture. Most of my Limbs were put out of Joint, and bruis'd in such a Manner, that I was unable, during some Weeks, to lift my Hand to my
Mouth;

Mouth; my Body being vaftly fwell'd, by the Inflammations caus'd by the frequent Diflocations. I have but too much Reafon to fear, that I fhall feel the fad Effects of this Cruelty fo long as I live; I being feiz'd, from time to time, with thrilling Pains, with which I never was afflicted, till I had the Misfortune of falling into the mercilefs and bloody Hands of the Inquifitors.

The Day of the *Auto da Fé* being come, I was made to walk in the Proceffion, with the other Victims of this Tribunal. Being come to St. *Dominic*'s Church, my Sentence was read, by which, I was condemn'd to the Galley (as 'tis term'd) during four Years.

Four Days after this Proceffion, I was conveyed to this Galley; and join'd, on the Morrow, in the painful Occupations of my Fellow Slaves. However, the Liberty I had of fpeaking to my Friends, after having been depriv'd of even the Sight of them, during my tedious, wretched Abode in the Prison of the Inquisition ; the open Air I now breath'd ; with the Satisfaction I felt in being freed from the dreadful Apprehensions which always overspread my Mind, whenever I reflected on the Uncertainty of my Fate ; these Circumstances united, made me find the Toils of the Galley much more supportable.

As I had suffer'd greatly in my Body, by the Tortures inflicted on me in the Prison of the Inquisition, of which the Reader has seen a very imperfect, tho' faithful Narrative, in the foregoing Sheets ; I was quite unfit to go about the painful Labour that was immediately allotted me, *viz.* the carrying Water (an hundred Pounds Weight) to the Prisons of the City. But the Fears I was under, of being expos'd to the Inhumanity of the Guards or Overseers who accompany the Galley-Slaves, caus'd me to exert myself so far beyond my Strength, that, twelve Days after, I fell grievously sick. I then

then was sent to the Infirmary, where I continued two Months. During my Abode in this Place, I was often visited by the *Irish* Friars belonging to the Convent of *Corpo Santo*, who offer'd to get my Release, provided I wou'd turn *Roman* Catholic. I assur'd them, that all their Endeavours would be fruitless; I expecting my Enlargement from the Almighty alone, who, if he, in his profound Wisdom thought proper, would point out other Expedients for my obtaining it, than my becoming an Apostate. Being unable, after this, to go through the Toils to which I had been sentenc'd, I was excus'd, by my amply rewarding the Overseers. 'Twas now that I had full Leisure, to reflect seriously on the Means of obtaining my Liberty; and, for this Purpose, desired a Friend to write to my Brother-in-law, Mr. *Barbu*, to inform him of my deplorable State; and to intreat him, humbly to address the Earl of *Harrington* in my Favour; my Brother-in-law having the Honour to live in his Lordship's Family. This Nobleman, whose Humanity and Generosity have been the Theme of infinitely abler Pens than mine, was so good as to declare, that he would endeavour to procure my Freedom. Accordingly, his Lordship spoke to his Grace the Duke of *Newcastle*, one of the Principal Secretaries of State; in order to supplicate for Leave, from our Sovereign, that his Minister at *Lisbon*, might demand me, as a Subject of *Great Britain*.

His Majesty, ever attentive to the Felicity of his Subjects, and desirous of relieving them in all their Misfortunes, was so gracious as to interpose in my Favour. Accordingly his Commands being dispatch'd to Mr. *Compton*, the *British* Minister at *Lisbon*; that Gentleman demanded my Liberty of the King of *Portugal*, in his *Britannic* Majesty's Name; which accordingly I obtain'd the latter End of *October* 1744. The Person who came and freed me from the

the Galley, by Order of the Inquisitors, took me before them. The President then told me, that Cardinal *da Cunha* had given Orders for my being releas'd. At the same time, he bid me return to the Holy Office in three or four Days.

I could perceive, during this Interval, that I was followed by the Spies of the Inquisition, who kept a watchful Eye over my Behaviour, and the Places I frequented. I waited upon our Envoy, as likewise upon our Consul, whom I inform'd of the Commands which had been laid upon me at the Inquisition; and those Gentlemen advis'd me to obey them. They caution'd me, however, to take a Friend with me, in order that he might give them Notice, in case I should be seiz'd again. I accordingly return'd to the Inquisitors five Days after, when the President declar'd; ' That the Tri-
' bunal would not permit me to conti-
' nue any longer in *Portugal*; and
' therefore

'therefore that I must name the City
'and Kingdom whither I intended to
'retire.'---' As my Family, (replied I)
'is in *London*, I design to go thither
'assoon as possible.'---They then bid
me embark in the first Ship that should
sail for *England*; adding, that the Instant I had found one, I must inform
them of the Day and Hour I intended
to go on board, together with the
Captain's Name and that of his Ship.

A Report prevail'd, some Days after, that one of the Persons, seiz'd by
the Inquisition for Free-Masonry; and
who obtain'd his Liberty by turning
Roman Catholic, had been so indiscreet
as to divulge the Cruelties exercised in
this Tribunal.

I now imagin'd that Prudence requir'd me to secure myself from a second Persecution. As there was, at
this time, no *English* Ship in the Port
of *Lisbon*, I waited upon Mr. *Vantil*,
the Resident of *Holland*, and besought
him to speak to the *Dutch* Admiral,

to

to admit me on board his Fleet. The Resident, touch'd with my Calamities, hinted my Request to the Admiral, who generously complied with it. I then went, together with a Friend, and inform'd the Inquisitor, that I designed to embark for *England*, in the *Damietta*, commanded by Vice-Admiral *Cornelius Screiver*, who was to sail in a few Days. Upon the Inquisitor's enquiring the exact time when I intended to go on board; I replied, at nine a-clock the next Morning. He then bid me come to him precisely at that Hour; adding, that he would send some Officers of the Inquisition to see me on Ship-board.

These Orders giving me great Uneasiness, I waited upon the several Gentlemen abovementioned; when telling them the Injunctions laid upon me, they advised me to act very cautiously on this Occasion. I therefore thought it would be safest for me to go on board immediately, without
giving

giving any Notice of it to the Inquiſitors. We lay at Anchor, after this, near three Weeks before *Liſbon*.

The Inquiſitor no ſooner found that I failed coming to him at the time appointed, in order to be conducted to the Ship, than he ſent out about thirty Spies. Nine of theſe coming to enquire after me, at the Houſe where I us'd to lodge, ſearch'd it from Top to Bottom; examining every Trunk, Cheſt of Drawers and Cloſet. But their Endeavours to find me being fruitleſs, ſome Officers of the Inquiſition getting into a Boat, row'd ſeveral times round the three *Dutch* Men of War lying at Anchor. Theſe Officers imagin'd, that if I was on board, and conſequently in a Place of Security, I ſhould not be afraid of ſhowing myſelf; a Circumſtance that would have put an End to their Search, which coſt them ſome Pains and Expence. As I did not gratify their Curioſity, and we weigh'd Anchor

Anchor a few Days after, I know not whether they continued it.

Their Search was fo open, both at the Houfe where I had lodg'd, as well as at other Places, that I was foon inform'd of it; at which I fhould have been delighted, had not my Joy been damp'd by the Apprehenfions I was under, left my dear Friend, Mr. *Mouton*, the Companion of my Sufferings and Tortures, merely on Account of Free-Mafonry, fhould likewife fall a Victim to their Barbarity. Speaking concerning him to the Admiral, he, with the utmoft Humanity, gave me Leave to fend for him on board. He coming accordingly next Day, was receiv'd, with great Satisfaction, by the whole Ship's Company, efpecially by myfelf; I having a peculiar Efteem for him, which I fhall ever entertain.

We fet fail two Days after. We had Occafion to obferve, during our whole Voyage, the true Pleafure which a generous Mind feels, in doing a humane Action,

Action, and in protecting the Unhappy. This was particularly conspicuous in the Admiral, he ordering the utmost Care to be taken of us, all the Time we were on board his Ship; he sometimes condescending to admit us to his Table, when he would talk to us with the utmost Familiarity. This Distinction won us the Civility of every Person in the Ship, which continued till our Arrival at *Portsmouth*, where we landed; without having been put to a Farthing Expence during the whole Voyage.

All these Favours, so generously bestowed by the Admiral, call aloud for the strongest Acknowledgments of Gratitude with regard to that Gentleman.

To conclude, I arriv'd in *London* the 15th of *December* 1744, after a long and dangerous Voyage.

I here return Thanks, with all the Powers of my Soul, to the Almighty, for his having so visibly protected me from that infernal Band of Friars, who

who employed the various Tortures mention'd in the former Pages, in order to force me to apoftatize from my holy Religion.

I return our Sovereign, King *George* II. (the Inftrument under Heaven for procuring me my Liberty) the moft dutiful and moft refpectful Thanks, for his fo gracioufly condefcending to interpofe in favour of an ill-fated Galley-Slave. I fhall retain, fo long as I have Breath, the deepeft Senfations of Affection and Loyalty for his Sacred Perfon ; and will be ever ready to expofe my Life, for his Majefty and his moft auguft Family.

PART II.

Origin of the Inquisition, and its Establishment in various Countries.

THE *Roman* Pontiffs employed every Expedient, and set every Engine at Work (among which none has serv'd their Purpose better than Religion) in order to increase their Authority. Pretending to be the Successors of St. *Peter*, they ascrib'd to themselves Characteristicks of Holiness superior even to that of the Apostles; and were so extravagant as even to boast their being infallible. Monarchs, infatuated with this pretended Sanctity of the Popes, whom they consider'd as Deities upon Earth, and Dispensers of celestial Blessings; strove to rival

one

one another in bestowing Territories, &c. upon these Pontiffs, in Hopes of obtaining their Favour; adding such extensive Privileges, that these Pontiffs became, at last, the Arbiters of crown'd Heads, who did not discover, till it was too late, that they themselves were become Slaves to the Papal Authority.

Some of these Princes being oppress'd with the Weight of their Chains, and desirous of throwing them off, resisted the Will of the Holy Father, and thereupon were declar'd Hereticks, and excommunicated. Nor did these Popes stop here; for, if these Kings persisted in their Obstinacy, they were dethron'd, and their Dominions given to others, who readily offer'd to pay the Obedience claim'd by the See of *Rome*.

The Emperors, jealous to see the *Roman* Pontiffs, and their Adherents, extend their Authority so far beyond its just Limits; did all that lay in their Power to restrain and reduce it within
narrower

narrower Bounds. About the Middle of the XI. Century, there broke out violent Contests between them, which rag'd above fifty Years.

The Emperors and Popes, being thus exasperated against each other, no longer acted in Concert, in order to suppress Heresy; so that these Commotions gave Occasion to the starting up of several new Heresiarchs. Hitherto the latter had oppos'd only the Mysteries; but now, leaving the Mysteries, they attack'd Morality and Discipline, and especially the Papal Authority. This was more than sufficient to open the Eyes of the Court of *Rome*, with regard to the Danger which threatned it, in case a speedy Remedy should not be found, in order to check these Hereticks, before the Contagion was become general; under Favour of the Disputes subsisting between the Emperor and the Pope.

But

But as thefe Heretics, or rather Enemies to the Pontifical Authority of *Rome*, were exceedingly numerous; not to mention their being fupported, clandeftinely, by Kings; the Popes were forc'd, at firft, to wink at, and even tolerate thofe Heretics, till fuch time as an Opportunity might offer, for fuppreffing, or rather rooting them out. For this Reafon, the *Roman* Pontiffs now contented themfelves with writing often to the Princes, Magiftrates and Bifhops; exhorting them to exert their utmoft Endeavours, in order to extirpate the Enemies of the See of *Rome*. However, Princes and Magiftrates took little pains to check them; whether it were that they did not care to facrifice a Set of People who were of fo much Ufe to them, in order for reftraining the Papal Authority, and increafing their own; or, whether they did not think them fo criminal as the Popes pretended; or whether Politics, which often vary according to Times and Interefts, terests, caus'd them to consider these Heretics as Persons whom it was incumbent on them to tolerate, for their own Advantage.

The Bishops, either through Indolence, or because they were not strong enough to oppose the Stream, were equally unsuccessful, whereby Heretics became so powerful, that they, at last, were able to make head against the See of *Rome*.

The *Arnaldists* †, who were among these, reduc'd the Popes to the greatest Distresses; they forcing them, more than once, to quit *Rome*, and to seek an Asylum elsewhere, in order to secure themselves from their Fury.

† So called from *Arnaldus* of *Brescia*, a Heretic in the Twelfth Century. He inveighed against the Temporalities of the Church; and even against Baptism and the Lord's Supper. This Heresiarch, after exciting many Troubles in *Brescia* and *Rome*, was hang'd in the latter City, anno 1155, and his Ashes thrown into the *Tyber*.---The Followers of *Anthony Arnauld* (the *Jansenists*) were also nam'd *Arnaldists*.

The

The *Waldenses* and *Albigenses*, (People of *France*) rifing up after them, were no lefs Enemies to the Authority ufurp'd by the *Roman* Pontiff, nor lefs zealous in attacking it : And the Protection indulg'd thofe People by *Raymond* Count *de Touloufe*, and by Counts *de Foix* and *de Comminges*, caus'd them to be ftill more enterprifing and more formidable.

Pope *Innocent* III. a Man of a great Spirit, and fortunate in his Enterprizes, form'd a Defign of promulgating a Crufade † againft them, which had been

---

† The Caufades were military Expeditions, eftablifh'd againft the Infidels, and firft preach'd by *Peter* the Hermit. Tho' the Glory of God was the pretended Motive for them ; yet many went merely out of venal Views, and others through Fear of being reproached with Cowardice. Such as defigned to enlift among the Crufaders, diftinguifh'd themfelves, from other People, by wearing Croffes of different Colours, on their Clothes, according to their Nation : The Croffes of the *Englifh* being white ; of the *French*, red ; of the *Germans*, black, &c. Eight Crufades were undertaken for the Conqueft of the Holy Land ; the firft *Anno* 1095, in the Coun-

been of such vast Service to his Predecessors, in order for increasing their Authority; however, he thought it necessary, before he carried Things to Extremities, to have Recourse to gentle Methods. For this Purpose, he sent into *Languedoc*, Missionaries, at whose Head were *Dominic*, a Native of *Old Castile*, who had lately founded an Order of Friars, called from his Name; together with the blessed *Peter* of *Chateauneuf* (as he is term'd by the *Romanists*) who was butcher'd at *Toulouse*, anno 1200. And now the Pope, resolving to employ temporal Weapons against them, published a Crusade, whereby Indulgences were granted to all such as should take up Arms, or fur-

cil of *Clermont*; and the last, under St. *Lewis* of *France*, *Anno* 1268. The *Cistercians* first form'd the Plan of these Crusades. A History, in *French*, of the Crusade against the *Albigenses*, was published at *Roan*, in 1703. About the Middle of the 12th Century, a Crusade of *Saxons* was establish'd against the Heathens of the North.—Religion was as much a Fashion, in these dark Times, as Clothes, &c.

nish Monies, &c. for assisting this Enterprize against the *Mahommedans*; for thus he call'd those People, to inflame still more the Crusaders against them †. The Papal Arms being successful, *Raymund* submitted himself (about the Year 1209) and gave, as a Pledge of his Word, seven of the chief Towns in *Provence* and *Languedoc*. On this Occasion several Cities were taken, and the most shocking Cruelties practic'd; numberless Multitudes of the Inhabitants being put to the Sword, without Distinction of Age or Sex. Counts *de Foix*, *de Comminges*, and *de Beziers*, afterwards followed the Example of *Raymund*. Count *Simon de Montfort*, General of the Church, signaliz'd himself but too much at the Head of these Crusaders.

The Origin of the Inquisition is thus related, by *Fleury*, in his Ecclesiastical

† This *Innocent* having been a famous Lawyer, he, by a Quirk, pronounc'd these Hereticks to be *Mahommedans*, viz. because both were Enemies to the Church.

Hiftory. 'In 1198, *Innocent* III.
'fent into the Southern Provinces of
'*France*, two *Ciftercian* Monks, *Rei-*
'*nier* and *Gui*, to convert the Mani-
'chees, with which thofe Parts fwarm'd;
'to excommunicate the obftinate; and
'to command the Lords to confifcate
'the Poffeffions of the Excommuni-
'cated; to banifh them, and punifh
'them with Severity: Impowering, at
'the fame time, *Reinier* to force the
'Lords likewife; to excommunicate
'them, and put their Lands under
'Sequeftration. Thefe Commiffioners,
'thus fent againft the Hereticks, were
'afterwards called Inquifitors.' The
Jefuits of *Trevoux* obferve, that 'the
'Council of *Narbonne*. held in 1235,
'and that of *Beziers* in 1246, gave
'the Dominicans (Inquifitors) in the
'Provinces of *Arles*, of *Aix*, of *Em-*
'*brun*, and *Vienne*, a Rule or Ordi-
'nance, confifting of 37 Articles;
'and thefe were the Bafis of the Pro-
'cedures which have been obferv'd,
'fince

'since that time, in the Tribunals of
'the Inquifition.'

Some imagine, that They find the Origin of the Inquifition, in a Conftitution made by Pope *Lucius*, in the Council of *Verona*, Anno 1184; becaufe that he commands Bifhops to examine perfonally, or by Commiffioners, People fufpected of Herefy; diftinguifhes the various Degrees of Perfons fufpected, convicted, penitent or relapfed, for All whom different Punifhments are enacted; and that, after the Church has employ'd, againft Criminals, fpiritual Weapons, It delivers them over to the fecular Arm, in order for corporal Punifhments to be inflicted on them; Experience having fhown, (fays my *Romifh* Author) that feveral Chriftians, and particularly the new Hereticks of this Age, little regarded Ecclefiaftical Cenfures, and defpis'd thefe fpiritual Punifhments.---
What bleffed Times were thefe, when

Ignorance, Superstition and Tyranny sway'd the Earth!

Dawn of the Inquisition in France, with the farther Contests between the Emperors and Popes.

THIS open War against the *Albigenses* and *Waldenses*, was followed by the Establishment of the Inquisition, which compleated the Destruction of the unhappy People in question. It had been founded, a little before, by Pope *Innocent* III. under the Direction of *Dominic*, on whom the Title of Saint was bestow'd.

This Pope, reflecting that, what open Force soever might be exerted against them, still vast Numbers would carry on their Worship in private, thought it necessary to establish a standing and perpetual Remedy; that is, a Tribunal compos'd of Men whose sole Occupation should be the searching after, and punishing Heretics. This Tri-

Tribunal was nam'd, *The Inquifition*, and *Dominic* was the firft Inquifitor.

Dominic having been fent, as was obferv'd, to *Touloufe*, to convert the Heretics, took up his Refidence at the Houfe of a Nobleman of this City, infected with Herefy. However, our Miffionary found Means to bring him back to the Church; after which the Nobleman devoted his Houfe, with his Family, to St. *Dominic* and his Order. The Tribunal of the Inquifition was eftablifhed in this Place, which is ftill call'd, *The Houfe of the Inquifition.*

It may hence be concluded, that *Dominic* was the firft Inquifitor, and *Touloufe* the firft City where the Inquifition was fettled. Some fay that this was in 1208, and others in 1212, or 1215; but whichfoever may be the true Æra, is of no great Confequence.

Thefe Inquifitors had, at firft, no particular Tribunal, their Function being only to enquire or fearch after Hereticks (whence the Former received their Name;)

Name;) to examine into their Number, Strength and Riches; which being done, they made a Report thereof to the Bishops, who, as yet, were the only Persons authoriz'd to take Cognizance of spiritual Matters. On these Occasions, the Inquisitors us'd to urge the Prelates to excommunicate and punish all Hereticks who should be impeach'd.

Pope *Innocent* being wholly dissatisfied with the Indolence of the Bishops, and their Officials (Judges) whose Zeal he thought much too lukewarm against Heretics; imagin'd that he perceiv'd, in the *Dominican* and *Franciscan* Friars, whose Orders were but lately founded, all the Qualities requisite for directing this new Establishment. The Monks of those Orders were fir'd with an implicit and boundless Zeal for the Court of *Rome*, and wholly devoted to its Interests. They had full Leisure to pursue that glorious Work, as this would be their only Business. They were descended from the Dregs of the People; and

and had no Kindred, as it were, or any other Tie which might check the Rigours of this Tribunal; they were severe and inflexible; the Solitude and austere Life profess'd by them, and of which they seem'd already tir'd; the Meanness of their Dress and Monasteries, so widely different from their present State; and especially the Humility and mendicant Life to which they, perhaps, had too heedlesly devoted themselves; these Things, I say, rendred them exceedingly fit for the Office in question, which, (in the Opinion of the Pontiffs) would soften the Asperity of their Vows, and sooth their Ambition, some Seeds whereof were still left in their Minds. The *Roman* Pope having thus made sure of a Set of People, so firmly devoted to his Service, and so admirably well qualified to exercise an Employment, whose chief Characteristicks are extreme Severity and Cruelty; sought for every Opportunity to increase their Authority, by by appointing them a particular Tribunal, where they were to fit, hear, and pronounce Sentence againſt Hereſies and Heretics, as Judges delegated by him, and repreſenting his Perſon.

This Pope firſt enlarg'd their Authority, by empowering them to beſtow Indulgences, to publiſh Cruſades, and to excite Nations and Princes to join the Cruſaders, and march forth in order to extirpate Hereſy.

In 1244, the Emperor *Frederick* II. increaſ'd their Power much more, by publiſhing four Edicts in *Pavia*. He therein declar'd himſelf Protector of the Inquiſitors; decreed, that the Clergy ſhould take Cognizance of Hereſy, and the Lay Judges proſecute Hereticks, after that the former had heard them. He likewiſe enacted, That all obſtinate Hereticks ſhould be burnt; and ſuch as repented, impriſon'd for Life. The Reaſon why *Frederick* teſtified ſo much Zeal for the Chriſtian Religion was, in order to deſtroy

ſtroy the Report which the Popes, with whom he had been engag'd in violent Conteſts, ſpread, throughout all the Courts of Chriſtendom, *viz*. that he intended to renounce the Chriſtian Religion and turn *Mahommedan*. This, very probably, induc'd him to exert himſelf with greater Severity againſt the Hereticks than any of his Predeceſſors; he being the firſt Emperor who ſentenc'd to Death all Hereticks without Diſtinction.

But whatſoever might be the Motive which prompted this Prince to act with ſo much Rigour againſt them, 'tis certain, that if he, at firſt, reap'd ſome little Advantage from this Conduct, it afterwards prov'd infinitely prejudicial both to himſelf and his Succeſſors; ſince the Court of *Rome* turn'd the Power with which he had inveſted the Inquiſitors, both againſt this Monarch and the Friends to the Empire, not only in *Italy* but in other Countries. In a word, the *Roman* Pontiffs us'd us'd their utmost Endeavours to increase this Authority, in order to make the Inquisitors still more formidable; they exerted this Power, with most Success, under the specious Pretence of Religion; by making all who presum'd to oppose the temporal Authority of the Popes, feel the dire Effects of it: A Circumstance so notorious, that 'twere almost needless to deduce Examples of it.

In 1322, Pope *John* XXII. caus'd the Inquisitors to prosecute *Matthew Visconti*, Sovereign of *Milan*. He accordingly was declar'd an Heretic; after which a most rigorous Bull was issued, forbidding all the Princes of *Italy* to have any Correspondence with him or his Subjects. 'Tis nevertheless well known, that his Heresy amounted to no more than his having too warmly espous'd, as a Vassal of the Empire, the Cause of the Emperor *Lewis* of *Bavaria*, with whom the

Pope was resolv'd to quarrel, on groundless Pretences.

The same Year the Bishop of *Ferrara*, a very zealous Inquisitor, prosecuted the House of *Este*, and declar'd it heretical; tho' it was guilty of no other Crime, than its having recover'd back *Ferrara*, which the Popes had seiz'd.

But, without going so far for Examples; 'tis well known that, whilst the Disputes subsisted between the *Spanish* Monarch *Philip* II. and Pope *Paul* IV. merely about Temporalities; this Pontiff did not scruple to declare openly, before his whole Court, that the above King of *Spain* was no less an Heretic than the Emperor *Charles* V. his Father. But not being able to enforce his Accusation by Arms, against so powerful a Prince; the Papal Reproaches serv'd to no other Purpose than to evince to the whole Earth, that all are consider'd as Heretics in *Rome*, who

who oppose the temporal Interests of this Court.

These Examples demonstrate, that *Frederick* II. did not know his true Interest; or else did not pursue it, when he so inconsiderately enlarg'd the Power of the Inquisitors; he having but too much Cause, some time after, to repent his Indulgence in this Particular. As this Monarch had been engag'd in Contests with many Popes, *Gregory* XI. was resolved to keep no Measures with him. Accordingly he excommunicated *Frederick* thrice; stirred up *Lombardy*, and Part of *Germany*; and issued a Crusade against him, as tho' he had been a Heretic and an Infidel. 'Tis even added, that he caus'd the Emperor's Son to rebel against his Father.

The Death of this Pope allow'd the Monarch a little Time for breathing. However, *Innocent* IV. would not give up any of the Pretensions which his Predecessors claim'd on the Emperor, tho'

tho' the former, when Cardinal, had profefs'd the ftricteft Friendfhip for him: A Circumftance which fhows, that Ambition is not to be reftrain'd by any Motive; that the Court of *Rome* ever purfues its Plans invariably; and that nothing can prevail with it to defift from an Enterprize wherein its Glory and Intereft are concern'd.

On the other hand, the Emperor being refolved not to make the leaft Ceffion, attack'd the new Pope fo very vigoroufly, before he had time to raife Money, that he was forc'd, at laft, to quit *Rome*, and remove to *Lyons*; where he fummon'd a General Council, to debate on the Excommunication and depofing of the Emperor. 'Twas to no Purpofe that the Kings of *England* and *France* interceeded for that Monarch. The Emperor did all that lay in his Power to prevent the ill Confequences with which this Step taken by the Pope might be attended; he fubmitting to Conditions that were moft pain-

painful to himself, and most satisfactory to the Pontiff; he promising, among other Things, to march an Army into the Holy Land, and never to return from thence. But now Part of *Germany* revolted from him. The General Council of *Lyons* confirm'd the deposing of the Emperor, and elected another, who died soon after. On Occasion of the Divisions which broke out in *Germany*, the opposite Factions elected two Emperors, who did not live long. Their Death was followed by an Interregnum during twenty Years, occasioned by the Feuds between the Princes of the Empire.

The Emperor *Frederick* lost his Crown, by giving up, through an inconsiderate Zeal, such Prerogatives as were his only Security; and the surrendring up of which occasion'd all his Misfortunes. The Interregnum was too advantageous to the Pope, for him to endeavour to put an End to it, which he might very easily have done. But
he

he pretended, on the contrary, that the *Roman* Pontiffs had a juft Claim to all the Imperial Rights, during this Interregnum; and, in Confequence thereof, that he himfelf had a Right to act, in *Lombardy*, and in many other Parts of *Italy*, as tho' he had been abfolute Monarch thereof.

Pope *Innocent* was too cunning not to fnatch the very favourable Opportunity which now offer'd. The *Dominicans* and *Francifcans* had ferv'd him fo very effectually; and difcover'd fo much Zeal, Courage and Intrepidity, by expofing themfelves to the utmoft Dangers in their Exercife of the Employment of Inquifitors; that the Pope thought it would be imprudent to intruft the Tribunal in queftion to any other Set of Men; a Tribunal he was determin'd to fettle in *Italy*, and in all other Countries into which his Authority might force it: A Bull was accordingly iffued for that Purpofe, which, however, met with ftrong Oppofition.

Here follows what other Authors say, concerning the Rise of the Inquisition in *France*. *Du Cange* tells us, that the Inquisitors were established in this Country about the Year 1229, against the *Waldenses*, by the Council of *Toulouse* ; which Inquisitors were chosen from among the *Dominicans* ; and some were appointed under *Francis* I. against the *Lutherans*; and established, by a Bull of Pope *Clement* VII. in 1525. Tho' the Tribunal of the Inquisition was never settled in *France*, after the same Manner as in *Spain* and *Italy*, yet Inquisitors were delegated to *France*, during many Years, by the Pope ; to preserve the Purity of Doctrine, and keep the People obedient to the Church. Twelve Years after the Death of St. *Dominic*, Pope *Gregory* IX. named two Friars of the same Order, *anno* 1233, to exercise the like Functions ; and this Apostolical Commission was perpetuated, not only in the Convent of *Toulouse*, but extended to several

several other Convents in the Kingdom. One of the Commissaries nominated in the Cause of the Templars, was the Inquisitor General in *France.* We find by *l'Histoire de la Pucelle d'Orléans* [the Maid of *Orleans*] that, *anno* 1430, *John Magistri* Vicegerent [Substitute] of *John Goverant,* Inquisitor of the Faith, was one of her Judges; that 35 Years after, *John Brehal* (who was an Inquisitor) and some Prelates, deputed by Pope *Calixtus,* declar'd her innocent. It does not appear that there were, from this Time till the Reign of *Francis* I. any Inquisitors (of this Sort) in *France*; whether it were that the Popes did not think them necessary, in an Age when Errors were in a great Measure rooted up; or that the then reigning Princes, being more jealous of the Regal Authority than their Predecessors, would not suffer any Infringement (as this seem'd to be) of the Liberties of the *Gallican* Church. See *Father* Bouhours'

Life of St. Ignatius, *Book* II. This Author obferves farther, that, under *Francis* I. *Matthew Ori,* was rais'd, by Pope *Clement* VII. to the Employment of Inquifitor, on occafion of the Herefies of *Germany.*---There are now no Footfteps of the Inquifition left in *France,* except in *Touloufe,* where there is an Inquifitor, a *Dominican*; but then his Authority relates only to the examining of Books concerning Doctrine.

The Inquifition would have been introduc'd into this Kingdom under *Francis* II. had not the excellent *Mighel de l'Hofpital,* Chancellor of *France,* ftrongly oppos'd that Defign. ' When
' the paffing the Edict of the Inquifition
' of *Spain* came before Chancellor *de*
' *l'Hofpital*; as he knew that the
' Members of the Privy Council and
' the Parliaments had confented to it,
' he drew up another Edict, in which
' he temper'd Matters fo happily, and
' gave fuch excellent Reafons for this,
' that

'that even the *Guises*, tho' strong Advocates for the Tribunal in question, approv'd his Opinion; and even brought over the *Spanish* Ministry to the same Way of thinking, notwithstanding that these were very desirous that *France* should be modell'd and govern'd as *Spain* was.' This was done in *May* 1560, in the Town of *Romorantin* †.

Establishment of the Inquisition in Italy.

THIS Affair being debated in the Pope's Council, such Difficulties were started in it, as could not easily be surmounted. The first was, that as the Bishops had a Right to take Cognizance of heretical Matters, and to decree ecclesiastical Punishments, they would be very loth to part with a Prerogative which they had enjoy'd from Time immemorial.

'Twas consider'd that these Prelates would not fail to represent;---That as

† *La Planche, Histoire de Francois* II. p. 361.

they,

they, in quality of Bishops, were invested with Authority and Means sufficient to force the Inquisition upon People; they consequently were better able to exercise it than Friars whose Orders were but lately instituted, and who were little known.---That they had been before but too much injur'd, by the Monks having been withdrawn from their Jurisdiction, to which those Monks, by the ancient Canons, and the Usages of the Church, were subject; so that the Bishops were not only forbid to be Judges over their respective Flocks, but perhaps even of themselves, in Articles of so much Importance as those of Doctrine and Belief:---That it would be using too much Violence, to endeavour to establish the Inquisition by Force, and in direct Opposition to the Prelates:---That tho' the common People paid the highest Reverence to the Holy See, they yet had no less for the Bishops; an indisputable Proof whereof was, the supreme Authority of the Church,

Church, which all Nations afcrib'd to General Councils. In fine, That the *Roman* Pontiff ow'd Part of his Authority to the Bifhops, thofe having divefted themfelves of theirs, in his Favour; and therefore, that it highly concern'd the See of *Rome*, to continue in the ftricteft Union and Friendfhip with the other Bifhops.

The fecond Obftacle was, that the Inquifition could not be fettled in the manner projected, without depriving the Lay Judges of the Power ever enjoyed by them, *viz.* of profecuting Hereticks; and which had been confirm'd to them by the laft Ordinances of the Emperor *Frederick* II. even at the Time that he increas'd the Authority of the Inquifitors. Hence there was Reafon to fear, that both Princes and Bifhops would not only declare ftrongly againft it, but excite their Subjects to oppofe the Eftablifhment of a new Tribunal, by which they were to be no longer fubject to their natural Judges, but

but to a Tribunal more harsh and more severe than that under which they were born.

Farther, it might naturally be expected, that the several Princes of Christendom would support their Magistrates in all the Authority with which they had invested them; and not permit the supreme Authority, to which the Power of Life and Death belongs, to be shar'd with the Inquisitors.

Tho' these Obstacles seem'd insurmountable at first Sight, they yet were not thought so by the Pope, who resolv'd to establish the Inquisition at all Events; and who, for this Purpose, hit upon such Expedients as seem'd to obviate all the Objections which had been rais'd against it.

The first Expedient was, that the Bishops should be declar'd Judges of Hereticks in Conjunction with the Inquisitors, and nothing be transacted without their Privity: That they should

should be present at Trials, whenever they thought proper. However, that the Inquisitors should take every Opportunity which offered, in order to draw the supreme Authority into their own Hands: That the Consequence of this would be, that as most of the Bishops were fonder of the Profits of their Ministry, than sollicitous to discharge its Duties, they would be contented with having their Authority divided in this Manner. To conclude, that the Bishops perceiving, insensibly, that nothing was left them except the bare Shadow or Name of Judges over Hereticks, they would resign their whole Authority to the Inquisitors, who then might be at full Liberty to act, dependent on, and under the sole Influence of the Court of *Rome*.

As to Princes and Magistrates, 'twas concluded, that it would be so much the easier to prevail with them not to oppose the Designs of the *Roman* Pontiff, as he, on Occasion of the Interregnum

regnum of the Empire, enjoy'd an almost absolute Authority in *Italy:* That it would be proper to seize this favourable Juncture, as such another might, perhaps, not present itself soon : That, in order to obtain the Consent of Magistrates, it would be requisite to make them a specious Satisfaction, in the same manner as had been done with regard to the Bishops. That, for this Purpose, the Magistrates should be permitted to chuse the subaltern Officers of the Inquisition ; should have leave to appoint an Assessor or Assistant-Judge to the Inquisitors, whenever these should search after Heretics, in Places subordinate to the Magistrate. In fine, that the Inquisitors might be more or less tenacious, according to the Opposition they should meet with, provided this related to Points of little or no Importance.

These Difficulties being removed, another started up, which was the greater, as Money was its Object ; and this

this was, to find out Means for defraying the various Expences of the Inquisition; such as the Salaries of the Inquisitors, with the Wages of the subaltern Officers and Goalers; to provide for the Subsistance of Prisoners, the Execution of Sentences, and other Matters, without which it would be impossible for the Inquisition to subsist with Honour. To supply what was wanting on this Occasion, 'twas resolved that the several Corporations in which this Tribunal might be introduc'd, should be tax'd certain Sums, in order to support it.

Matters being thus far adjusted, cunning and trusty Persons were sent into the Provinces, to pave the Way to, and win the Approbation of the several Inhabitants with regard to this intended Tribunal. The *Dominicans* were appointed Inquisitors in *Lombardy*, *Romagna*, and *Marca Anconitana*.

As the Motives, for establishing the Inquisition, were represented in the most favourable

favourable Colours ; as People had not yet experienc'd its Cruelties, nor even suspected them, it was introduc'd with little Opposition. This gave an Opportunity to the Pope, who had an admirable Talent at taking Advantage of such Conjunctures as favour'd his Designs, to direct a Bull † to the Magistrates and Communities of the various Towns where the Inquisition had been settled. This Bull consisted of thirty one Chapters, which were so many Statutes or Regulations for establishing the Tribunal in question. The Pontiff added two express Orders on this Occasion ; First, for registring, without Delay, these Regulations in all the Offices where Records are kept, notwithstanding any Opposition to the contrary ; he

† Bulls are properly Letters, with a Leaden Seal, issued out of the Chancery of *Rome* ; and answer to the Letters Patents, Edicts, &c. published by Order of temporal Princes. When these Bulls are by Way of Grant or Favour, the Leaden Seal is dependant from silken Strings ; but if it relates to some judicial or executory Act, the Seal hangs by a hempen Cord.

reserving

reserving to himself the Power to judge of the Validity of these Oppositions. By the second Order, the Inquisitors were empower'd to put Places under an Interdict, and to excommunicate all Persons who should refuse submission to those Regulations. However, as the Pope was afraid of hazarding too much his Authority, he endeavour'd, at first, to settle the Inquisition in the abovemention'd Provinces only. Nevertheless, the Bull in question was so much oppos'd, both in his Lifetime, and after his Decease; that his Successor was oblig'd to renew it, during seven Years successively, by softning it, in certain Particulars, which the People had objected against, and refus'd to comply with. But spite of all these Mitigations, and the Censures which the Inquisitors were permitted to thunder out against the Refractory, new Oppositions started up. This obliged Pope *Clement* IV. in 1265, to renew these Bulls for six Years together: And four Popes, his Successors,

Succeſſors, did all that lay in their Power to get them receiv'd, but without Succeſs. 'Twas therefore found neceſſary to apply Lenitives. People complain'd of the exceſſive Severity of the Inquiſitors, which was the more intolerable, as the former were unus'd to it. The Parties aggriev'd had not forgot the extraordinary Rigour with which the Officers of the Inquiſition rais'd the Revenues aſſign'd them; and they were even accus'd of extorting conſiderable Sums, on this Pretence. Cities and Corporations refus'd abſolutely to furniſh any longer the Sums neceſſary for the Support of the Inquiſition and its Officers. Now whether theſe Oppoſitions, and the Complaints on which they were grounded, appear'd juſt; 'tis certain the Court of *Rome* reſolved to make ſome Conceſſions, in order to leſſen the Averſion which People had to this new Yoke.

Cities and Corporations were therefore diſpens'd with contributing towards the

the Expences of the Inquisition, which the Pontiff was resolv'd to provide for, in such a Manner as should be no Burthen to the Public; whence 'twas naturally suppos'd, that all Complaints with regard to the Exactions of the Inquisitors, would cease.

And to remove the Outcries made against the shocking Rigour of the Inquisitors, in the Exercise of their Employment; the Bishops were allow'd a little more Power, in the Prosecutions of the Inquisition, than hitherto had been indulg'd them.

The Pope gain'd two considerable Advantages by this Condescension. First, as the Inquisitors no longer depended on the People for their Support, they were the more strongly attach'd to the Court of *Rome*. Secondly, the Inquisition was now receiv'd in *Lombardy*, *Romagna*, *Marca Anconitana*, *Tuscany*, *Genoa*, and all Parts of *Italy*; the Kingdom of *Naples*, and the Republic of *Venice*, excepted.

I shall

I shall obferve, that the Inquifition of *Rome* is compos'd of twelve Cardinals, and fome other Officers. The Pope prefides perfonally in this Affembly. The Inquifition is the chief Tribunal of *Rome*. The Congregation of the Inquifition was firft eftablifhed in 1545. The above Cardinals affume to themfelves the Title of Inquifitors General throughout the Chriftian World; but they have no Jurifdiction in *France*, and fome other *Romifh* Countries. They are impower'd to deprive or remove all inferior Inquifitors, at leaft thofe of *Italy*.

Popes *Innocent*, *Alexander*, *Urban*, *Clement*, and the feven Pontiffs their Succeffors, exerted their utmoft Endeavours, but to no Purpofe, to prevail with the *Venetians* to follow the Example of the other States of *Italy* in this Particular.

The Conduct of the Inquifitors, were Circumftances which ftrongly induc'd the Republic of *Venice* to refufe Ad-

of the INQUISITION. 115

Admiffion to that Tribunal in its Territories. The only Topic of Difcourfe, in all Places, was the Diforders and Seditions caus'd by the Sermons, as well as the imprudent Behaviour of the Inquifitors: For thefe Zealots would, upon any Caprice, publifh Crufades againft the Hereticks; when the Crufaders in queftion, who had been drawn together on a fudden, inftead of affifting the Caufe of Religion, only revenged themfelves of their Enemies; and feiz'd the Poffeffions of a numberlefs Multitude of innocent Perfons, upon the falfe Pretence of their being Hereties. *Milan* and *Parma* were very near ruin'd by the Seditions rais'd in them on thefe Occafions; and nothing was heard, all over *Italy*, but bitter Complaints againft the Inquifition and the Inquifitors. The Senate of *Venice*, who underftand their Intereft as well as any Body of Men in the World, took Advantage of the Diforders abovemen-

I 2   tion'd

tion'd, to justify their constant Refusal of this Tribunal.

However, Pope *Nicholas* IV. being noways disheartned at all the fruitless Attempts made by his Predecessors, renewed them; when the Senate perceiving that they, in case they persisted in their Refusal, would, at last, be forc'd to admit an Inquisition dependant on that of *Rome*; they establish'd one by their own Authority, compos'd of both Ecclesiastical and Lay Judges. This Inquisition has its own Laws, which differ from those of the Tribunals of this kind settled in *Italy*, and is far less rigorous. The utmost Precautions were taken by those who established this Inquisition, to prevent such Disorders as had broke out in all other Places where it had been admitted.

The Senate having thus taken the Resolution to admit the Inquisition, an Act or Instrument for that Purpose, was drawn up the 4th of *August* 1289, in the most authentic manner, and
sent

sent to the Pope. Tho' the Pontiff was not pleased with the Modifications introduc'd by the Senate, he nevertheless express'd, in outward Show, his Approbation of the Instrument presented to him; and ratified it by a Bull dated the 28th of *August* abovemention'd; in Hopes that the *Venetians* might afterwards be prevail'd upon to comply with the Desires of the Court of *Rome*, which, however, they have not yet done. On the contrary, this sage Republic, so far from repealing the old Laws, establishes new ones, whenever it is apprehensive that the Court of *Rome* intends to lessen its Authority, by enlarging that of the Inquisition. How glorious is it for this Republic, to see, in its Territories, the Tribunal of the Inquisition, subject to the Ordinances and Laws which the Senate formerly prescrib'd, and still prescribe to it; at a time that this Tribunal governs and commands, in the most despotic manner, in all the other

other States where it was received without Restriction; and is now become the most formidable, the most dreadful, and most cruel Tribunal in the Universe; insomuch that even Kings themselves are not secure from its Prosecutions, at least from its Resentment!

With regard to the Kingdom of *Naples*, the Inquisition has never been received there. This was owing, at first, to the almost perpetual Dissentions which reign'd between the *Neapolitan* Kings and the *Roman* Pontiffs. From the time that the *Spanish* Monarchs have possess'd that Kingdom, how great a Harmony soever might subsist between them and the Court of *Rome*, yet Things have always continued on the same Foot, and this from a singular Circumstance, *viz.* that the Popes themselves oppos'd it; and for this Reason, because the Kings of *Spain* insisted perpetually, that the *Neapolitan* Inquisitors ought to be dependant on the Inquisitor General of *Spain*,

Spain, and not on the general Inquisition of *Rome*, as the Popes asserted. This the latter would never consent to; and from this Argument, that as the Kingdom of *Naples* held, of the See of *Rome*, and not of *Spain*; the Inquisition should consequently hold likewise of the Pope. But as these two Courts were never able to agree about this Matter, the *Neapolitan* Bishops have always enjoy'd the Privilege of judging Heretics. However the Pope may, in certain Cases, depute Commissaries to *Naples*, to judge of heretical Matters; but this happens seldom or never. In 1544, Don *Pedro* of *Toledo*, Viceroy of *Naples* under the Emperor *Charles* V. endeavour'd to settle the Inquisition in that Kingdom; but the People mutinying during several Days, the Viceroy's Design was defeated.

The Inquisition established in Spain.

THO' the Inquisition had been so strongly oppos'd in *France* and *Germany*, it yet gain'd Footing in *Spain*; the Kings of *Arragon* admitting it into the several States dependant on their Crown. Endeavours were us'd, but to no Purpose, to force it into the western Parts of *Europe*; the People opposing it with the utmost Vigour, whereby it lost a considerable Part of its Power in the Kingdom of *Arragon*; till *Ferdinand*, King of that Country, and *Isabella* of *Castile*, uniting under one Monarchy, by their Marriage, almost all the *Spanish* Dominions; restor'd the Tribunal in question to its pristine Authority in *Arragon*, and afterwards in all *Spain*, which was not properly brought under the Yoke of the Inquisition, till about the Year 1484.

of the INQUISITION.

The Court of *Rome* was indebted for this to *John de Torquemada*, a *Dominican*. This Friar, who was Confessor to *Isabella*, had made her promise, before she came to the Throne, that, in case she should be rais'd to it, she would use all possible Methods to extirpate Hereticks and Infidels. As she afterwards was Queen, and brought the Kingdom of *Castile*, by Way of Dower, to *Ferdinand*; they finding themselves exceedingly powerful, resolv'd to conquer the Kingdom of *Granada*, and to drive back the *Moors* into *Barbary*. The *Moors* were accordingdingly subdued; and all the Territories possess'd by them in *Spain* seiz'd, so that prodigious Multitudes of them were forc'd to return into *Africa*. Nevertheless, great Numbers still continued in *Spain*; a Circumstance owing to their having Possessions or Wives in this Country, or their being settled in Traffic there.

As

As *Ferdinand* and *Isabella* consider'd that, in case they should banish these *Moors* from *Spain*, they thereby would depopulate the Countries conquer'd by them; their Majesties consented that they, as well as the *Jews*, should continue in it, provided they would turn Christians; upon which those People, finding that all Resistance would be vain, embrac'd the Christian Religion, in outward Appearance.

But now *Torquemada* assuring the Queen, that this Dissimulation would be of infinite Prejudice both to the Church and State, was urgent with her to perform the Promise she had made him, *viz.* of prosecuting the Infidels and Heretics assoon as she should be seated on the Throne. He enforc'd his Intreaties with all the Arguments which false Politicks and false Religion could suggest; concluding, that the best Expedient would be, to introduce and settle the Inquisition under the Authority of their Majesties. In a Word,
the

the Queen, after many Sollicitations, promis'd to ufe her utmoft Endeavours to get the King's Confent; which fhe afterwards obtaining, their Majefties demanded and procur'd, from Pope *Sixtus* IV. *anno* 1478, Bulls for the Purpofes abovemention'd.

Torquemada had been of fuch important Service to the See of *Rome*, that 'twas natural he fhould be rewarded by it; the Pope raifing him to the Purple. He afterwards was appointed by *Ferdinand* and *Ifabella*, Inquifitor-General of the whole Monarchy of *Spain*; and he difcharg'd the Functions of his Employment, fo much to their Expectation, that he profecuted, in 14 Years, above 100,000 Perfons, 6000 of whom were fentenc'd to the Flames.

Matters were afterwards carried to fuch a Height, by the barbarous Zeal of Princes, that *Philip* II. King of *Spain*, eftablifhed the Inquifition even on board of Ships of War. This bigotted Monarch would, doubtlefs, have introduc'd introduc'd it into the Skies, had it been in his Power. In 1571, he fitted out a Fleet call'd the *Invincible*, commanded by Don *John* of *Austria*; and, as it had been found necessary to employ Sailors of all Nations, *Philip* fearing, that a Mixture of Religions would corrupt the *Romish* Faith, consulted Pope *Pius* V. on this Occasion; when the Pontiff sent one of the Inquisitors of *Spain*, who had been appointed by the Inquisitor-General of that Monarchy, as Inquisitor of the Fleet; with Power to preside in the several Tribunals; and solemnize *Auto da Fes* in all Places they might put into. The first *Auto da Fé* was held in the City of *Messina*, where various Punishments were inflicted on many Persons.

This Tribunal was introduc'd into *Sicily* and *Sardinia*, at the time that those Islands were subject to the Crown of *Spain*.

I am

I am to observe, that the Post of chief Inquisitor, is one of the first in *Spain*; that he is commonly a *Dominican* Friar, and often an Archbishop or Cardinal. He is nominated by the King, and confirm'd by the Pope. There is no Appeal from this Inquisitor to *Rome*.

The Inquisition established in Portugal.

THE Account of the Manner in which the Inquisition was brought into *Portugal*, seems a little fabulous; however, we shall give it in few Words.

This Tribunal is said to have been introduc'd by the Artifice of *John Peres de Saavedra*, a Native of *Corduba*, or *Jaen*, in *Spain*. We are told that he, having found the Secret to counterfeit apostolical Letters, amass'd, by that means, about thirty thousand Ducats, which were employed by him in order to bring the Inquisition into *Portugal*, and that in manner following. He assum'd the Character of Cardinal-Legate from the See of *Rome*; when forming his Houshold, of one hundred and fifty Domesticks, he was receiv'd, in the abovemention'd Quality, at *Seville*, and very honourably lodged in the Archiepiscopal Palace. Advancing, after this, towards the Frontiers of *Portugal*, he dispatch'd one of his Secretaries to the King, to acquaint him with his Arrival; and to present him with fictitious Letters from the Emperor, the King of *Spain*, the Pope, and several other Princes both ecclesiastical and secular; who all intreated his Majesty to favour the Legate's pious Designs. The King, overjoy'd at this Legation, sent a Lord of his Court to compliment him, and attend him to the Royal Palace, where he resided about three Months. The Mock-Legate having succeeded in his Designs, by laying the Foundation of the Inquisition, took Leave of his Majesty; and

and departed, greatly satisfied with his Atchievement: But, unluckily for himself, he was discovered on the Confines of *Castile*, and known to have been formerly a Domestic of a *Portugueze* Nobleman. He was then seiz'd, and sentenc'd ten Years to the Gallies, where he continued a very long Time till, at last, he was released from thence *anno* 1556, by a Brief from Pope *Paul* IV. This Pontiff, who us'd to call the Inquisition, *the grand Spring of the Papacy*, wanted to see him.

We are told, that the Inquisition of *Portugal*, was copied from that of *Spain*, and introduc'd in the former, *anno* 1535. But Mr. *de la Neuville*, in his History of *Portugal*, Tom. I. Pag. 59, declares, that the Inquisition was introduc'd there *anno* 1557, under *John* III. and settled in the Cities of *Lisbon*, *Coimbra* and *Evora*.

The Inquisition has subsisted ever since in *Portugal*, and is the most severe, the most rigid, and cruel of any in the World.

The Tribunal in question rose, afterwards, with the *Spanish* and *Portugueze* Names; and shar'd, as it were, in their Acquisitions: For those two Nations, making boundless Conquests in both the *Indies*, established the Inquisition, in the several Countries won by their Arms, after the same Methods, and under the same Regulations, as in their Dominions in *Europe*.

Attempts made to introduce the Inquisition into Germany *and the* Netherlands.

THE Court of *Rome*, after settling the Inquisition in *Italy*, attempted to establish it in *Germany*; but the Spirit and Rigour of this Tribunal, no ways suiting the brave Temper of the *Germans*, they oppos'd it so vigorously, that the Pope was forc'd to lay aside his Design. He nevertheless was persuaded, that Time, and Artifices, would,

would, at laſt, crown his Endeavours. However, Time only prov'd, that the *Germans* were too heroic a People ever to ſubmit to ſo horrid a Yoke, and of this he had the ſtrongeſt Proof; this Tribunal being baniſhed out of ſeveral Cities, where inexpreſſible Pains had been taken to introduce it;. not to mention, that the Inquiſitors had behaved in them with greater Lenity than in any other Place. This was before the Popes attempted to ſettle the Inquiſition in *France*.

With regard to the *Netherlands*, the Conformity of the Temper of its Inhabitants, with thoſe of the *Germans* and *French*, between whom they are ſituated; made the *Roman* Pontiff conclude, either that it would be impoſſible to ſettle the Inquiſition among the People in queſtion, or that it would not be long ſuffer'd in their Country; for which Reaſon, few Attempts were made for this Purpoſe, till the Emperor *Charles* V. finding that

K   vaſt

vast Numbers of Hereticks had made the *Low Countries* their Asylum, published an Edict in 1550, whereby the Inquisition was order'd to be establish'd there, after the same Manner as in *Spain*: But this Edict was not put in Execution in the former Country, occasioned by the Remonstrances of *Mary* Queen of *Hungary*, Governess of the *Netherlands*, and Sister to that Emperor.

However, after his Decease, *Philip* II. his Son, resolv'd, if possible, to set up an Inquisition in the *Netherlands*; when the People making an Insurrection, long and bloody Wars ensued. The Result of these Wars was, seven of the Provinces of the *Low Countries* were dismemred from the *Spanish* Monarchy, and these form the Republic of the United Provinces. 'Twas with Difficulty that *Philip* preserv'd the rest.

The Popes had, long before, been desirous of introducing this Tribunal into *Great Britain*: But the Genius and Temper of its Inhabitants, still more abhorrent of all violent Remedies, and more prone to Insurrections than either the *Germans* or *French*; seem'd so opposite to the Spirit and Conduct of the Inquisition, that 'twas imagin'd every Endeavour for that Purpose would be fruitless. 'Twas also concluded, that tho' the *Roman* Pontiffs, by their being more rever'd in *England* than in any other Part of *Europe*, might have Interest to get it introduc'd into that Kingdom, it yet would be impossible for it to continue long there.

We find, however, that Endeavours were us'd to introduce the Inquisition here, under the Reign of Queen *Mary*, Sister to Queen *Elizabeth*. ' The Ju-
' stices of Peace (says Bishop *Burnet*)
' were now every where so slack in the
' Prosecution of Hereticks, that it
' seem'd necessary to find out other
' Tools. So the Courts of Inquisition
' were thought on. These were set
' up

'up first in *France* against the *Albi-*
'*genses*, and afterwards in *Spain*, for
'discovering the *Moors*; and were
'now turn'd upon the Hereticks.
'Their Power was uncontroulable;
'they seiz'd on any Thing they pleas'd,
'upon such Informations, or Presump-
'tions as lay before them. They ma-
'manag'd their Processes in secret, and
'put their Prisoners to such Sorts of
'Torture, as they thought fit for ex-
'torting Confessions or Discoveries
'from them. At this time [in 1557]
'both the Pope and King *Philip*, tho'
'they differ'd in other Things, agreed
'in this, that they were the only sure
'Means for extirpating Heresy. So,
'as a Step to the setting them up, a
'Commission was given to *Bonner*,
'and twenty more, the greatest Part
'Lay-men, to search all over *Eng-*
'*land* for All suspected of Heresy, that
'did not hear Mass, go in Processions,
'or take Holy Bread or Holy Water:
'They were authorized three being a
'Quorum,

'Quorum, to proceed either by Pre-
'fentments, or other politick Ways:
'They were to deliver all they dif-
'covered to their Ordinaries; and
'were to ufe all fuch Means as they
'could invent; which was left to
'their Difcretions and Confciences, for
'executing their Commiffion. Many
'other Commiffions, fubaltern to theirs,
'were iffued out for feveral Counties
'and Diocefes. This was looked on
'as fuch an Advance towards an *In-*
'*quifition*, that all concluded it would
'follow ere long. The Burnings were
'carried on vigoroufly in fome Places,
'and but coldly in moft Parts; for
'the Diflike of them grew to be al-
'moft univerfal †.' How greatly are
we indebted to fuch of our generous
Anceftors, as under the immortal
Queen *Elizabeth*, refcued us, at the
Hazard of their Lives and Fortunes,

† *Abridgment of the Hiftory of the Church of England*, Book III. p. 312. *London* 1682, 8vo.

from that diabolical Yoke, the Inquifition. And hence, what *Englifhman* but muft read, with the utmoft Deteftation, the following Words, fpoke by a Recorder of *London*, at the Trial of the celebrated Quakers, *William Penn* and *William Mead* †. ' Till
' now, I never underftood the Reafon
' of the Policy and Prudence of the
' *Spaniards*, in fuffering the Inquifi-
' tion among them. And certainly it
' will never be well with us, till fome-
' thing like the *Spanifh* Inquifition be
' in *England*.' Nothing fure can be more horrid than thefe Words! which muft throw eternal Infamy round the Name of this Recorder (Sir *John Hovel*).--The *Britons*, 'tis to be hop'd, will never fall fo low, as to let the Inquifition take Footing among them.

† *An Anfwer to the feditious and fcandalous Pamphlet*, entitled, *The Trial of* W. Penn *and* W. Mead, p. 3. *London* 1670, 4*to*.

--- *The*

*— The baleful Dregs
Of these late Ages, the inglorious Draught
Of Servitude and Folly have not yet,
Blest be th'eternal Ruler of the World,
Defil'd to such a Depth of sordid Shame
The native Honours of the human Soul,
Nor so effac'd the Image of its Sire.*
Pleasures of the Imagination, B. II.

We find (by Bishop *Burnet*) that previous to the Persecution under Queen *Mary*, hinted at above, there were Consultations concerning the Methods to proceed against Hereticks. Cardinal *Pool* had been suspected to bear some Favour to them formerly, but he took great Care to avoid all Occasions of being any more blamed for this: And indeed he lived in that Distrust of all the *English*, that he open'd his Thoughts to very few: For his chief Confidents were two *Italians* who came over with him, *Priuli* and *Ormaneto*.

Secretary *Cecil*, who in Matters of Religion complied with the prefent Time, was obferved to have more of his Favour than any *Englishman* had. *Pool* was an Enemy to all fevere Proceedings; he thought Churchmen fhould have the Tendernefs of a Father, and the Care of a Shepherd; and ought to reduce, but not devour the ftray Sheep. He had obferv'd, that Cruelty rather inflamed than cured that Diftemper. He thought the better and furer Way, was to begin with an effectual Reformation of the Manners of the Clergy, fince it was the Scandal given by their ill Conduct and Ignorance, that was the chief Caufe of the Growth of Herefy; fo he concluded, that if a primitive Difcipline fhould be revived, the Nation would, by Degrees, lay down their Prejudices, and might, in time, be gained by gentle Methods. *Gardiner*, on the other hand, being of an abject and cruel Temper himfelf, thought the ftrict Execution of the Laws

Laws against the *Lollards*, was that to which they ought chiefly to trust. If the Preachers were made public Examples, he concluded the People would be easily reclaimed; for he pretended, that it was visible, if King *Henry* had executed the Act of the six Articles vigorously, all would have submitted. He confessed a Reformation of the Clergy was a good Thing, but all Times would not bear it. If they should proceed severely against scandalous Churchmen, the Hereticks would take Advantage from that, to defame the Church the more, and raise a Clamour against all Clergymen.—The Queen was for joining both these Counsels together; and intended to proceed, at the same time, both against scandalous Churchmen and Hereticks †.—In the Course of the Persecutions, Endeavours were us'd, by the different Parties, to urge the Queen to continue them,

† *Burnet*, ubi supra, 269, 270, 271.

and to diffuade her from thefe Barbarities. 'At this time (fays Bifhop *Burnet*) a Petition was printed beyond
' Sea; by which the Reformers addref-
' fed themfelves to the Queen; they
' fet before her the Danger of her be-
' ing carried by a blind Zeal, to de-
' ftroy the Members of Chrift, as St.
' *Paul* had done before his Conver-
' fion. They remembred her of *Cranmer*'s interpofing to preferve her Life
' in her Father's Time. They cited
' many Paffages out of the Books of
' *Gardiner, Bonner* and *Tonftall*, by
' which fhe might fee that they were
' not acted [actuated] by true Prin-
' ciples of Confcience, but were tur-
' ned as their Fears or Intereft led
' them. They fhowed her how con-
' trary Perfecution was to the Spirit of
' the Gofpel; that Chriftians tole-
' rated *Jews*: And that the *Turks*,
' notwithftanding the Barbarity of their
' Tempers, and the Cruelty of their
' Religion, yet tolerated Chriftians.
                                      ' They

'They remembred her, that the first
'Law for burning in *England*, was
'made by *Henry* IV. as a Reward to
'the Bishops, who had helped him to
'depose *Richard* II. and so to mount
'the Throne. They represented to
'her, that God had trusted her with
'the Sword, which she ought to em-
'ploy for the Protection of her People,
'and was not to abandon them to the
'Cruelty of such Wolves. The Peti-
'tion also turned to the Nobility, and
'the rest of the Nation; and the Dan-
'ger of a *Spanish* Yoke, and a bloody
'Inquisition were set before them.---
'Upon this the Popish Authors writ se-
'veral Books in Justification of these
'Proceedings. They observed, that the
'*Jews* were commanded to put blas-
'phemers to Death; and said the He-
'reticks blasphemed the Body of Christ,
'and call'd it only a Piece of Bread.
'It became Christians to be more zea-
'lous for the true Religion, than Hea-
'thens were for the false. St. *Peter*,
'by

'by a divine Power, struck *Ananias*
'and *Sapphira* dead. Christ, in the
'Parable, said, *Compel them to enter
'in.* St. *Paul* said, *I would they were
'cut off that trouble you.* St. *Austin*
'was once against all Severities in such
'Cases, but changed his Mind, when
'he saw the good Effect which some
'Banishments and Fines had on the
'*Donatists.* That on which they in-
'sisted most, was, the Burning of the
'Anabaptists in King *Edward*'s Time.
'So they were now fortified in their
'cruel Intentions; and resolved to
'spare none, of what Age, Sex or
'Condition soever they might be †.'
The Reader of good Sense, of what
Religion soever, will see at once the
Weakness of the Arguments on the Po-
pish Side, compar'd with those of the
Protestants; and yet the former, (so
horrid was this Ministry) prevailed.

† Idem, P. 276, 277.

The Inquisition has not enlarg'd its Jurisdiction since the Attempts made to force it into the *Netherlands*. Such Countries as had admitted this Tribunal before, are still subject to it; and those which had refus'd it, have been so happy as to keep it out; so that it is now confined to a great Part of *Italy*, and the Dominions subject to the Crowns of *Spain* and *Portugal*; yet its Power extends over a larger Extent of Ground than all *Europe*; and, in the several Places where it is establish'd, the sad Marks thereof are but too apparent.

Come! by whatever sacred Name disguis'd,
OPPRESSION, *come! and in thy Works rejoice!*
See Nature's richest Plains to putrid Fens
Turn'd by thy Rage. From their unchearful
 Bounds
See raz'd th' enliv'ning Village, Farm, and Seat.
First rural Toil, by thy rapacious Hand
Robb'd of his poor Reward, resign'd the Plow;
And now he dares not turn the noxious Glebe.
'Tis thine entire. The lonely Swain himself,
Who loves at large along the grassy Downs
His Flocks to pasture, thine abhorrent flies.
Far as the sick'ning Eye can sweep around
          'Tis

'Tis all one Desart, desolate and grey,
Graz'd by the sullen Bufalo alone ;
And where the rank unventilated Growth
Of rotting Ages taints the passing Gale.
Beneath the baleful Blast the City pines,
Or sinks enfeebled, or infected burns.
Beneath it mourns the solitary Road,
Roll'd in rude Mazes o'er th'abandon'd Waste ;
While antient Ways, ingulph'd, are seen no
 more.
 Such thy dire Plains, thou Self-destroyer ! Foe
To Human-kind.
  THOMSON'S LIBERTY, Part I.

PART III.

A Distinct Account of the Inquisition, and of the several Things appertaining to it.

THERE are, in the Dominions of the King of *Portugal*, four Inquisitions, *viz.* at *Lisbon, Coimbra, Evora* and *Goa*, in the *East Indies*. The Jurisdiction of the last mention'd, extends over all the Countries possess'd by his *Portugueze* Majesty on the other Side of the Cape of *Good-Hope*.

Besides these four Inquisitions, there is a supreme Council held in *Lisbon*, to which all the other *Portugueze* Inquisitions are subordinate. This Tribunal consists of an Inquisitor-General, who is appointed by the King, and confirm'd by the Pope. He is empower'd to nominate the Inquisitors in all the Countries dependent on the Crown of *Portugal*. Under him are five Counsellors, a Fiscal Proctor †, a Secretary of

---

† *Proctor* is well known to be much the same, in Ecclesiastical Courts, as an Attorny is in Lay ones. His Business is to see that the Church Discipline be maintain'd ; and to bring to Punishment the Disobedient. *Fiscal* signifies properly what belongs to the Exchequer, or King's Treasury ; here it is said to imply a Proctor, who, for the sake of, and in the Name of the Public, is to prosecute Delinquents with regard to Matters Ecclesiastical.

The Author of the *Relation of the Inquisition of Goa*, p. 89, & *seq*. Paris 1688, 12*mo*. writes as follows concerning the Officers of the Inquisition.

' There are at *Goa* two Inquisitors : The first call'd
' *Inquisidor mor* [I suppose this should be *Mayor*] or
' the great *Inquisitor*, is always a secular Priest ;
' and the second a *Dominican* Friar. There like-
' wise are Officers call'd *Deputados*. These are numerous, and of all Religious Orders. They as-
' sist at the Judgment of Prisoners, and the draw-
' ing up of their Prosecutions ; but never come to
' the Tribunal, unless sent for by the Inquisitors.
' There are other Officers stil'd *Calificadores*, who
' examine such Propositions as are look'd upon to
' be contrary to the Purity of Doctrine. These do
' not assist at the Judgments; they only making
' their Report with regard to Actions committed.
' There also is a Proctor, an Attorney, and Advo-
' cate

of the King's Bed-Chamber, two Secretaries of the Council, an Alcayde or Goaler, a Receiver, two Reporters,

' cates or Counsellors for such Prisoners as may de-
' sire them. However, these Counsellors are rather
' their Betrayers than Defenders; their chief Endea-
' vours being only to draw their Secrets out of them.
' Besides, tho' there were no Reason to suspect their
' Fidelity, yet their Favour would be of little Bene-
' fit to the Prisoners; these Counsellors being never
' allowed to speak to them, except before the Judges,
' or some Persons deputed by the latter, in order to
' be present at these Conferences.

' There are other Officers of the Inquisition, cal-
' led *Familiares*, who are, as it were, the Serjeants
' or Bailiffs of this Tribunal. Persons of all Condi-
' tions, not excepting Dukes and Princes, glory in
' being Familiars. These are employed in seizing
' Persons impeach'd; and the usual Rule is, to
' send a Familiar of the same Rank or Condition
' with the Person who is to be seiz'd. These Offi-
' cers have no Salary, they thinking it honour suffi-
' cient to serve so holy a Tribunal. They wear a
' Medal on which the Arms of the Inquisition is en-
' grav'd. They go alone, to seize a Prisoner; and
' when such an one is told, that the Inquisitors have
' sent for him, he is oblig'd to follow the Familiar
' instantly; for, were he to make the least Resist-
' ance, every one would assist the above Officer.

' There likewise are Secretaries, Apparitors cal-
' led *Meirinhos*, an *Alcayde* or Goaler; and Guards
' or Attendants to look after the Prisoners, carry
' them Food, and other Things necessary.'

two Qualificators, and a great Number of subaltern Officers.

This supreme Council has an unlimited Authority over all the Inquisitors of *Portugal*; they not being permitted to solemnize an *Auto da Fé* without its Permission. This is the only Tribunal of the Inquisition from which there is no Appeal. It may enact new Laws at Pleasure. It determines all Suits or Contests arising between the Inquisitors. It punishes the Ministers and Officers of the Inquisition. All Appeals are made to it. In fine, the Authority of this Tribunal is so great, that there is scarce any one but trembles at its bare Name; and even the King himself does not dare to oppose it.

We observ'd that, besides the supreme Council, there are four other Tribunals of the Inquisition. Each of them is compos'd of three Inquisitors or Judges, a Fiscal Proctor, two Secretaries, a Judge, a Receiver, and a Secretary

tary of confiscated Possessions, Assessors, Counsellors, an Executor, Physicians and Surgeons, a Goaler, a Messenger, Door-keepers, Familiars, and Visitors.

There are, in the *Romish* Church, two Sorts of Judges in Matters of Faith. The first are so by virtue of the Employment with which they are invested; such is the Pope and the Bishops; who, immediately after their Consecration, are supposed to receive, from Heaven, a Right and an absolute Jurisdiction over Hereticks.

The second sort of Judges, are those delegated by the Pope, who sets himself up as supreme Judge in Matters of Faith; and gives the Judges in question an entire Jurisdiction over all Hereticks and Apostates. These are called Apostolical Inquisitors.

This Employment is of such Eminence, that those who are rais'd to it have the same Title with Bishops: And *Clement* IV. to do them the greater Honour, and enlarge their Power, freed them from the Jurisdiction of the Bishops

Bishops where they reside; making them dependant only on the General Inquisitor of the Kingdom. They likewise may publish Edicts against Hereticks; heighten their Punishment; excommunicate, or take off the Excommunication from such as have incurr'd it, except these are dying.

The Inquisitors may seize a Heretic, tho' he should have fled for Refuge into a Church; which the Bishop must not oppose, on any Pretence whatsoever; a Circumstance that gives the Inquisitors greater Power than is enjoy'd by the Kings of the Countries where the Inquisition is establish'd.

No Prelate, or Legate from the See of *Rome*, can pronounce Sentence of Excommunication, Suspension or Interdict, against the Inquisitors and their Secretaries, without an express Order from the Pope; to prevent, as is pretended, the Affairs of Religion from being injur'd, and Hereticks from going unpunish'd.

The

The Inquisitors may forbid the secular Judges to prosecute any Person, even in a Prosecution carried on, at first, by their Order.

Any Person who shall kill, or employ another to kill, abuse or beat an Inquisitor and Official of the Inquisition, shall be deliver'd over to the secular Arm, in order to be severely punish'd.

Pope *Urban* IV. granted them likewise the Privilege, of absolving one another, and their Assistants, with regard to any Faults committed by them, arising from human Frailty; and for which they may have incurr'd the Sentence of Excommunication. They, farther, may grant an Indulgence of twenty or forty Days, (as they may think proper) to Persons whom they shall think penitent.

They are impower'd to absolve all Friars, Companions, and Notaries of the Inquisition, from the Penance which may have been enjoin'd them during three Years; provided such had en-

endeavour'd sincerely, and personally aided and insisted in the Prosecution of Hereticks, and of all who favour, defend or conceal them. And if any of the Persons in question should die in the Pursuit of so pious (as 'tis strangely term'd) a Work, the Inquisitors may give them full Absolution, after such Persons shall have made a Confession of all their Sins.

To these Privileges we shall add such as relate more immediately to the Prosecution of Persons impeach'd. All Affairs relating to the pretended Holy Office, are manag'd by the Inquisitors, who, by virtue of the Denunciations, Informations, and Accusations, brought against all Sorts of Persons; issue their Orders for citing, seizing, imprisoning, and laying in Irons, those who are accus'd.

Run, with your Nose to Earth:
Run, Blood-Hound, run; and scent out Royal
  Murder.
You second Rogue, but equal to the first,
Plunder, fly, hang: Nay, take your Tackling
  with you,

of the INQUISITION.

For thefe fhall hold them faft: (*hang, hang the Slaves*)
To the mid Region in the Sun.
Plunder, be gone, Vipers, Afps and Adders.
  DRYDEN's Tragedy of the Duke of *Guife,* Act III. Scene I.

The Inquifitors receive the Confeffions and Depofitions of thofe Perfons, and appoint the various Tortures, in order for extorting from them whatever they defire fhould be confefs'd. In fine, they condemn definitively, all who have the fad Fate to be their Prifoners, without any Appeal whatfoever. The Inquifitors may, for their own Eafe, appoint Perfons to affift as Judges, in their Names, in cafe of Sicknefs or Abfence; and thefe are allowed much the fame Prerogatives with thofe who eftablifhed them; and can be remov'd by none but the Inquifitors by whom they were nominated. They likewife may appoint more Affiftants or Com-miffaries, proportionably to the Cities or Towns in the Provinces dependant on this Tribunal. There muft be one Commiffary, at leaft, in every Town.

The second Officer of the Inquisition is the *Fiscal Proctor*. This Man, upon Informations made against Persons, receives the Depositions of the Witnesses; and addresses the Inquisitors, in order for their being seiz'd and imprison'd. In a word, he is their Accuser, and pleads against them, after their being taken up. The Secretaries keep an exact Register of the Prisoners from the Time of their Commitment; of the principal Articles of the Indictment; with the Names of the Witnesses who swore against them. In a word, they write down the Proceedings in all Causes, and the Defence made by the Prisoner. They likewise register all the Orders given by the Executor, and other Officers of the Tribunal in question. All Writings must be carefully lock'd up, to prevent their being perus'd by any Persons except those acquainted with the Secrets of the Inquisition. The Judge of the Goods and Chattels confiscated, is
Judge

Judge between the Fifc or Exchequer, and private Perfons, in all Caufes relating to the Effects of Prifoners.

The *Receiver* is to take exact Care of the confifcated Poffeffions; muft fell them, and apply the Monies purfuant to the Orders given him. He likewife muft be prefent, when the Executor, and the other Officers, fequefter the Poffeffions of Prifoners; which is not done without an exprefs Command from the Inquifitor. The Secretary of the Sequeftrations, takes an exact Inventory of all the Effects belonging to the Prifoners found in their Poffeffion; or in the Hands of other Perfons, who, fhould they alienate the leaft Part of them, would be expos'd to the utmoft Rigours of this Tribunal. All the Effects and Poffeffions belonging to the Prifoners, are lodged with the Receiver of the Sequeftrations; together with an exact Inventory, figned by the Executor, who, as well as the Secretary, has a Copy thereof.

The Duties of the *Executor*, is to execute the Orders of the Inquisitors, and particularly to take Criminals, and go in pursuit of them, if they are at a Distance ; to look carefully after them, when in their Hands ; and even to fetter them, *&c.* in order to convey them, with the greater Security, to the Prisons of the Inquisition.

The *Familiars* are the Bailiffs or Catchpoles of the Inquisition. Tho' this is a most ignominious Employment in all other criminal Courts, it yet is look'd upon as so honourable in the Inquisition, that every Nobleman in *Portugal* is a Familiar of this Tribunal. 'Tis not surprizing, that Persons of the highest Quality should be sollicitous for this Post, since the Pope has granted, to these Familiars, the like plenary Indulgences as the Council of Lateran gave to such Persons as should go to the Succour of the Holy Land against the Infidels. They are the *Satellites* of the Inquisitors ; they attending

ing on them and defending them if neceffary, againft the Infults of Heretics. They accompany the Executor, whenever he goes to feize Criminals; and muft obey all Orders given them by the chief Officers of the Inquifition. Several Privileges are allowed them, efpecially the carrying Arms; but they are order'd to ufe thofe with Difcretion.

Affeffors and Counfellors are Perfons fkill'd in the Canon and Civil Law. The Inquifitors confult them in all difficult Points, but follow their Opinions no farther than they think proper. They commonly make Ufe of thofe Perfons to give the greater Weight to their Sentences, by the fpecious Precautions they take; but in no other view than to impofe on Mankind.

The *Vifitor* is a Perfon appointed by the Inquifitor-General, to infpect all the Towns, Cities and Provinces where Commiffaries are eftablifhed. They muft inform him of the Care which thefe these Commissaries take in searching after Heretics; and make a Report thereof, in order that he, with his Council, may use such Measures as may be thought fitting: The Visitor must pay the most exact Obedience to the Instructions of the Inquisitor: He is forbid to lodge at the Houses of those over whose Conduct he has an Eye; to receive the least Present from them, or any one sent in their Name. The Number of these Visitors is always in Proportion to that of the Towns, and the Extent of the Provinces where the Inquisition is established.

The several Officers of this Tribunal must make Oath, before the Inquisitors, to discharge faithfully the Duties of their Employment; not to divulge the most minute Particular relating to Inquisition or its Prisons, on any Pretence whatsoever, upon Pain of being turn'd out, and punished with the utmost Severity. The Inquisitors admit of no Excuse on these Occasions; Secrecy

crecy being the Soul, as it were, and the mighty Support of this Tribunal.

Besides thefe feveral Officers of the Inquifition, the Popes have likewife commanded, by their Bulls, Magiftrates in general, to give all the Affiftance in their Power, not only to the Inquifitors; but likewife to their various Subaltern Officers, who may ftand in Need thereof, in the Exercife of their Employments, upon Pain of their being fubject to Ecclefiaftical Punifhments.

The Inquifitors being, as was obferv'd, Judges delegated by the Pope, for enquiring into Matters of Faith, and for extirpating Herefy; they, upon this fpecious Pretence, are impower'd to profecute all Sorts of Friars, of what Rank or Condition foever, either in their own Names, by the fupreme Council of the Kingdom, or by the Pope. 'Tis fo much the Intereft of the *Roman* Pontiff to fupport the Inquifitors, that he exerts his whole Authority

rity for this Purpose; some Examples whereof will be given hereafter.

In fine, they may prosecute indiscriminately, any Layman infected with Heresy, not excepting Princes or Kings. However, the Inquisitors, to secure themselves from any ill Consequences which might attend their attacking Persons in such exalted Stations, consult the Pope on these Occasions, and proceed as he may direct. This Precaution is not us'd out of Respect to Persons of high Eminence and crown'd Heads; but, for Fear lest a severe Treatment shou'd exasperate them, and cause them to oppose the Inquisition in Places where it is poor, and not powerfully established. No Persons wou'd be exempt from the Prosecutions of this Tribunal, how great soever his Privileges might otherwise be, shou'd he presume to speak contemptuously of this Tribunal; this being an infinitely worst Crime than the most pernicious Heresy.

Having

Having thus mention'd the Privileges, &c. of the Inquisition, let us now specify the Cases or Circumstances which subject a Person to this Tribunal.

The first is Heresy. Under the Name of Heretics are comprehended all Persons who have spoke, writ, taught or practis'd any Tenets contrary to the Scriptures, to the Articles of the Creed; and, especially, to the Traditions of the Church of *Rome*. Likewise such as have denied the Catholic Faith, by going over to some other Religion; or who, tho' they do not quit the *Romish* Communion, praise the Customs and Ceremonies of other Churches; practice some of them; or believe that Persons may be sav'd in all Religions, provided they profess them with Sincerity.

They likewise consider as Heretics, all who disapprove any Ceremonies, Usages, or Customs receiv'd, not only

only by the Church, but even by the Inquisition.

All who think †, say, or teach any Thing contrary to the Opinion recceiv'd at *Rome*, with Regard to the Pope's supreme, unlimited Authority, and his Superiority over General Councils; as likewise such as speak, teach or write any Thing contrary to the papal Decisions, on what Occasion soever, are look'd upon as Heretics.

A Suspicion of Heresy, which is the second Case, is still more extensive; for to incur such Suspicion, 'tis enough that a Person only starts some Proposition which may offend the Hearers; or does not impeach those who advance any such. That Person is likewise suspected of Heresy, who contemns, insults or mutilates any Images. Likewise all those who read Books condemn'd by the Inquisition, or who lend them to others.

† How can other Persons know their Thoughts?

That

That Person also incurs a Suspicion of Heresy, who deviates from the ordinary Customs relating to Religion, practic'd by the *Romanists*; such as letting a Year pass, without going to Confession and Communion; the eating Meat on Fish Days; or the neglecting to go to Mass at the Times enjoin'd by the Church.

Those also are suspected of Heresy, who, being in holy Orders, repeat such Sacraments as should not be repeated; endeavour to enter into the Marriage-State; or marry two or more Wives.

In fine, such incur a Suspicion of Heresy, as go but once, to the Sermons of Hereticks, or to any other of their public Exercises. Likewise those who neglect to appear before the Inquisitors, when summon'd; or procure Absolution, the same Year they were excommunicated. Also, the contracting a Friendship with Hereticks; the lodging such; the making them Presents, or even visiting them; especially the preventing their being imprifon'd in the Inquifition; the furnifhing them with Opportunities of efcaping, tho' induc'd thereto by the ftrongeft Ties of Blood, of Gratitude or Pity. This Article is carried to fuch Lengths by the Inquifitors, that Perfons are not only forbid to fave Hereticks; but are obliged to difcover them, tho' a Father, Brother, Hufband, or Wife; and this upon Pain of Excommunication; of incurring a Sufpicion of Herefy; and of being obnoxious to the Rigours of the Tribunal in queftion, as Fautors or Abettors of Herefy. How unnatural, how cruel is fuch an Injunction! Thefe conftitute the third Cafe, fubject to the Judgment of the Inquifition. Under the Name of Fautors, are comprehended all who favour, defend, or give Advice or Affiftance, of what kind foever, to thofe whom the Inquifitors have begun to profecute.

Thofe likewife become obnoxious, who, knowing Perfons to be Hereticks, or or to have escap'd out of the Prisons of the Inquisition; or who, upon their being cited to appear, refused to obey the Summons; conceal, or give them Advice or Assistance in order for their escaping; likewise such as molest, by Threats or otherwise, the Agents of this Tribunal in the Execution of their Office; or who, tho' they don't obstruct it themselves, aid or abet such as oppose them.

Under the Name of Fautors of Heresy, are also included those who speak, without Permission, to the Prisoners; or who write to them, either to give them Advice, or merely to comfort them. Such as prevail upon, by Money or otherwise, Witnesses to be silent, or to favour the Prisoners in their Depositions; or who conceal, burn, or get Possession, in what Manner soever, of Papers which may be of Use in convicting Persons accus'd.

The fourth Case subject to the Judgment of the Inquisition, includes Magicians,

gicians, Wizards, Soothsayers, and such like, of whom there are suppos'd to be (very idly sure) more in *Italy* than in any other Country, the *Italian* Women being strangely curious and credulous. We shall not specify the various Accusations brought on those Occasions; they consisting of ridiculous Superstitions, arising from a heated Imagination and blind Credulity, rather than from a deprav'd Will and a corrupt Heart. We will only observe, that, among the several Cases subject to the Inquisition, none fill its Prisons with a greater Number of Women of all Conditions.

Blasphemy, (the fifth Case) tho' very common, and one of the greatest Crimes, yet the Inquisitors do not take Cognizance of it, except it contain some Heresy. We shall forbear giving Instances thereof here, it being much better for Mankind, that such Things should be buried in Oblivion.

Tho' neither *Jews, Mohammedans,*
or

or such like, are subject to the Inquisition, in many Things, they yet are obnoxious to it, in all the Cases abovemention'd; those Crimes not being tolerated in *Jews* and *Mohammedans*, &c. more than in Christians. Farther, the Abovemention'd become subject to the Inquisition, if they assert, write, or publish any Particulars contrary to the *Romish* Communion. Thus, for Instance, should a *Jew* or *Mohammedan* deny the Trinity, or a Providence, he would be punished as an Heretic; as also, was he to hinder a Person professing any of those Religions from turning Christian; or convert a *Romanist* to theirs, or favour such a Design.

Jews are not allow'd to vend, publish, or even keep the *Talmud*; or any Book, which speaks contemptuously of the Christian Religion, or is prohibited by the Inquisition †.

† The Decrees of the Inquisition, with regard to Books, are not consider'd as infallible, as appears from

In fine; *Jews* are not permitted to have Christian Nurses, or to do any Thing in Contempt of the *Romish* Religion. The Inquisitors take Cognizance of all such Cases; and punishes Offenders in them with the utmost Severity; so that the Dread of this obliges those unhappy People to become Converts to Popery. However, such a

---

from the Petition presented, by the Jesuits of the Province of *Toledo*, to the King of *Spain*. These Fathers observed, that the Petition which had been address'd to him by the *Carmelites*, was unjust; its Drift being to silence both Parties, after that the Inquisition of *Toledo* had condemn'd fourteen Volumes of *Acta Sanctorum*. These Jesuits show, among other Things, that pursuant to the Practice of the Holy Office, Persons may object to its Decrees; and that, 'tho' the Inquisitors condemn a Book, they yet will permit the Author of it to justify his Opinion. This is exemplified in the Case of *John Nicholas de Diana*, a Jesuit, who having preached a Sermon on St. *Lucifer*, it was condemned by the Inquisitors of *Sardinia*. The Jesuit appealing to *Diego Arze-Reynoso*, Inquisitor-General of *Spain*, the latter revok'd the Proceedings of the Inquisition of *Sardinia*; and re-instated our Jesuit in his Reputation. *John Nicholas de Diana* spent thirteen Years in this Contest. See his Article in *Bayle*'s Dictionary.

Con-

Converſion does not make them better Men. Theſe are always diſtinguiſhed by the Title of New Chriſtians, a Name which is ſo much deteſted, that the old Chriſtians can ſeldom be prevail'd upon to marry among the New, tho' the Families of the latter had been Chriſtians from their Great Grandfathers. The utter Abhorrence in which theſe new Converts are held, makes them unite more cloſely one with the other, in order to perform mutual Services, which they could not expect from the old Chriſtians: But this very Union is commonly the Source of their Misfortunes. To illuſtrate this, I need but obſerve that, if a new Chriſtian, who is ſincerely ſuch, happens to contract a very ſtrict Intimacy with other new Chriſtians, this alone would be ſufficient to make him ſuſpected of practicing *Jewiſh* Ceremonies with them, in ſecret. In conſequence of this Suſpicion, ſuch Perſon is ſeized by Order of the Holy Office; and accus'd, by the Depofition of fome Perfon, of being a *Jew*. Being confcious of his Innocence, he flatters himfelf that nothing will be eafier for him than to prove it publickly ; whence he makes no Difficulty to comply with the Cuftom eftablifh'd by the Inquifitors, *viz.* of giving in immediately a complete Inventory of all his Effects, &c. upon the firm Perfuafion that they'll be reftored to him, the Inftant he fhall have juftified himfelf. But he is miftaken ; for, prefently after he has given in fuch Inventory, the Inquifitors feize his Effects, and fell them publickly by Auction. The bare Accufation pronounces him guilty ; and he has no other Way to efcape the Flames, than by making a Confeffion, conformably to the Articles of the Indictment. As his Accufer, the Witneffes, and himfelf, are not brought Face to Face, his Innocence is of no Service. His Riches prove his Ruin, thofe being certainly feized ; and his Life would inevitably fall

fall a Sacrifice, fhould he not acknowledge himfelf a relapfed *Jew*, tho' he had always been a zealous *Romanift*.

The fixth and laft Cafe fubject to the Judgment of the Inquifition, is of thofe who refift its Officers, or any way oppofe its Jurifdiction. As one of the chief Maxims of this Tribunal, is to ftrike Terror, and to awe fuch as are fubject to it; it punifhes with the utmoft Severity all who offend its Agents and Officers. On thefe Occafions, the flighteft Fault is confider'd as a heinous Crime. Neither Birth, Employment, Dignity or Rank, can protect. To threaten ever fo little the loweft Officer belonging to the Inquifition, its Informers, or Witneffes, would be punifhed with the extremeft Rigour.

Such are the Cafes which fubject a Perfon to the Inquifition; and there are four Ways, by which fuch a One ufually, becomes fo. Firft, by common Fame, which declares him to be guilty

guilty of one or more of the Crimes specified above: Secondly, by the Deposition of Witnesses, who impeach him: Thirdly, by his being inform'd against by the Spies of the Inquisition, who are dispers'd every where: Lastly, by the Confession of the Prisoner, who accuses himself, in Hopes of being treated with greater Humanity, than if he had been inform'd against by others.

We shall now proceed to the Manner of prosecuting a Person impeach'd; and this, sometimes, upon the slightest Suspicion. First, he is summon'd, three several times, to appear before the Inquisitors; when, if through Fear or Contempt, he should neglect to do this, he would be excommunicated, and sentenc'd, provisionally, to pay a considerable Fine; after which, should he be seiz'd, a more severe Sentence would inevitably be pass'd upon him.

The safest Course therefore, for a Person impeach'd, is, to obey the first Summons.

Summons. The longer he delays on this Occasion, the more criminal he makes himself, in the Eye of the Inquisitors, tho' he should really be innocent. To disobey the Command of the Inquisitors, is ever consider'd by them, as a Crime. They always look upon Delays to be certain Indications of Guilt, as showing a Dread to appear before the Judges. When, therefore, a Person is reduc'd to this sad Extremity, nothing can secure him from the most rigorous Punishment, but a voluntary and perpetual Exile: Nothing is forgot by the Inquisitors; Time cannot obliterate any Crime; and Prescription is a Thing unknown to them.

It frequently happens, that the Inquisitors, either from their considering the Crime of which a Person stands impeach'd, as enormous, and that they have sufficient Evidence against him; or from their apprehending that he may escape; immediately issue their Orders,

ders, without first sending a Summons, for his being seiz'd, in any Place whatsoever. When this is the Case, no Asylum or Privilege can stop, a single Moment, the Prosecution, nor abate its Rigours. The Inquisitors give an Order, under their own Hands, to the Executor, who takes a sufficient Number of Familiars along with him, to prevent a Rescue.

Words could scarce describe the Calamity of a Man under these Circumstances. He, perhaps, is seiz'd, when in Company with his Friends, and surrounded by his Family; a Father by his Son's Side; a Son by that of his Father, and a Wife in Company with her Husband. No Person is allowed to make the least Resistance, or even to speak a single Word in favour of the Prisoner; who is not indulg'd a Moment's Respite to settle his most important Affairs.

Hence the Reader may judge, of the continual Apprehensions with which

which Persons, inhabiting Countries where the Inquisition is established, must necessarily be fill'd; since, in order to secure themselves from it, one Friend is oblig'd to sacrifice another; Sons their Parents; Parents their Children; Husbands their Wives, and Wives their Husbands, by accusing them to the pretended Holy Office. How horrid a Source have we here of Perfidy and Inhumanity! What kind of Community must that be, whence Gratitude, Love, and a mutual Forbearance with regard to human Frailties, are banish'd! What must that Tribunal be, which obliges Parents, not only to eraze from their Minds the Remembrance of their own Children; to extinguish all the Sensations of Tenderness and Affection, which Nature inspires for them; but even to extend their Inhumanity so far, as to force them to become their Accusers, and consequently the Cause of the Cruelties inflicted on them.

What Idea ought we to form to ourselves of a Tribunal, which obliges Children, not only to stifle every soft Impulse of Gratitude, Love and Respect due to those who gave them Birth; but even forces them, upon the most rigorous Penalties, to be Spies over their Parents; and to discover to the merciless Inquisitors, the Crimes, the Errors, and even the little Lapses to which human Frailty so often urges: In a Word, a Tribunal which will not permit Relations, when imprison'd in its horrid Dungeons, to give each other the Succours, or to perform the Duties which Religion enjoins. What Disorder and Confusion must such a Conduct give rise to, in a tenderly-loving Family! An Expression, innocent in itself, and perhaps but too true, shall, from an indiscreet Zeal, or a panic Fear, give infinite Uneasiness to a Family; shall ruin it intirely; and, at last, cause one or more of its Members to be the innocent, sad Victims of the most barbarous of all Tribunals.

What Distractions must necessarily break out, in a Family where the Husband and Wife are at Variance, and the Children loose and wicked! Will such Children scruple to sacrifice a Father who endeavours to restrain them by his Exhortations, by Reproaches or paternal Corrections? Alas no! These will plunder his House, to support themselves in their Extravagance and Riot; and afterwards deliver up their unhappy Parent to all the Horrors of a Tribunal, whose Proceedings are founded on the blackest Injustice.

A riotous Husband, or a loose Wife, have likewise an easy Opportunity, by Means of the Prosecutions in question, to rid themselves of any one who is a Check to their Vices, by delivering up him or her to the Rigours of the Inquisition. Every detestable Expedient, such as false Oaths and Testimonies, are employ'd, with Impunity, to sacrifice

crifice an innocent Person. Very justly, therefore, might an ingenious *French* Author, a *Romanist*, write thus (speaking of the various Courts in *Lima :*) " The most formidable of all the Tribunals is that of the Inquisition, whose bare Name strikes Terror universally. I. Because the Informer is admitted as a Witness. II. As the Persons impeach'd never know those who inform against them. III. As the Witnesses are never confronted.--Hence innocent People are daily seiz'd, whose only Crime is, that certain Persons are bent upon their Destruction †."

When a Person is once imprisoned by the Inquisitors, his Treatment is still more cruel. He is thoroughly search'd, to discover, if possible, any Books or Papers which may serve to convict him; or some Instrument he may employ to put an End to his Life, in order to es-

† *Relation du voyage de la Mer de Sud, par Mr. Frezier*, p. 201. *Paris*, 1732, 4to.

cape the Torture, &c. Of this there are but too many sad Examples; and some Prisoners have been so rash, as to dash their Brains out against the Wall, upon their being unprovided with Scissars, a Knife, a Rope, and such like.

After a Prisoner has been carefully search'd; and that his Money, Papers, Buckles, Rings, &c. have been taken from him, he is conveyed to a Dungeon, the bare Sight of which must fill him with Horror. Torn from his Family and his Friends, who are not allowed Access to, or even to send him one consolatory Letter; or to take the least Step in his Favour, in order to prove his Innocence; he sees himself instantly abandon'd to his inflexible Judges, to his Melancholy, to his Despair; and even often to his most inveterate Enemies, quite uncertain of his Fate. Innocence, on such an Occasion, is as a weak Reed, nothing being easier than to ruin an innocent Person.

Being come to Prison, the Inquisitor, attended by the Officers of this mock holy Tribunal, goes to the Prisoner's Abode; and there causes an exact Inventory to be taken of all his Papers, Effects, and of every Thing found in his House. They frequently seize all the Prisoners other Possessions; at least the greatest Part of them, to pay themselves the Fine to which he may be sentenc'd; for very few escape out of the Inquisition without being half ruin'd, unless they happen to be very wealthy indeed.

The House of the Inquisition in *Lisbon* is a very spacious Edifice. There are four Courts, each about forty Foot square, round which are Galleries (in the dormitory Form) two Stories high. In these Galleries are the Cells or Prisons, being about three hundred. Those on the Ground-Floor are allotted for the vilest of Criminals (as they are term'd;) and are so many frightful Dungeons, all of Free-Stone, arch'd over,

over, and very gloomy. The Cells on the first Floor are fill'd with less guilty Persons; and Women are commonly lodg'd in those of the second Story. These several Galleries are hid from View, both within and without, by a Wall above fifty Foot high; and built a few Foot Distance from the Cells, which darkens them exceedingly. The House in question is of so great an Extent, and contains so vast a Variety of Turnings, that I am persuaded a Prisoner could scarce find his Way out, unless he was well acquainted with its Windings; so that this horridly-spacious Prison may be compar'd to *Dædalus*'s Labyrinth.

Here Rooms within themselves incircled lie,
With various Windings to deceive the Eye.
. . . .
Such is the Work, so intricate the Place,
That scarce the Workmen all its Turns could
     trace;
And Dædalus *was puzzled how to find*
The secret Ways of what himself design'd.
   Ovid's Metamorph. Book VIII. translated by Dr. Croxall.

The Apartments of the chief Inquisitor, which likewise are very large, make Part of this House. The Entrance to it is through a Coach-Gate †, which leads to a large Court or Yard, round which are several spacious Apartments, where the King and his Court commonly stand, to view the Procession of the Prisoners the Day of the *Auto da Fé*.

The Furniture of these miserable Dungeons is, a Straw-bed, a Blanket, Sheets, and sometimes a Mattress. The Prisoner has likewise a Frame of Wood about six Foot long, and three or four wide. This he lays on the Ground, and spreads his Bed upon it. He also has a great earthen Pot to ease Nature in; an earthen Pan for washing himself; two Pitchers, one for clean and

† These are very common in *France*, and are made to give an Air of Grandeur to a House, and to serve as a Passage for Coaches to enter the Court or Yard of it. As low Persons are fond of imitating those in high Life, we often see, in *Paris*, a Coach-Door to the House of an insignificant Tradesman.

the

the other for foul Water; a Plate, and a little Veffel with Oil to light his Lamp. He is not, however, allow'd any Books, not even thofe of Devotion.

With regard to Provifions, the Inquifitors allow every Prifoner a Teftoon, [Seven Pence Half-penny *Englifh* Money] *per* Day for his Subfiftance. The Goaler, accompanied by two other Officers, vifits, at the End of every Month, all the Prifoners, to enquire of them how they would have their monthly Allowance laid out. The Prifoner ufually expends nine Teftoons for Part of his Provifions; that is, for a Porringer of Broth, and half a Pound of boil'd Beef daily; eight Teftoons for Bread, four for Cheefe, two for Fruit, four for Brandy, and the reft for Oranges, Lemons, Sugar and Wafhing. The Goaler's Secretary, who accompanies him, takes an exact Account of what Particulars every Prifoner requefts to be provided with during the Month; which

which Orders are punctually obferv'd; the Perfon who is appointed to furnifh the Prifoners on thefe Occafions being punifhed, in cafe he infringes them. Such as have a great Appetite, or defire Wine, (as Foreigners particularly do) petition for an Audience, in order to fet forth their Wants; and thefe are ufually fupplied, provided fuch Indulgence does not foment Intemperance, or is too expenfive. I myfelf addrefs'd the Inquifitors for this Purpofe, and my Requeft was granted.

"Tis only on fuch Occafions, or in Sicknefs, that the Inquifitors fhow fome little Humanity. Thefe excepted, nothing is found in them, but Severity and Barbarity. They are quite inflexible; for when once a Perfon has the Misfortune to be their Prifoner, he is not only forbid all Correfpondence with his Family and Friends, (as was obferved above) but even to make the leaft Noife, to complain, figh, addrefs Heaven aloud, to fing Pfalms or Hymns.

Hymns. These are capital Crimes, for which the Guards or Attendants of the Inquisition, who are ever walking up and down the Passages, first reprove him severely; but if he happens to make any Noise a second Time, they open his Cell, beat him severely; and this, not only to punish the Prisoner himself, but likewise to intimidate the others, who, by reason of the horrid Silence which reigns, and the Proximity of the Cells, hear the Blows and Cries of the wretched Victim. I shall here give an Instance of this Barbarity, attested by several Persons. A Prisoner having a violent Cough, one of the Guards came and ordered him not to make a Noise: He replied, that 'was not in his Power to forbear; when his Cough increasing, he was commanded, a second time, to be silent; but this being impossible, they stripp'd the poor Creature naked, and beat him so unmercifully, that his Cough grew worse;

and the Blows being again repeated, he died soon after.

By this Silence which the Guards or Keepers force Prisoners to keep, they not only deny them every little Consolation, but prevent such as are Neighbours from making the least Acquaintance; for, the Instant this should be found, they would be remov'd to other Cells.

They never lodge two Prisoners in the same Ceil; to prevent, (as the Inquisitors pretend) their consulting together, in order to suppress or conceal the Truth, or to baffle the Interrogatories; but the chief Motive for keeping those unhappy Persons apart, is to extort from them, by the dread Solitude of their Confinement, a Confession of whatever the Inquisitors may require from them.

However, on some Occasions, two Prisoners are lodged together in the same Cell; as, for Instance, when a Husband and Wife are imprison'd for

the

the like Crime; and that there is no room to fufpect, that one of them will prevent the other from freely confeffing the feveral Articles of which he or fhe may ftand indicted. When a Prifoner is fick, a Companion is given him, in order to affift him, as he is told. Likewife, when the Inquifitors have not been able to prevail with a Prifoner to plead guilty, and that there are not Proofs fufficient to convict him; they then fend him a Companion, who has been taught his Leffon before hand, by the Officers of the Inquifition; and this Companion artfully glides into the Confidence of the Prifoner; wins his Friendfhip; and inveighs ftrongly againft the Inquifitors; accufes them of Injuftice, Cruelty and Barbarity; and, infenfibly, caufes the unhappy Victim to join his Reproaches, againft the Inquifitors and the Inquifition. This is a black and unpardonable Crime; and fhould the Prifoner fall inadvertently into this Trap, he would

would be inevitably undone; for then his Companion immediately defires to be admitted to Audience; appears as a Witnefs againſt him; and is no longer his Fellow-Prifoner.

A Day or two after a Prifoner is brought into his Cell, his Hair is cut off, and his Head ſhav'd. On thefe Occafions no Diftinction is made in Age, Sex, or Birth. He then is order'd to tell his Name, his Profeffion; and to make a Difcovery of whatever he is worth in the World. To induce him to do this the more readily, the Inquifitor promifes, that, if he be really innocent, the feveral Things difclos'd by him will be carefully reſtor'd; but that, fhould any Effects, &c. conceal'd by him, be afterwards found, they all will be confifcated, tho' he may be clear'd. As moſt of the *Portugueze* are fo weak, as to be firmly perfuaded of the Sanctity and Integrity of this Tribunal, they don't fcruple to difcover even fuch Things as they might

might most easily conceal; from a firm Belief that every Particular will be restor'd to them, the Moment their Innocence shall be prov'd. However, these hapless Persons are impos'd upon; for those who have the sad Fortune to fall into the merciless Hands of these iniquitous Judges, are instantly bereav'd of all their Possessions. In case they plead their Innocence with regard to the Crimes of which they stand accus'd, and yet should be convicted by the Witnesses who swore against them, they then would be sentenc'd as guilty, and their whole Possessions confiscated. If Prisoners, in order to escape the Torture, and in Hopes of being sooner set at Liberty, own the Crime or Crimes of which they are impeach'd, they then are pronounced guilty by their own Confession; and the Public, in general, think their Effects, &c. justly confiscated. If such Prisoners come forth as repentant Criminals, who had accus'd themselves volun-

voluntarily, they yet dare not plead their Innocence; since they thereby would run the Hazard of being impris'on'd again, and sentenc'd, not only as hypocrite Penitents; but likewise as Wretches who accuse the Inquisitors of Injustice; so that, what Course soever these Persons might take, they would certainly lose all such Possessions belonging to them, as the Inquisitors had seiz'd.

Sometimes a Prisoner passes several Months in his Cell, without hearing a single Word of his being brought to Trial; without his knowing the Crime of which he stands impeach'd, or a single Witness who swore against him. At last the Goaler tells him, as of his own Accord, that it will be proper for him, to sue to be admitted to Audience. He then is conducted, for the first time, bare-headed to the Judges; an Under-Goaler walking first, himself next, and lastly the Goaler. Being come to one of the Doors of the Inquisition, quifition, the firft mention'd knocks thrice; upon which the Door is open'd by one of the Attendants on, or Porter of the Inquifition. The Prifoner, &c. are then commanded to ftay in this Anti-chamber, till the Porter has knock'd three Times at the Door of the great Hall of the Inquifition. This is done in order to give the Inquifitors Time to prepare for, and to receive the Prifoner; that is, for him to difmifs all Perfons to whom he may be giving Audience; thereby to prevent the Prifoners from feeing, or being feen, by them.

Every Thing being ready, purfuant to the Orders given for that Purpofe, the Judge who prefides in the great Hall, anfwers by a little Bell; upon which the Porter of the Hall in queftion opens the Door. The Prifoner then enters, guarded by the two Officers above-mention'd; when thefe, advancing towards the Table, give the

Prifoner

Prisoner a Stool; after which they retire, bending the Knee.

Then the President bids the Prisoner kneel; ordering him, at the same time, to lay his right hand on a Book, which is shut. He then addresses these Words to him: " Will you promise " to conceal the Secrets of the Holy- " Office, and to speak the Truth?"--- The Prisoner answering in the Affirmative, the President commands him to sit down; and afterwards asks him a great Variety of Questions with regard to all such Crimes, as may be committed, cognizable by the Inquisition.

The Secretary writes down very accurately the several Interrogatories and Answers; which being done, he rings the little Bell, when the Prisoner is convey'd back to his Cell, in the same Manner as he had been brought from it; but not till after he has been exhorted, to recollect all the Sins he may have committed, ever since his being come to Years of Discretion.

In

In case the Prisoner has made an ingenuous Confession, and complied with all the Customs and Orders of the Inquisition, the Goaler and Under-Goaler make him a low Bow, and assume an Air of Mildness: But if, on the contrary, the Prisoner will not answer directly to all such Interrogatories as are put to him, but employs ambiguous Expressions or Evasions (as they are suppos'd;) such as, *I know not*, *I cannot call to Mind*, *I have forgot*, he then is taken back, with Indignation, to his Cell.

Some Days after this first Audience, the Prisoner is again brought before his Judges, with the abovemention'd Formalities. He then is ask'd, whether he may have seriously examin'd into his past Life, and has some Things farther to divulge. In case he accuses himself of some other Crime or Crimes, his Declaration is receiv'd, and drawn up: But if he refuses to make any Confession, the Judge endeavours, by a thousand ensnaring Questions, to draw from him such Answers as may condemn him. This Snare is laid with the utmost Subtlety, and can scarce be escap'd; for should the Prisoner be seiz'd merely on such a random Report as is not sufficient to convict him; the Judges would be greatly puzzled, in case he did not fall, one Way or other, into the Snares spread for him; nor furnish, by his Answers, wherewithal to find him guilty. Farther, as the Inquisitors promise to treat the Prisoners with great Lenity, and even to release them, provided they will accuse themselves, before their Crime has been prov'd; Prisoners are thus overreach'd, and plead guilty to the Crimes of which they stand impeach'd, in Hopes of obtaining, by a voluntary Confession, their speedy Release, which is solemnly promis'd them. They often go farther, and even declare themselves guilty of Crimes of which they are wholly innocent; a Circumstance that

of the INQUISITION.

is infinitely pleasing to the Inquisitors, when these have not Matter sufficient to convict a Prisoner.

But if the Prisoner, either because he is really innocent, or too artful to be impos'd upon, persists in pleading not guilty; then a written Copy is given him of his Indictment, wherein the Inquisitors intermix many false Accusations, relating to the most enormous Crimes, with those of which he stands indicted; all such Circumstances, sworn to by the Witnesses, as might be of Service to the Prisoner, being suppress'd. The blending of Truth and Falshood, in this Manner, is another Trap laid for the wretched Victim; for as he does not fail to inveigh bitterly against the horrid Crimes with which he is falsely charg'd; his Judges take occasion, from thence, to suppose, (most unjustly) that those concerning which he complains least, are true. How false soever this Consequence may be, be, it yet is turn'd greatly to the Disadvantage of the Prisoner.

After the Prisoner has received the Articles of the Indictment in Writing, he is ask'd whether he desires to have a Counsellor. However, he is not at Liberty to chuse one; a Counsellor not being allowed to defend the Cause of a Heretic, upon pain of his being declared infamous. This Counsellor is appointed by the Inquisitors, who secure him to themselves by an Oath. Such a Counsellor must consequently be of little Service to the Prisoner, as he is not permitted to be his Advocate; to give him Advice; or to search for Proofs of his Innocence, except before the Inquisitors. Thus the Prisoner is reduc'd to the sad Necessity of defending himself, against Accusers and Witnesses who are wholly unknown to him. The Fiscal Proctor is his Accuser, and the only Person he knows.

'Tis to no Purpose that he insists upon knowing, and being confronted with

with the Witnesses who have sworn against him. The only Circumstance in his Power is to guess at them, and to ask if such and such People are not his Enemies; to which no Answer either affirmative, or negative, is returned. The Inquisitors then proceed in the Interrogatories, when, if he still continues to deny, he is remanded back to his Cell. In fine, after being sometimes conducted from the Prison to Audience, and from the Audience to Prison, for several Years together, his Trial is at last prepar'd, and ended definitively. For this Purpose he is taken before the Inquisitors, who deliver him a Copy of the Depositions of the several Witnesses; but not till they have expung'd every Particular which might serve to his Justification; as likewise all such Circumstances concerning Persons and Places, as might give the Prisoner some Light, with regard to the Witnesses who have sworn against him.

If the Prisoner is not prepar'd to reply to the Articles of which he stands accus'd; he is allow'd three or four Days to consider of them; and, for this Purpose, is remanded back to his Dungeon. On this Occasion, the unhappy Victim racks his Brain, in order to find out his Accusers; with respect to whom he yet often remains in doubt, even after all his Reflexions.

This Time being elapsed, he again is summon'd before his Judges. He then is heard, with regard to any Exceptions he may make as to the Witnesses who have sworn against him, tho' he knows neither their Names, Professions or Characters†. But, if he should happen to pitch upon the real Persons; and give Reasons why he supposes they endeavoured to wreak all their Malice on him, by false and unjust Accusations; tho' this might weaken their Testimony, it yet would not invali-

---

† What Inconsistencies are here!

date

date it, especially if he should be charg'd with any black and infamous Crime.

Such are the Prerogatives of the Witnesses in this Tribunal, who are never nam'd, confronted or known, by which Means Crowds of them are to be had. In the Case of Heresy, the Inhumanity of the Inquisitors is so great, that every Person, how infamous soever his Character may be; tho' a false Swearer, a Thief, or a *Mohammedan* †; yet his Testimony would be receiv'd, and this would suffice to cause a Prisoner to be sentenc'd to the Flames.

The Prisoner having given in his Answers, in case the Inquisitors are not satisfied with them; if the Indictment is not sufficiently prov'd; or that the

† This Ranking of a *Mahommedan* with a Thief, &c. is very unjust; for, surely a *Mohammedan* may be a Man of the greatest Probity and Virtue. But the Particulars in the Text are extracted from a *Romish* Writer, tho' an Enemy to the Inquisition; and many *Romanists* look upon *Mohammedans* in general, on account of their Religion, as the most horrid of Wretches.

Judges want to discover any Accomplices the Prisoner may have; they order him to be tortur'd, at a Motion made by the Fiscal Proctor for that Purpose; and this is done immediately.

If the Tortures force, from the Prisoner, a full and entire Confession of all the Articles of which he stands accus'd, he then is convey'd back to a frightful Dungeon; where he is left a Prey to his Melancholy; to the violent Anguish caus'd by the Tortures; and to his dreadful Expectation of still greater Barbarities. But, in case the Tortures have not been able to force a Confession from him, he then is remanded back to his sad Abode, when the basest Artifices and Snares are employ'd. Upon Pretence of succouring him in this deplorable Condition he is reduc'd to, by his Sufferings, he is allow'd a Companion in his Cell, (as was hinted at above) who, after gaining his Confidence, by pretending that he he also is imprison'd for the like Crimes with himself; exclaims against the Inquisition, its Injustice, Rigour and Cruelty; and thus make the Prisoner fall into Snares, which are the more difficult to be shunn'd, as they are disguis'd under the deceitful Appearances of Friendship, Compassion, and Sympathy in Misfortunes. Some Familiars of the Inquisition don't scruple to confine themselves four or five Months in a Cell, merely to entrap a Prisoner.

In fine, if the Person impeach'd is found guilty, either from Evidence or his own Confession, he is sentenc'd to be whipt, to perpetual Imprisonment, to the Galley, or to Death; according as the Crime committed by him, is thought more or less enormous. One sure Circumstance is, the best Part of his Effects, if not all, are confiscated, as was said before.

I must observe, that the Inquisitors don't confine their Power merely to the Living, or to those who die in their Prisons.

thrown into it, and thefe were foon confum'd. Not long after, *Brookes*, Bifhop of *Glocefter*, gave the like Treatment at *Oxford*, to the Corps of *Catharine*, Wife of *Peter Martyr*, who dying a few Years before, had been buried in *Chrift-Church*, near the Remains of St. *Fridifwide*, who was greatly venerated in that College: For the above *Catherine* being convicted, of imbibing her Hufband's Herefy, fhe was condemn'd; her dead Body was dug up, carried upon Men's Shoulders, and caft upon a Dunghill. However, in Queen *Elizabeth*'s Reign, her Corps, by Order of Archbifhop *Parker*, and other Commiffioners, was taken from the Dunghill, and buried in its former Place.---

After Judgment has pafs'd on all the Prifoners, a mock religious Ceremony is perform'd; when they all walk in difmal Proceffion to St. *Dominick*'s Church, and there hear their Articles of Impeachment read, together with
the

the Sentences. This Ceremony is call'd *Auto da Fé*, or Act of Faith.

Here follows a succinct Description of one solemniz'd at *Madrid* in 1682.

The Officers of the Inquisition, preceded by Trumpets, Kettle-Drums, and their Banner, march'd, *May* 30, 1682, in Cavalcade to the Palace of the great Square; where they declar'd, by Proclamation, that on the 30th of *June*, the Sentences of the Prisoners condemn'd to the Flames, and to other Punishments, would be put in Execution. There had not been a Spectacle of this Kind, in *Madrid*, during forty Years before, for which Reason it was expected, by the Inhabitants, with as much Impatience as tho' it had been the merriest Holiday. The 30th of *June* being come, numberless Multitudes of People appear'd, as splendidly dress'd as for a Royal Wedding. In the great Square was rais'd a high Scaffold: Into this Square, from seven in the Morning, till nine at Night, came

came Criminals of both Sexes; all the Inquisitions in the Kingdom having sent their Prisoners to *Madrid*. The Prosecutions and Sentences were read aloud. There were twenty *Jews*, Men and Women, and one Renegado *Mohammedan*, who were all burnt. Fifty *Jews* and *Jewesses* having never been imprison'd before, and repenting of their Crimes, were sentenc'd to a long Imprisonment, and to wear a yellow Scapulary. Ten more, indicted for Bigamy, Witchcraft, and other Crimes, were sentenc'd to be whipt, and afterwards sent to the Gallies; these wore large Paste-board Caps on their Heads, with Inscriptions on them; having Halters about their Necks, and Torches in their Hands.

The whole Court was present; the King, the Queen, the Embassadors, Courtiers, and numberless Multitudes of People. The Inquisitor's Chair was plac'd in a Sort of Tribunal, far above that of the King. The unhappy

py Victims were executed fo near to the Place where the King ftood, that he could heard their Groans; the Scaffold on which they ftood, touching his Balcony. The Nobles of *Spain*, acted here the fame Part as the Sheriffs Officers in *England*. Thofe Noblemen led fuch Criminals as were to be burnt; and held them when they were faft bound with thick Cords; the reft of the Criminals being conducted by the *Familiars*, or common Servants of the Inquifition. Several Friars, both learned and ignorant, argued with great Vehemence, to convince thefe unhappy Creatures of the Truth of the Chriftian Religion. Some of thofe Criminals (*Jews*) were perfectly well fkill'd in their Religion; and made the moft furprizing Replies, and that without the leaft Emotion. Among them was a young Maiden of exquifite Beauty, and but feventeen Years of Age; who being on the fame Side with the Queen, addrefs'd her, in Hopes
of

of obtaining her Pardon, as follows:
"Great Queen! Will not your Ro-
"yal Presence be of some Service to
"me in my miserable Condition?
"Have Regard to my Youth; and
"consider that I profess a Religion
"which I imbib'd from my Infancy."
The Queen turn'd away her Eyes; and
tho' she seem'd to greatly pity her Distress, she yet did not dare to speak a
Word in her Behalf.

Now Mass began, in the Midst of which the Priest came from the Altar, and seated himself in a Chair prepared for that Purpose. The chief Inquisitor descended from the Amphitheatre, dress'd in his Cope, and having a Mitre on his Head; when, after bowing to the Altar, he advanced towards the King's Balcony; went up to it by the Stairs, at the End of the Scaffold; attended by some Officers of the Inquisition, carrying the Cross and the Gospels; with a Book containing the Oath by which the Kings of *Spain* oblige them-

themselves to protect the Catholic Faith; to extirpate Heretics; and to support, with all their Power, the Prosecutions of the Inquisition.

The King standing up, bareheaded, having, on one Side, the Constable of *Castile*, who held the Royal Sword lifted, swore to maintain the Oath, which was read by a Counsellor of the Royal Council. His Majesty continued in this Posture till the Inquisitor returned to his Place; when a Secretary of the Inquisition mounted a Sort of Pulpit, and read the like Oath, administring it to the Counsellors and the whole Assembly. Mass began about Twelve, and did not end till nine at Night, because of the Sentences of the several Criminals; they being all read, aloud, one after another. The Intrepidity with which those hapless Prisoners suffer'd Death was very astonishing. Some threw themselves into the Fire; others burnt their Hands, and afterwards their Feet, thrusting them into the

the Flames, and holding them therein with so much Resolution, that many were sorry such heroic Souls were not enlightned by the Gospel. I myself (says the Author) did not go to see the Execution; for besides its being Midnight, and at a considerable Distance from my Abode, I was so deeply struck with the Sight of them in the Day-Time, that it put me very much out of Order. The King could not be absent from this horrid Spectacle, as it was a religious one; he being obliged to give a Sanction, by his Presence, to all Acts of the Inquisition. However, this extreme Severity does not contribute to the Conversion of the *Jews*, it not making the least Impression on them. There are great Numbers of these in *Madrid*, who are known to be such, and yet enjoy Posts in the Treasury, and live unmolested. When they are very rich, the Government only terrifies them, in order to make them pay a large Ransom for their
Lives,

Lives, whereby considerable Sums are rais'd: These Persons, provided they have but Money, secure themselves from the Flames, tho' they merit them no less than the poorest Wretch †. Thus far this Author, who was a Romanist. If so many of These exclaim against the Inquisition, what Moderation can be expected from a Protestant?

The learned Dr. *Geddes*, Vol. I. Pag. 447, & *seq.* of his Tracts, thus describes an *Auto da Fé* in *Lisbon*, of which he himself was a Spectator.---The Prisoners are no sooner in the Hands of the civil Magistrate, than they are loaded with Chains, before the Eyes of the Inquisitors; and being carried first to the secular Goal, are, within an Hour or two, brought from thence before the Lord Chief Justice, who, without knowing any Thing of their particular Crimes; or of the Evidence that was

† *Memoires de la Cour d'Espagne.* Part 2. p. 50, & seq. Hague 1691. Second Edit. 12mo.

given in against them, asks them one by one, *In what Religion they intend to die?* If they answer, that they will die in the Communion of the Church of *Rome*; they are condemn'd by him, *to be carried forthwith to the Place of Execution, and there to be first strangled and afterwards burnt to Ashes*:---But if they say, *they will die in the Protestant*, or in any other Faith that is contrary to the Romish, they then are sentenc'd by him *to be carried forthwith to the Place of Execution, and there to be burnt alive.*

At the Place of Execution, which at *Lisbon* is the *Ribera*, there are so many Stakes set up, as there are Prisoners to be burnt, with a good Quantity of dry Furze about them. *The Stakes of the Professed,* as the Inquisitors call them, may be about four Yards high; and have a small Board, whereon the Prisoner is to be seated, within half a yard of the Top. The Negative and Relaps'd being first strangled and burnt; the Professed go up a Ladder, betwixt

of the INQUISITION.

the two Jesuits, who attended Them all Day; and when they are come even with the forementioned Board, they turn about to the People, and the Jesuits spend near a Quarter of an Hour, in exhorting the Professed to be reconcil'd to the Church of *Rome*; which, if they refuse to be, the Jesuits come down, and the Executioner ascends; and having turned the Professed off the Ladder upon the Seat, and chained their Bodies close to the Stake, he leaves them; and the Jesuits go up to them a second Time, to renew their Exhortation to them, and at Parting tell them; *That they leave them to the Devil, who is standing at their Elbow to receive their Souls; and carry them with him into the Flames of Hell-fire, so soon as they are out of their Bodies.* Upon this a great Shout is raised; and assoon as the Jesuits are got off the Ladder, the Cry is; *Let the Dogs Beards be made, let the Dogs Beards be made*; which is done by thrusting flaming Furzes faftned to a long Pole, againft their Faces. And this Inhumanity is commonly continued until their Faces are burnt to a Coal; and is always accompanied with fuch loud Acclamations of Joy, as are not to be heard upon any other Occafion; a Bullfeaft, or a Farce being dull Entertainments, to the ufing a profefs'd Heretic thus inhumanly.

The profeffed Beards being thus made, or trimm'd as they call it in Jollity; Fire is fet to the Furze, which is at the Bottom of the Stake, and above which the Profeffed are chained fo high, that the Top of the Flame feldom reaches higher than the Seat they fit on; and if there happens to be a Wind, to which that Place is much expos'd, it feldom reaches fo high as their Knees. So that if there is a Calm, the Profeffed are commonly dead in about half an Hour after the Furze is fet on Fire; but if the Weather proves Windy, they are not, after that, dead

in

in an Hour and half, or two Hours; and so are really roasted and not burnt to Death. But tho', out of Hell, there cannot possibly be a more lamentable Spectacle than this, being joined with the Sufferers (so long as they are able to speak) Cries, *viz. Miserecordia por amor de Dios,* " Mercy for the " Love of God;" yet it is beheld by People of both Sexes, and all Ages, with such Transports of Joy and Satisfaction, as are not, on any other Occasion, to be met with.---Thus far Dr. *Geddes,* who observes, p. 450, (a very remarkable Circumstance) " That this " inhuman Joy is not the Effect of a " natural Cruelty, but arises from the " Spirit of their Religion; a Proof " of which is, that all public Male- " factors, except Hereticks, are no " where more tenderly lamented than " by the *Portugueze*; and even when " there is nothing in the Manner of " their Deaths that appear inhuman " or cruel.

A short, but moving Description, is likewise given of an *Auto da Fé*, by Dr. *Wilcox*, afterwards Bishop of *Gloucester*, in a Letter to Bishop *Burnet*, quoted in *Chandler's Limborch*, Page 302. The Letter is dated from *Lisbon*, *January* 15 *N. S.* 1706, and is as follows:

My Lord,

"IN Obedience to your Lordship's Commands, of the 10th *ult.* I have here sent all that was printed concerning the last *Auto da Fé*. I saw the whole Process, which was agreeable to what is published by *Limborch* and others upon that Subject. Of the five Persons condemned, there were but four burnt; *Antonio Tavanes*, by an unusual Reprieve, being saved after the Procession. *Heytor Dias*, and *Maria Penteyra*, were burnt alive, and the other two first strangled. The Execution was very cruel. The Woman was

"was alive in the Flames half an Hour, and the Man above an Hour. The prefent King and his Brothers were feated at a Window fo near, as to be addreffed to, a confiderable Time, in very moving Terms, by the Man as he was burning. But tho' the Favour he begg'd was only a few more Faggots, yet he was not able to obtain it. Thofe who are burnt alive here, are feated on a Bench, twelve Feet high, faftned to a Pole, and above fix Feet higher than the Faggots. The Wind being a little frefh, the Man's hinder Parts were perfectly wafted; and as he turn'd himfelf, his Ribs open'd before he left fpeaking; the Fire being recruited as it wafted, to keep him juft in the fame Degree of Heat. But all his Intreaties cou'd not procure him a larger Allowance of Wood, to fhorten his Mifery and difpatch him."---How hard muft his Heart be, who can read this without Horror? I fhall

I shall now give a Relation of that in which I myself had the ill Fate to walk. A Fortnight before the Solemnization of this *Auto da Fé*, Notice was given in all the Churches, that it would be celebrated on *Sunday* the 21st *June* 1744. At the same Time, all who intended to be Spectators thereof, were exhorted not to ridicule the Prisoners, but rather pray to God for their Conversion. On *Saturday* the 20th of the Month abovementioned, we were all ordered to get ready by next Morning; and, at the same Time, a Band was given each of us, and old black Clothes to such as had none.

Those accused of *Judaism*; and who, thro' Fear of the Torture, confess'd their being such, were distinguished by large Scapularies call'd *San Benidos*. This is a Piece of yellow Stuff, about two Ells long; and in the Middle of which a Hole is made, to put the Head thro': On it were sowed Stripes of red Stuff, and this falls behind

of the INQUISITION.

hind and before, in Form of a St. *Andrew's* Crofs. Thofe who are condemned for Sorcery, Magic, and fuch like, wear the fame Kind of Scapulary, defcrib'd above. They are diftinguifhed only by wearing a Pafte-board Cap, about a Foot and half high, on which Devils and Flames are painted; and, at the Bottom, the Word WIZARD is writ in large Characters.

I muft obferve, that all fuch Perfons as are not fentenc'd to die, carry a lighted yellow Wax-Taper in their Hands. I was the only Perfon to whom one was not given, on Account of my being an obftinate Proteftant.

The relaps'd *Jews*, and fuch heretical Roman Catholicks, as are fentenc'd to die for refufing to confefs the Crimes whereof they are accus'd, are drefs'd in grey Samaras, much fhorter than the *San Benidos* abovementioned. The Face of the Perfon who wears it, is copied (before and behind) from the Life, ftanding on Firebrands ; with Flames

Flames curling upwards, and Devils round it. At the Bottom of the Samara, their Names and Sirnames are writ.

Blasphemers are dress'd as above, and distinguished only by a Gag in their Mouths.

The Prisoners being thus habited, the Procession open'd with the Dominican Friars, preceeded by the Banner of their Order. Afterwards came the Banner and Crucifix of the Inquisition, which was followed by the Criminals, each whereof walked between two Familiars, who were to be answerable for them; and bring back, to Prison, such as were not to be executed, after the Procession was ended.

The accompanying Prisoners on these dismal Occasions is thought so great an Honour, that such as attend, to Execution, these unhappy Victims, and even lean upon them, are always the first Noblemen of the Kingdom; who are so proud of acting in this Character, that they wou'd not resign that Honour

Honour for any other that fhou'd be offered them, fo cruelly blind is their Zeal.

Next came the Jewifh Converts, followed by fuch as were indicted for Witchcraft and Magic, and had confefs'd their Crimes.

The Proceffion clos'd with the unhappy Wretches who were fentenc'd to the Flames.

The March then began, when the whole Proceffion walk'd round the Court of the chief Inquifitor's Palace, in Prefence of the King, the Royal Family, and the whole Court, who were come thither for this Purpofe. The Prifoners being all gone thro' the Court juft mentioned, proceeded along one of the Sides of *Rocio* Square; and went down *Odreyros* Street; when, returning by *Efcudeyros* Street, and up another Side of *Rocio* Square, they came, at laft, to St. *Dominick*'s Church, which was hung, from top to bottom, with red and yellow Tapiftry.

Before

Before the High-Altar was built an Amphitheatre, with a pretty confiderable Number of Steps, in order to feat all the Prifoners and their Attendant-Familiars. Oppofite was rais'd another greater Altar, after the Romifh Fafhion, on which was placed a Crucifix furrounded with feveral lighted Tapers, and Mafs-Books.. To the Right of this was a Pulpit, and to the Left a Gallery, magnificently adorn'd, for the King, the Royal Family, the great Men of the Kingdom, and the foreign Minifters, to fit in. To the Right of this Gallery was, a long one, for the Inquifitors; and between thefe two Galleries, a Room, whither the Inquifitors retire to hear the Confeffions of thofe who, terrified at the Horrors of impending Death, may be prompted to confefs what they before had perfifted in denying; they fometimes gladly fnatching this laft Moment allowed them to efcape a cruel Exit.

Every

Every Perfon being thus feated in the Church, the Preacher afcended the Pulpit, whence he made a Panegyric on the Inquifition; exhorted fuch Prifoners as were not fentenc'd to die, to make a good Ufe of the Clemency indulg'd them; by fincerely renouncing, that Inftant, the Herefies and Crimes of which they ftood convicted. Then directing himfelf to the Prifoners who were to be burnt, he exhorted them to make a good Ufe of the little Time left them, by making a fincere Confeffion of their Crimes, and thereby avoiding a cruel Death.

During the Sermon, the Prifoners have fome Refrefhments; the open Air having a very ftrong Effect on moft, and the Length of the March fatiguing them greatly. On this Occafion dry Fruits are given them, and as much Water as they can drink.

The Preacher being come from the Pulpit, fome Priefts belonging to the Inquifition afcended it fucceffively, to read

read the Trial of each Prisoner, who was standing all the Time, holding a lighted Taper. Each Prisoner, after hearing it, return'd to his Place. This lasted till Ten at Night.

The Trials of all the Prisoners not sentenc'd to die, being read, the President of the Inquisition, drest in his sacerdotal Vestments, appear'd with a Book in his Hand; after which five or six Priests, in Surplices, tapp'd, with a Sort of Wands, the Heads and Shoulders of the Prisoners in question: saying certain Prayers us'd in the Romish Church, when the Excommunication is taken off.

Then another Priest went up into the Pulpit, to read the Trials of the ill-fated Persons sentenc'd to the Flames; after which these sad Victims were delivered up to the secular Power, whose Officers take them to the *Relaçaon* †, whither the King comes. Thus the

† A Senate House, or Court of Judicature.

Inquisition, to conceal its Cruelties, calls in the secular Arm, which condemns the Prisoners to die; or rather ratifies the Sentence past by the Inquisitors. This lasted till six in the Morning.

At last these miserable Creatures, accompanied by the Familiars and Priests, were conducted, under the Guard of a Detachment of Foot, to *Campo da Laa*, or the Wool-field. Here they were fastned, with Chains, to Posts, and seated on Pitch-barrels. Afterwards the King appear'd, in a sorry Coach, at which were Ropes, instead of Harnesses. He then ordered the Friars to exhort each of the Victims in question, to die in the Romish Faith, upon Pain of being burnt alive; but to declare, that such as complied with the Exhortation of the Priest, should be strangled before they were committed to the Flames. His Majesty staid till all the Prisoners were executed.

In the *Auto da Fè*, in which I walk'd, were burnt the following Persons:

1. Father *Joseph de Seguira*, a Priest, convicted of various Heresies, and obstinate.
2. *Theresa Carvalha*, a Widow, found guilty of different Heresies, and confessing them.
3. *Francis Dias Cabaço*, a Scrivener, convicted of Heresy, and obstinate.
4. *Charles Joseph*, a Barber, convicted of Heresy, and obstinate.
5. *Gabriel Roderiguez Bicudo*, a Shoemaker, who, after publickly abjuring Judaism in a former *Auto da Fé*; and being taken up a second Time for committing the like Crime, was convicted, and proved obstinate.
6. *Pedro de Rates Henequim*, living on his Estate, condemn'd for inventing, writing, following and defending the Doctrines of Hereticks; for turning

turning Heresiarch with execrable Blasphemies; convicted, false, dissembling, confident, varying and impenitent.

7. *Josepha Maria*, Spinster, Daughter of *Gabriel Rodriguez Bicudo*, abjuring in the same Manner as her Father (above) and convicted a Second Time; false, dissembling, and impenitent.

8. *Mecia da Costa*, a Widow, reconcil'd in a former *Auto da Fé* for the Crime of Witchcraft, and living a-part from the Catholic Faith; making a Contract with the Devil, whom she worshipped as God; convicted, denying, obstinate and relaps'd †.

The Instant the sad Victims abovementioned were delivered up to the

† The above is extracted and translated from the original Sheet of Paper, dated at *Lisbon*, 21st *June* 1744, (brought by me from that City, and which any Person may peruse) containing the Names of the several Persons, and their pretended Crimes, who walk'd in the *Auto de Fé*, of the above Date.

secular

secular Arm, all the rest of the Prisoners were led back, with the like Ceremony, about ten at Night, from St. *Dominick*'s Church to the Inquisition. Being arrived there, we were carried thro' several Galleries, till we came to the Abode allotted Us. Here were several Chambers, the Doors of which were open; when each of us chose that which he lik'd best. There then were given to each a Straw-bed, a Blanket, and Sheets which had been laid in. Most of these Things were far from clean, there not having been an *Auto da Fé* for two Years before. The Women were lodg'd a Story above us.

Being thus settled, to the best of our Power, we thought ourselves the happiest Persons upon the Earth, tho' we had little to boast of. However, we were now together, and breath'd the fresh Air; we enjoy'd the Light of the Sky, and had a View of a Garden: In a Word, we knew that we should not be put to Death; all which Circumstances

cumstances prov'd a great Consolation. The Alcaide or Goaler, and his Brother-Keeper brought each of us a Loaf, a Cake, and Water sufficient for the whole Company; permitting us, at the same Time, to divert ourselves, provided we did not make a Noise. This was the first Time we had supp'd, in the Inquisition, with any Satisfaction. Having been greatly fatigued, by the Ceremony describ'd in the foregoing Pages, I slept very soundly.

I am to observe that, from the Time of our returning from the Procession, we were supported at the Expence of the Cardinal-Inquisitor, and not at that of the mock holy Office. We were soon sensible of this Change of Masters, not only by the Advantages describ'd above; but also by the Permission allowed us, of sending, to our Relations and Friends, for such Provisions as we might want, if we did not like those given us; or had not enough to satisfy our Appetites. 'Twould

'Twould be the highest Ingratitude in me not to mention the very essential Favours which I myself, as well as the three Brethren, my Fellow-Prisoners, receiv'd from the Free-Masons at *Lisbon*. These cou'd not be easy till they had obtain'd Leave to visit us, which gave us inexpressible Joy; and their Bounty prov'd of the most signal Advantage to us. We imagin'd, at first, that the Reason why the Cardinal order'd us to be confin'd, during some Days, in this Part of the Prison, was to accustom us, by insensible Degrees, to the open Air; and to dispel the dreadful Melancholy which had so long oppress'd us. However, the true Cause of it was, that each of us might be the more easily convey'd to the Places to which he was doom'd by his Sentence; to put into our Hands a Bill of the Expences the Inquisitors had been at; and to give the various Officers the Instructions necessary, for conveying us afterwards to the several Places appointed by the Inquisitors. Dur-

of the INQUISITION.

During the Courfe of the Week in queftion, fome of the Prifoners were banifh'd: Such as had more Hufbands or Wives than one were whipt thro' the Streets of *Lifbon*, and others fent to the Galley, among whom I was.

The *Portugueze* Galley, is a Prifon ftanding by the River Side, and confifts of two very fpacious Rooms built one over the other. That on the Ground-Floor is the Apartment of the Slaves, and the other is for the Sick, and the Officers of this Prifon; It being the Receptacle, not only of fuch as are condemn'd by the Inquifitors, but likewife by the Lay Judges. Among thefe Prifoners are *Turks* and *Moors*, taken on Board the *Corfair* Veffels; together with fugitive Slaves, and bad or villainous Servants, whom their Mafters fend to this Galley, as a Chaftifement.

Thefe feveral Prifoners, of what Quality foever, are employ'd in Toils equally low and grievous. Some work in the Dock-yards; they carrying Timber to the Carpenters, unloading the Ships, and providing Water and Provisions for victualling such as are outward bound. They likewise carry Water to the Prisons in *Lisbon*; and to the King's Gardens, in order for refreshing them: In a Word, they are obliged to submit to any Labours, how ignominious and painful soever, for the Service of his *Portugueze* Majesty, or of the Officers who command over them. These Slaves are treated with the greatest Severity and Cruelty, except they find Means to bribe their Overseers to Gentleness, by giving them, at Intervals, a little Money.

In this Galley, all the Slaves are fastned two and two, by one Foot only, with a Chain eight Foot long. At their Girdle is an Iron Hook, by which they shorten or lengthen their Chain, to make the Weight of it less troublesome. Their Heads and Beards are shav'd once a Month. They wear coarse

coarse blue Cloaths, Caps and Coats; and have a great Coat, made of coarse Serge of the same Colour, which serves them as a Cloak in the Day Time, and a Coverlet at Night. They lie in a Sort of Frame of Boards rais'd a little from the Ground, over which a Matt is spread.

To every Galley-Slave is given, each Day, a Pound and half of very dry, black Biscuit; with six Pounds of Salt Meat every Month, and a Bushel of Pease, Lentils or Beans, which they are allowed to sell; in order to purchase better Provisions, if they can afford it.

They are led early every Morning, a few Festivals excepted, whithersoever their Drudgery may be wanted. They then toil incessantly till Eleven, when they leave work, in order to eat and rest themselves till One; after which they again renew their miserable Labours, and these they carry on till Night, when they are conducted back to the Galley.

Such is the Life which thefe unhappy Wretches lead daily.

When any of them fall fick, they are remov'd to the other great Room, where proper Care is taken of them by the Phyficians, Surgeons, &c. It is incumbent on me to do Juftice to them in this Particular. The Sick are here treated with all imaginable Care and Humanity. Thofe whofe Stomachs are too weak to digeft ftrong Aliments, have good Broth, on which Occafion Chickens are not fpar'd. But 'tis far otherwife with Regard to Punifhments; the Tafk-Mafters exercifing great Cruelty towards all fuch as commit a Fault: Thofe unhappy Slaves, being laid on their Bellies, are faftned to a Ladder; when two Men whip alternately, their bare Pofteriors, with a Bull's Pizzle, or a thick pitch'd Rope. The Sufferers often receive two or three hundred Lafhes in this Manner, whereby their Skin is not only flead, but Pieces of Flefh are torne away; fo that the

the Surgeons are obliged to make deep Incisions, in order to prevent a Mortification; which frequently prevents their working during a long Time. These Wounds often become ulcerous, and many are disabled for Life. In short, the Barbarities exercis'd by this Tribunal are so great, and so various, that *Oldham* might justly put the following Words into the Mouth of *Ignatius Loyola*:

Let th' Inquisition Rage, fresh Cruelties
Make the dire Engines groan with tortur'd Cries:
Let Campo Flori *every Day be strew'd*
With the warm Ashes of the Lutheran *Brood:*
Repeat again Bohemian *Slaughter o'er;*
And Pie'mont *Vallies drown with floating Gore:*
Swifter than murth'ring Angels when they fly
On Errands of avenging Destiny.
Fiercer than Storms let loose, with eager Haste
Lay Cities, Countries, Realms, whole Nature waste.
Sack, ravish, burn, destroy, slay, massacre,
Till the same Grave their Lives and Names inter.
  SATYR III. (*against the* Jesuits.)

PART

PART IV.

Examples of the Injustice and Cruelty of the Inquisition.

THE pretended Zeal of the Inquisitors, for preserving Religion in all its Purity, is merely a Cloak to hide their boundless Ambition, their insatiable Thirst of Riches, and their vindictive Spirit.

The Emperor *Frederic*, mentioned in the foregoing Pages, who first invested the Inquisitors with great Privileges, was the first who made the most cruel Abuse of them. All who oppos'd his Will were deemed Hereticks, and judged and burnt as such. He committed

mitted to the Flames, upon the falfe Pretence of Herefy, fo great a Number of *Romanifts*, that Pope *Gregory* could not forbear reprefenting to him, in the moft ferious Terms; that it became him to extirpate Heretics only, and not the true Sons of the Church.

The Monarch in queftion, did not forefee that the Court of *Rome* might turn thofe very Weapons againft him, which he had employed fo unjuftly againft a Multitude of Chriftians. This Emperor was afterwards fenfible of his Error, but too late; for he himfelf was in 1239 impeach'd as a Heretic; and being judg'd, was excommunicated as fuch; and his Subjects freed from the Allegiance they had fworn to him; though his Herefy was no more, than his having oppofed the unlimited Power which the Popes pretended to exercife over all Chriftians, not excepting even crown'd Heads.

Elezine, Lord of *Padua*, whofe Herefy was only his too great Attachment
to

to the Emperor *Frederic*, was likewise excommunicated, and Inquisitors appointed to prosecute him for this pretended Crime. Accordingly he was summon'd to appear in *Rome*, whither he sent Persons of Reputation to declare his Innocence. However, these were not allowed to be heard, the Pope insisting that he should appear in Person; and, upon his refusing to obey this Order, the *Roman* Pontiff sent the Bishop of *Treviso* to inform *Elezine*, that he would render himself obnoxious to all the Punishments inflicted on Heretics, in case he refused to appear personally in *Rome*, sometime in *August* 1251: And further, that if he did not submit to all the Pope's Injunctions, he would be declared infamous, and a Heretic; himself and his Possessions seiz'd, and a Crusade sent against him and his Adherents. In fine, Sentence was pass'd against this Lord in 1254, whereby he was pronounced a Heretic, and all his Possessions

Poffeffions confifcated in favour of his Brother *Albert*.

About the fame Time, Count *de Touloufe* fell a Victim to the cruel Power of the *Roman* Pontiffs and their wicked Agents. His Dominions were fack'd by Crufaders, whom the Pope had fent out againft him. In fine, this Count, though a zealous *Romanift*, could find no other Way to extricate himfelf, than by making a Submiffion, too mean and fevere for a Prince, whofe only Crime was his ftrong Attachment to *Frederic*, then at Variance with the Court of *Rome*; and his not perfecuting his own Subjects, who were accus'd, by that Court, of Herefy.

When once the Tribunal of the Inquifition had gain'd a certain Afcendant, by the Weaknefs of the Emperors and other Sovereign Princes, who feem'd to vie with one another, in enlarging its Authority and Privileges; the Inquifitors prov'd to the Princes in queftion, and to their Succeffors, that they all

were

were subject to this Tribunal. Afterwards, throwing off every Restraint, and being aided by the Thunders of the Vatican, which these weak Princes dreaded prodigiously; the Inquisitors carried their Insolence to such a Height, as would have appear'd incredible to Protestants, in this Age, was it not solemnly vouch'd by famous Authors of acknowledg'd Veracity, who liv'd in those Times.

The *Spanish* Inquisitors cited *Jane*, Daughter of the Emperor *Charles* V. to appear before their Tribunal; in order to be examined concerning another Person, with regard to some Articles of Faith, which the Inquisitors declared were heretical. The Emperor himself stood in such Awe of the Inquisition, that he commanded his Daughter, in case she thought the Person accus'd ever so little guilty, not to delay her Information, in order to avoid the Sentence of Excommunication, levelled not only against other Persons, but even against

against himself. The Princess, in Compliance with this Command, immediately gave in her Deposition to *Valdes* Archbishop of *Seville*, then Inquisitor-General.

The Inquisition of *Arragon* proceeded to still greater Lengths; it having the Insolence to prosecute Don *Carlos*, eldest Son to Don *John* II. King of *Arragon* †.

The Inquisition of *Castile* distinguish'd itself in a Manner equally daring and horrid; this Tribunal attempting to prosecute the Memory of the Emperor *Charles* V. and to sentence his Will to the Flames, as heretical; together with all those Persons who had had the greatest Share in this Monarch's Friendship.

Here follows a succinct Account of this Incident, as related by *Thuanus*, *d'Aubigné*, and *le Laboureur*.

† Cabrera Hist. de Don Juan.

This Emperor's Retreat had given rife to various Reports. One of thefe was, that he had contracted, by his almoft continual Correfpondence with the Proteftants of *Germany*, an Inclination for their Opinions; and yet the fole Motive of his withdrawing to a Solitude, was, that he might have an Opportunity of ending his Days in Exercifes of Piety conformable to his fecret Difpofition. 'Twas likewife affirm'd, that his ill Treatment of feveral of thofe brave Proteftant Princes, whom he had fubdued by Force of Arms, extorted from him fuch an Admiration of their Conftancy in ill Fortune, as made him almoft blufh for his Conquefts; and rais'd in him, by infenfible Degrees, an Efteem for their Religion.

A Circumftance which added to the Probability of thefe Reports, was, his making Choice of Perfons fufpected of Herefy to be the Companions of his Retreat, and the Directors of his Con-

Conscience. Doctor *Caculla* was his Preacher; and his Confessors were the Archbishop of *Toledo*, and especially *Constantine Pontius*, Bishop of *Drossin*. This Report was strengthened by the great Number of Passages, writ with the Emperor's own Hand, on the Walls of his Cell at St. *Justus'* where he died; these agreeing pretty nearly with the Tenets of the Protestants, on Justification and Grace.

But a Circumstance which confirm'd this Opinion still more, was, his Will not being drawn up after the Manner of the *Roman* Catholicks; I mean that no pious Legacies were read therein, nor any Monies bequeathed for saying Masses, which gave Offence to the Inquisitors. However, they did not dare to speak openly on this Occasion, till they should first know the Sentiments of *Philip* II. and whether he would not be offended at the Prosecution in question; but this Prince, on his ascending the Throne, signaliz'd himself by persecuting all those who had shook off the papal Yoke; so that the Inquisitors, in Imitation of him, first persecuted the Archbishop of *Toledo*, Primate of *Spain*, afterwards *Caculla*, and last of all *Constantine Pontius*.

As the King permitted them to be imprisoned, this was considered as an undoubted Proof of his Zeal for the *Romish* Religion: But the most judicious were struck with Horror, when they saw the Emperor's Confessor, in whose Arms he died, delivered up, by his own Son, to a most ignominious and cruel Punishment.

The Inquisitors could not forbear showing, that they were prompted, to this horrid Act, by no other Views than those of Interest; since, in the Trials of the three Persons abovementioned, they charg'd them with being concern'd in drawing up the Emperor's Will; and sentenc'd both It, and Them, to the Flames.

Philip,

Philip, who hitherto had beheld with the utmoſt Indifference, the Conduct of the Inquiſitors, now rouz'd as from a Lethargy; when reflecting on the bad things the World would ſay of him, in caſe he did not ſtop a Proſecution ſo injurious to the Memory of his Royal Father, and which might likewiſe be attended with fatal Conſequences, he endeavoured, ſecretly, to ſtop the Proſecution; but employ'd, at the ſame time, gentle Expedients, for fear of angering the Inquiſitors.

Don *Carlos*, only Son to King *Philip*, being a Prince of great Vivacity; and entertaining the utmoſt Veneration for his Grandfather's Memory, was highly offended at this Inſult put upon it. Not knowing all the Extent of the Power of this horrid Tribunal, he inveighed againſt it; and, after blaming his Father's Weakneſs, ſpoke publickly of this Deſign of the Inquiſitors, as a ſhocking and unheard of Attempt. He even went ſo far, as to threaten to extirpate,

extirpate, one Day or other, the Inquisition, and all its Agents, for this abominable Outrage. But this generous Prince paid dear for these passionate Expressions; the Inquisitors being determin'd to sacrifice him to their Vengeance, and hasten his End.

However, this Dispute between the King and the Inquisition was afterwards adjusted. *Caculla* was burnt alive, with the Effigy of *Constantine Pontius*, who died in Prison some Days before. The Archbishop of *Toledo* appealed to *Rome*; and extricated himself by Money and Friends. After this, no farther mention was made of the Emperor's Will.

Tho' this Reconciliation might pacify the Prince of *Spain*, the Inquisitors were far from being appeas'd; it being one of their chief Maxims, never to forgive. In this View they rais'd so great a Spirit of Discontent among the common People, that the King was forc'd to remove Don *Carlos* from Court;

Court; together with Don *John* his Brother, and the Prince of *Parma*, his Nephew, who had fhar'd in Don *Carlos*'s juft Refentment againft the Inquifitors.

This cruel Tribunal had not yet fatiated its Revenge. Some Years after it imputed to this young Prince, as a Crime, the Compaffion he had extended to the Inhabitants of the *Netherlands*, who were treated barbaroufly. They declared, that as all the People in queftion were Hereticks, the Prince muft neceffarily be One, fince he fet up for their Defender. In fine, they gain'd fo ftrange an Afcendant over the King's Mind, that he, infpired by a moft unnatural Spirit of Bigottry, and being afraid of quarrelling with the Inquifitors, fentenc'd his Son to die. The only Indulgence the latter met with on this Occafion, was to have the Species of Death left to his Choice. The ill-fated Prince, *Roman* like, had recourfe to the hot Bath; when opening the Veins of his Arms and Legs, he died gradually. Thus did this excellent young Prince fall a Martyr to the mercilefs Inquifitors.

The Year 1580 furnifhes us with another very remarkable Inftance, of the affuming Spirit of this pretended holy Tribunal.

Cardinal *Charles Borromeo*, Archbifhop of *Milan*, who afterwards was canoniz'd, going his Vifitation of certain Places, in his Diocefe, fubordinate to him, as to Spirituals, and to the *Swifs* Cantons as to Temporals; thought it neceffary to make fome Regulations for the good of thefe Churches.

The *Swifs* took Umbrage at this Conduct; when, without addreffing the Archbifhop, they fent an Embaffador to the Governor of *Milan*, intreating him not to let the Prelate continue his Vifitation in the Places fubject to them; and to affure him, that in cafe of refufal, they would employ Force; which muft break the Harmony ny it so highly concern'd his Sovereign, the King of *Spain*, to preserve.

The Embassador being arrived in *Milan*, lodg'd at a rich Merchant's House of his Acquaintance. The Inquisitor was no sooner inform'd of this, than, disregarding the Law of Nations, and the fatal Consequences with which so great an Outrage might be attended; he went, with all his Officers, to the Embassador's Abode; when causing him to be shackled in his Presence, he hurried him away to the Prison of the Inquisition. Though all Persons were struck with Horror, at such an Insult offer'd to a State in the Person of its Embassador, yet no one dar'd to make the least Opposition. The Merchant was the only Person who interested himself in his Favour; for he, waiting upon the Governor of *Milan*, told him the cruel Usage the Embassador had met with. The Governor sent for the Inquisitor, and obliged him to release the Embassador that Inftant; which being done, he paid him all imaginable Honours, and complied with his feveral Demands. Thus the *Swifs* were inform'd of their Embaffador's Releafe, almoft at the fame Time with the News of his Imprifonment, otherwife they would have feiz'd the Cardinal, and ufed him exactly as the Inquifitors had treated their Embaffador. The Governor afterwards inform'd the Archbifhop, by a Letter, that the Intereft of his Catholic Majefty requir'd abfolutely, that he fhould difcontinue his Vifitations; which being done, things were quiet.

The Inftances here given, prove fufficiently, that if the Inquifitors had kept within the Bounds which the Popes pretended to fet to them, in eftablifhing their Tribunal; (I mean the rooting up of Herefy) and had not concerned themfelves with Politicks; they would not have behav'd fo infolently towards Monarchs, &c. Let us now fee fome other Examples of their

Treat-

Treatment of Persons distinguish'd by their Birth and Employments.

Mark Antonio de Dominis was of a most illustrious *Venetian* Family. He first entered among the Jesuits; was afterwards Bishop of *Segni*, and at last Archbishop of *Spalatro* and Primate of *Dalmatia*. He was thought the best skill'd of any Man of his Age, in every Branch of Literature; especially in Divinity and History, both sacred and prophane. This Prelate was consulted as an Oracle, on every Subject, and gave the highest Satisfaction to all Querists. Imbibing Protestant Principles, he defended them with the utmost Vigour, in his *Republica Ecclesiastica*; and, at the same Time, wrote with greater Vehemence against the Pope and the Court of *Rome*, than its most inveterate Enemies had ever done.

The passionate Desire the Prelate had to print this Work in his Life-time; and the little Probability there was of his being able to stay in *Italy* after its

Publication, made him retire to *Germany*; where he afterwards went to *England*, whither he was invited by *James* I. King of *Great-Britain*. *Mark Antonio* met with a gracious Reception from this theological Monarch; he giving him an honourable Support; and doing all that lay in his Power, to engage him to renounce the Errors of the Church of *Rome*.

On the other Hand the Pope, whether he was unwilling to leave a Man of so exalted a Character, in the Hands of the Enemies to the *Romish* Church; or rather, as it afterwards appear'd, had resolved to be revenged of, and make a public Example of him; set every Engine at Work, to induce him to return to his native Country. At last, Don *Diego Sarmiento da Cunha*, the *Spanish* Embassador at the *British* Court, made *Mark Antonio* such splendid Offers, that he was prevailed upon to return to *Italy*.

This

This unhappy Prelate then forgot the Maxims he had so frequently inculcated in his Works, *viz.* That no Person can offend the Court of *Rome* with Impunity, and that it never pardons an Injury: For *Mark Antonio*, spite of the strong Exhortations of his Friends in *England*, who were for ever representing to him the Dangers to which he would inevitably expose himself; set out for *Rome*, where he was no sooner arrived than he found his Mistake too late. The Pontiff did not keep one of the Promises made to *Mark Antonio*, but obliged him to abjure publickly the pretended Heresies advanc'd in his Books. He now was left, seemingly, at Liberty; but was ever followed by Spies, who, at last, falsely swore that he carried on a secret Correspondence with *England*. Immediately the Inquisitors seiz'd this great Man; but carrying on his Prosecution with their usual Dilatoriness, he died in Prison, either thro' Grief for the wrong Steps taken by him; or thro' Fear of the shameful and cruel Punishment which he was sensible awaited him.

The Enemies to Duke *d' Ossona*, prime Minister of *Spain*, having conspir'd his Destruction, thought the most effectual Means to do it, would be the impeaching him to the Inquisitors. Neither the vast Favour of his Prince, nor his Character of first Minister to so great a Monarch, cou'd secure him from the Hands of the most horrid of Tribunals. This great Man being seiz'd, fell a Victim to its Cruelty, None of the numberless Multitude of Persons, on whom he had heap'd his Bounty during his Prosperity, and whose Fortune was inseparable from his, daring to speak for him, thro' Fear of falling a Prey to the Inquisitors.

Lewis de Carvajal, tho' Governor and Captain General of the Provinces of *Tampico* and *Pamico*, was sentenc'd to to do Penance, publickly, for not impeaching, to the Inquifition, four young Ladies his Neices, who fecretly profefs'd *Judaifm*. This Gentleman being feiz'd, the following Sentence was pronounced publickly againft Him, *viz.* " That he fhould be removed from " all his Employments under the King, " and his Poffeffions confifcated." This Governor being afterwards reduc'd to the Extremes of Mifery, died with Grief.

Alphonfo Nobre, born in *Villa Viziofa*; and defcended from one of the moft ancient and moft illuftrious Families of that City, many of whom had fill'd thofe Pofts, which, in *Portugal*, are beftowed on none but noble Perfons; and all whofe Anceftors cou'd not be reproach'd with the leaft Tincture of *Judaifm*; was feiz'd and carried to the Prifons of the Inquifition of *Coimbra*, upon the Information of Perfons who fwore that he was not a Chriftian. Some Time after, his only Son and

and Daughter were seiz'd and confin'd in the same Prison. These Children, who were very young, impeach'd their Father; whether excited thereto by evil Counsellors, or that the Tortures had extorted the Impeachment from them. At last the unhappy Father was sentenc'd to be burnt alive, on the Depositions of his Children. The Day of the *Auto da Fé* being come, the Son drew near to his Parent, to crave Forgiveness and his Blessing, but the ill fated Father replied: " I pardon you " both, tho' you are the sole Cause of " my ignominious and cruel Death: " As to my Blessing, I cannot give it " you; for he is not my Son, who " makes a pretended Confession of " Untruths; and who, having been a " *Roman Catholic*, shamefully denies " his Saviour, by declaring himself a " *Jew*.---Go, (adds he) unnatural Son! " I beseech Heaven to pardon you!" Being come, at last, to the Stake, he discover'd such great Courage and Resolution;

solution; made such pathetic Discourses, and address'd himself with so much Fervour, to the Almighty, as fill'd all his Hearers with Admiration, and caus'd them to look upon his Judges with Horror.

In the same *Auto da Fé* were likewise burnt Donna *Beatrix Carvalho*, of a noble Family of *Elvas*, and Wife to *Jacomo de Mello*; she being sentenc'd to die for *Judaism*, on the Oaths of her Children. There is no doubt but that, had the Inquisitors acted with Sincerity and Equity, and with a real Intention to find out the Truth, they might have discovered the Innocence of the Lady in Question; as well as that of the above Signior *Nobre*, by comparing the Confessions which each of their Children had made separately, with the Depositions of the Witnesses. A wide Difference wou'd certainly have been found, on this Occasion, in the Facts and Circumstances. Truth admits of no Variation; and is ever the same,

same, in the Mouths of those who follow its Dictates. Thus by confronting them, new Lights must have been struck out; but then the doing this wou'd not have brought on the Confiscation of the Possessions of the two Victims in question, the swallowing up of which was the sole View of the Inquisitors.

How strongly is the Folly and Inhumanity of the *Romish* Church, in forcing People's Consciences painted by Mr. *Bayle!* " In what Light soever
" the *Romanists* exhibit their Religion,
" they will prove no other Certainty of
" their Cause, than the Certainty of
" their Persuasion; I mean, they will
" never be able to prove, to a De-
" monstration, that their Principles
" are founded on Truth; only, that
" they imagine them to be true;
" which Circumstance is common with
" the most ridiculous Sects. If the
" *Romanists*, in consequence of their
" Persuasion, shou'd imagine, that
" they

"	they have a Right to extirpate o-
"	ther Sects; every Sect ought to be
"	equally authoriz'd, in consequence
"	of its Persuasion, to root out all
"	those which differ from it in Opi-
"	nion. Now, as nothing wou'd more
"	contribute to make the Earth a
"	Scene of Confusion and Slaughter,
"	than the establishing it as a Princi-
"	ple, *That All who are perswaded of*
"	*the Truth of their Religion, have a*
"	*right to extirpate all the rest*; as this
"	would be bringing back Mankind to
"	the State of Nature spoken of by the
"	Politicians, when every Man was
"	his own Master; and had a Right
"	to every Thing, he cou'd possess
"	himself of, by Force; 'tis plain that
"	true Religion, which soever it may
"	be, ought not to assume a Privilege
"	of tyrannizing over the Rest; nor
"	pretend that such Actions as are done
"	by it, degenerate into Crimes when

"	com-

"committed by other Religions †." Let us hear this excellent Author, arguing against those who will allow but one Religion in a Country: "The
"Reason of this (will the *Romanists*
"say) is because ours is the true Religi-
"on.--Say rather, (observes Mr. *Bayle*)
"because you imagine yours to be the
"true Religion; whence your Maxim
"will be reduc'd to this; *There must*
"*be but one Religion in a Kingdom*;
"*and this Religion ought to be that*
"*which is suppos'd to be the true one.*
"But, pursuant to this Maxim, the
"*English* and *Dutch* have a Right to
"extirpate Dissenters; the *Grand*
"*Seignior* to persecute all the Chri-
"stians in his Empire; the *Chineze*,
"the *Indians*, and the *Japoneze*, to
"stifle Christianity in its Birth; the
"old *Romans* must have acted very
"justly, in persecuting the Church;

† *Critique generale de l' histoire du Calvinisme de Mr.* Maimbourg, *Tom.* I. p. 224, 225. *Ville-Franche* 1684, 12mo.

"and

of the INQUISITION. 259

" and, if they are blame-worthy, 'tis
" for their not having Art or Power
" sufficient to extirpate it. In a
" Word, the Maxim of tolerating
" only one Religion, gives a Sanction
" to the most horrid Abominations ‡.

Here follows another Instance of the brutal Injustice of the Inquisitors: *Joseph Pereira Meneses*, Captain General of his *Portugueze* Majesty's Fleets in *India*, was ordered by the Governor of *Goa* to sail, with his Fleet, to the Succour of the City of *Diu*, then besieg'd by the *Arabs*. Proceeding on his Voyage, he was detain'd by contrary Winds, at *Baçaim*; whereby the *Arabs* had an Opportunity of plundering *Diu*, and of coming back loaden with rich Spoils, before the Arrival of the Succours brought by *Pereira Meneses*. This Commander being return'd to *Goa*, was immediately seiz'd by Order of *Antonio de Mello de Castro*,

‡ Idem, p. 294, 295.

Governor of that Place, and a sworn Enemy to *Pereira*. His Prosecution was then order'd, when he was accus'd of loitering at *Baçaim*, purposely to avoid engaging the Enemy; and thus to have caus'd, by his Neglect and Cowardice, the Ruin and Plunder of *Diu*. However, as Governors are not permitted to put Commanders to Death, without first obtaining an express Order from the Court of *Portugal*; *Antonio de Mello* cou'd not take away his Enemy's Life; for which Reason he pronounc'd such a Sentence upon him, as was more intolerable than Death itself to a Man of Honour. *Pereira*, pursuant to the Judgment pass'd upon him, was led by the common Executioner thro' the Streets, with a Halter about his Neck, and a Distaff at his Side. A Herald walking before, cried aloud, That this Punishment was inflicted on him, by the King, for his being a Coward and Traytor. *Pereira* was then carried back to Prison, where
a Fa-

a Familiar of the Inquisition came and demanded him. This fresh Step surpriz'd every one, who knew that he cou'd not justly be accus'd of *Judaism*, as he was of an ancient Christian Family, and had always behaved with Honour. The Day of the *Auto da Fé* was therefore expected with Impatience by the People, in order that his Crime might be made known to them: But how great was their Surprize, when the Prisoner did not come forth in the Procession!

Pereira had long been engaged in a Quarrel with a Gentleman, once his intimate Friend, and who was seemingly reconcil'd to him before this Misfortune. This false Friend, harbouring a secret Resolution to revenge himself whenever an Opportunity should offer, thought this Imprisonment of *Pereira* the most favourable for his Purpose, that cou'd have happen'd. He now suborn'd five of *Pereira*'s Domesticks, who accus'd their Master, to the Inquisitors, of Sodomy; making Oath that they had seen him perpetrate that abominable Crime with one of his Pages, Who thereupon was seiz'd. The Latter, having less Courage than his Master; and dreading a cruel Death, in case he shou'd not do all he was commanded; and finding no other Way to save his Life than by pleading guilty, charg'd himself with a Crime of which he was entirely innocent; and thus became, pursuant to the Practice of the Inquisitors, a fresh Witness against his Master. The Servant, by this Confession, saved his own Life, and was banished to *Mozambique* in *Africa*.

In the mean Time, as *Pereira* persisted in declaring himself innocent, he was condemned to be burnt alive; and wou'd have been committed to the Flames, had not his continual Protestations of his Innocence; or rather a secret Esteem which the Inquisitors ever entertained for him, made them suspend his Execution; in order to try whether

whether they might not, in Time, prevail with him to make a Confession; or find Opportunities to clear up the Affair. For this Reason he was ordered to remain in Prison till next *Auto da Fé.*

During this Interval, the Inquisitors examined the Prisoner and his Witnesses several Times; when interrogating the Latter, separately, whether the Moon shone the Night in which, pursuant to their Oath, their Master committed the detestable Crime in question, they varied in their Answers. Being now put to the Torture, they denied all they before had swore against their Master. The Accusers were then seized, and *Joseph Pereira* being declared innocent, came out of Prison, next *Auto da Fé,* stripp'd of all his Possessions and quite ruin'd. His chief Accuser was banished during nine Years to *Africa,* and the Witnesses were sentenc'd to the Galley for five Years.

The above Advantages, and many more might be gain'd by confronting Witnesses; and these the Inquisitors wou'd not neglect, did they make Justice and Equity the Foundation of their Prosecutions. But, unhappily for those who fall into their Hands, they find that Avarice, Ambition, and a vindictive Spirit, have banish'd every generous Impulse from the Breasts of these iniquitous Judges.

The abovemention'd Example shows, that the Inquisitors make Heresy a Pretence, merely to seize upon the Wealth of the Innocent; and that this Tribunal gives a wicked Man the finest Opportunity possible, to satiate his Vengeance.---The Spirit which animates the Inquisitors established in the *East-Indies*, must really be horrid, since even the *Jesuits* themselves thus speak of them, in their *universal* Latin and French *Dictionary*, printed at *Trevoux*. " The Inquisition (say these " most righteous Fathers) is vastly se-
" vere

"vere in *India*. 'Tis true, indeed,
"that seven Witnesses are required to
"swear against a Man, in order for
"his being condemn'd; but then the
"Depositions of a Slave, or of a
"Child, are admitted. The Prisoner
"must accuse himself; and 'he never
"sees, nor is confronted, with those
"who swear against him. A Person
"who happens to let drop the least
"Word against the Church; or does
"not speak, with sufficient Reverence
"of the Inquisition, shall be im-
"peach'd.---The Standard or Banner
"of the Inquisition is of red Silk, in
"which a Cross is painted; having an
"Olive-bough on one Side; and on
"the other a Sword, with these
"Words of the Psalmist round it:
"*Arise, Lord, and judge thy Cause.*"
What a solemn Mockery have we here
of Scripture, and how detestable a Use
is made of a Supplication of the Psalmist!---Is this Religion? Does this
Spirit descend from above? Surely no;
but

but seems dictated rather by the black Chiefs of *Milton*'s infernal Council.

The following Instance proves, that the Inquisitors will condemn an innocent Person, rather than permit any of their Accusations to be disprov'd.

A Major in a *Portugueze* Regiment was charg'd with professing *Judaism* privately, and hurried away to the Prison of the Inquisition in *Lisbon*. Being descended of a Family distinguished by the Name of *New Christians*, this was a strong Prejudice against him. He then was ask'd, several Times, the Cause of his Seizure, tho' he himself was an utter Stranger to it. After he was kept in Prison two Years, the Inquisitors told him, that he was accus'd and duly convicted, of being a relaps'd *Jew*, which he utterly denied; protesting that he had been always a true and faithful Christian. In a Word, they cou'd not prevail with him, either by Threats or Promises, to plead guilty to any one Article of
which

which he ftood impeach'd: He declaring refolutely to his Judges, that he wou'd die with Innocence, rather than preferve his Life by an Action, which muft cover him with eternal Infamy.

Duke *d'Avéyro*, then Inquifitor-General, who was defirous of faving this Officer, being one Day upon his Vifitation, ftrongly exhorted him to embrace the Opportunity he had of extricating himfelf; but the Prifoner continuing inflexible, the Inquifitor was fir'd, and fpoke thus to him: " Doft " thou imagine that we'll have the " Lie on this Occafion?" The Inquifitor then withdrew, leaving the Prifoner to his Reflections on what he had heard. Surely thefe Words imply'd a Meaning inconfiftent with the Character of an upright Judge, and ftrongly fpoke the iniquitous Spirit of this Tribunal.

To conclude, the *Auto da Fé* approaching, our Victim was condemn'd to the Flames, and a Confessor sent to him. Terrified at this horrid Death, he, though entirely innocent, declar'd himself guilty of the Crime laid to his Charge. His Possessions were then confiscated; after which he was made to walk in the Procession, in the Habit of one relaps'd; and, lastly, was sentenc'd to the Gallies for five Years.

William Lithgow, a *Scotchman*, had ever retain'd a strong Inclination for Travel. To gratify it, he first went to *Malaga*, and there agreed with the Captain of a *French* Ship, to carry him to *Alexandria*. Before this Ship set sail, an *English* Fleet, fitted out against the *Algerines*, came and cast Anchor before *Malaga*, the 7th of *October* 1620; which threw the whole City into the utmost Consternation; these Ships being suppos'd to belong to *Mahommedans*. However, next Morning they found their Mistake; when the Governor seeing the *British* Cross in the Flags, went on board the Ship of the

the Admiral, Sir *Robert Manſel*, who received him with the greateſt Politeneſs; ſo that at his Return, he removed the Fears of the Inhabitants, and made them lay down their Arms. On the Morrow, ſeveral of the Crew came on Shore; and being *Lithgow*'s particular Friends, ſpent ſome Days in viewing the Curioſities of the City, and in otherwiſe diverting themſelves; and then inviting him on board, they preſented him to the Admiral, from whom he met with all imaginable Civility. They kept *Lithgow* on board next Day, after which he returned to *Malaga*, and the Fleet ſet ſail.

As *Lithgow* was returning to his Quarters through Bye-Streets, in order to carry all his Things on board the *French* Ship, which was to ſail that Night for *Alexandria*; he was ſeiz'd by nine Catchpoles, or Officers, who took him before the Governor, to whom he complain'd of the Violence which had been done him. The Governor answered only by a Nod; and bid certain Persons, with the Town-Secretary, go and examine him. This was to be transacted with all possible Secrecy, to prevent the *English* Merchants, residing in *Malaga*, from hearing of his Arrest.

The Council assembling, he was examined; and being suspected to be an *English* Spy, they did all that lay in their Power to make some Discovery to that Purpose, but in vain. They afterwards ask'd the Names of the Captains of the Fleet; whether *Lithgow*, before his leaving *England*, did not know of the fitting out of this Fleet? Why he refus'd the Offer which the *English* Admiral made, of taking him on board his Ship? In a Word, they affirm'd that he was a Spy; and that he had been nine Months in *Malaga*, in no other View than to give Intelligence, to the *English* Court, of the Time when the *Spanish* Fleet was expected from *India*. They then observ'd, serv'd, that his Intimacy with the Officers, and a great many more of his Countrymen on board this Fleet, who had fhewed him the higheft Civilities, were ftrong Indications of his Guilt.

As *Lithgow* found it impoffible to eraze thefe bad Impreffions, he intreated them to fend for a Bag, containing his Letters and other Papers; the perufal of which, he declared, would prove his Innocence. The Bag being accordingly brought, and the Contents of it examin'd, they were found to confift chiefly of Paffports, and Teftimonials from feveral Perfons of Quality; a Circumftance which, inftead of leffening their Sufpicions, ferved only to heighten them. Prefently a Subaltern Officer came into the Room to fearch him, and took eleven Ducats out of his Pocket. Stripping him afterwards to his Shirt, they found in the Waiftband of his Breeches, the Value of 548 Ducats, in Gold. *Lithgow* putting on his Cloaths again, was conducted to a fe-a secure Place, and from thence removed to a horrid Dungeon, where he was allow'd neither Bed nor Bedding; and only an Ounce and half of musty Bread, and a Pint of Water daily.

As he wou'd confess nothing, he was put to the Torture three Days after. The Wretches had the Inhumanity to make him undergo, in the Space of five Hours, fifty different Sorts of Torture; after which he was remanded back to Prison, where two Eggs were given him, and a little hot Wine, just to keep him alive.

On this Occasion he received from a *Turk*, Favours which he cou'd not have hoped from Persons who style themselves Christians. This *Turk* administer'd to him all the Consolation possible, and wept to see the Cruelties exercis'd on *Lithgow*. He then informed him, that certain *English* Priests belonging to a Seminary, together with a *Scotch* Cooper, had been some-

sometime employed, by the Governor's Order, in tranflating, into *Spanifh*, all his Books, and the Obfervations made by him in his Travels. The *Turk* added, that it was publickly reported, that he was a moft notorious Heretic. 'Twas then *Lithgow* naturally fuppofed that every Engine would be fet at work, in order to ruin him.

Two Days after, the Governor, with the Inquifitor and two *Jefuits*, came to *Lithgow* in Prifon; when, after afking him feveral Queftions, and ftrongly urging him to change his Religion, they declared; that, having firft feiz'd him as a Spy, they had difcovered, by the Tranflation of his Papers, that he ridiculed the bleffed Lady of *Loretto*; and fpake very irreverently of his Holinefs, Chrift's Vicegerent upon Earth: That Informations had been lodg'd againft him before the Inquifitors; that he fhould be allowed eight Days to return to the Pale of the Church; during which the Inquifitor him-

himself, and other Priests, wou'd give him all the Instructions necessary, to extricate him from his miserable State. They visited him again several Times, but without Success. In fine, the eighth Day being come, he was sentenc'd to undergo eleven different Tortures; when, in case he survived them, he was to be carried to *Granada*, and burnt there, after *Easter* Holidays. The same Evening he was put to the Torture, and bore it with great Resolution, tho' the utmost Cruelty was practis'd on this Occasion. He then was remanded to his Dungeon, where some *Turkish* Slaves brought him, secretly, Refreshments, which he was took weak to take. One of these Slaves, tho' educated in the *Mahommedan* Religion from his Infancy, was so strongly affected with the deplorable Condition to which *Lithgow* was reduced, that he fell sick for several Days. However, a Moorish She-Slave amply compensated for the kind *Turk*'s Absence; she being

being allowed more Liberty in the Prison. The She-Slave brought *Lithgow*, daily, Provisions with a little Wine; and this Courtesy continued six Weeks.

To conclude, at the Time that *Lithgow* expected, every Instant, to die in the most cruel Torments, he was released by a very unexpected Accident. A *Spaniard* of Distinction being at Supper with the Governor, the Latter inform'd him of every Thing that had happen'd to *Lithgow*, since his Imprisonment. As he had describ'd, minutely, the various Tortures he underwent; a young *Flemish* Servant, who used to wait on the *Spanish* Gentleman at Table, mov'd to Compassion at the sad Relation of the Barbarity exercis'd on *Lithgow*, and his being sentenc'd to the Flames; fell into such Agonies that he could not sleep the whole Night. Getting up next Morning by Day-break, he went, unknown to any one, to an *English* Factor; and informed him

him of the Conversation which had pass'd between the Governor and his Master. The Servant being gone, the *Englishman* sent for the other six Factors, his Countrymen, residing in *Malaga*; when consulting together, they resolved to write to *Madrid*, to Sir ----- *Aston*, the *English* Embassador; who presenting a Memorial to the *Spanish* King and Council, *Lithgow* was releas'd and put on board Sir *Robert Mansel*'s Fleet, then lying at Anchor before *Malaga*. The poor Victim was so vastly weak, that they were forced to carry him, upon Blankets. The Admiral afterwards demanded *Lithgow*'s Books, Papers, Money, &c. but no other Answer was return'd him than mere Compliments †.

'Tis no Wonder that the *Romanists* shou'd treat the Persons of Protestants, and other Hereticks (as they term them)

---

† See *Lithgow*'s Travels; and *Limborch*'s History of the Inquisition, translated by the Rev'd Mr. *Samuel Chandler*, Vol. II. pag. 223. *London*, 1731, 4to.

so unmercifully, since they are such bitter Enemies even to their very Names, on which they will not suffer the least Encomium to be bestow'd. "The Author *de papistarum In-*" *dicibus Librorum prohibitorum &*" *expurgandorum* (says a great Wri-" ter †,) gives us the Rules which the" Inquisitors are obliged to observe," in licensing Books; whereby it ap-" pears, among other Things, that" they have positive Orders to blot out," indiscriminately, all Praises which" may be bestow'd on a Heretic. This" is scarce credible; few Persons ima-" gining, that Religion is capable of" giving so unjust a Bias to the Mind." *Bellarmin* was so firmly persuaded," that it was one Part of an orthodox" Character never to praise a Heretic," that our Author [Mr. *Bayle*] laughs" at him for asserting positively [*de*

† *Nouvelles de la Republique des Lettres,* for *July,* 1685. Art. 2. pag. 776, *&c.*

" *No tis*

" *Notis Eccles.* c. 6. art. 1.] *That it
" does not appear, that the Catholicks
" ever commended the Doctrines or
" Actions of Hereticks*; and yet *Bayle*
" proves, in Opposition to *Bellarmin*,
" that his Touchstone or Criterion is
" not very much to be depended upon,
" since *Cochleus, Æneas Sylvius, Pog-
" gius* of *Florence, Clavius* the *Jesuit*,
" Monsieur *de l'Aubespine* Bishop of
" *Orleans*, and *Caramuel*, have be-
" stow'd great Elogiums upon Here-
" tics. However, this lets us into the
" true Genius of the Inquisition. A
" remarkable Circumstance is, the In-
" quisitors give Orders for erazing,
" from all Sorts of Books, the Prefaces,
" Dedications; and absolutely all which
" may be ever so little honourable to
" Persons separated from the Church
" of *Rome*, not excepting even Kings.
" Hence 'tis commanded, in the *In-
" dices Expurgatorii*, that if an Histo-
" rian says; *Such a Day was born
" Christopher the illustricus Duke of
                                    " Wir-

" Wirtemberg, *(Præclarus Dux Wer-
" tenbergensis;)* the Title *præclarus*
" (illustrious) shall be eraz'd; which
" Title is yet of so little Consequence,
" that 'tis frequently bestowed on an
" indifferent Scholar. They likewise
" enjoin, that all Capital Letters, usu-
" ally prefixed to proper Names, sig-
" nifying, that an Heretic is styl'd,
" *Doctor, a celebrated Divine, vir cla-*
" *rissimus, vir reverendus,* shall be in-
" stantly expung'd. *Serrarius* the
" *Jesuit* asserts, in his *Minerval: That*
" *the Praises of a Heretic, in the Book*
" *of a* Romanist, *are an Abomination*
" *unto the Lord; in the same Manner*
" *as the abominable Offerings, spoken*
" *of in* Deuteronomy xxiii. v. 18."
What an irreligious Rant have we
here!

We are told by *Gonsalvius* ‡, that
the Inquisitors of *Seville*, seiz'd and

‡ This Work is entitled, Reginaldi Gonsalvii Montani sanctæ Inquisitionis Hispanicæ artes aliquot detectæ ac palam tradictæ. Heidelbergæ 1567. 8vo.

imprisoned *Jane Bohorquia*, Wife to the Lord of *Higuera*, of noble Extraction. She was taken up on the Information (forc'd by Torture) of *Mary Bohorquia*, her Sister, burnt afterwards as an Heretic. *Mary* depos'd, that she had frequently discours'd with her Sister *Jane*, on religious Subjects. The Lady in question was six Months gone with Child, when she was seiz'd, for which Reason they treated her with less Cruelty at first. However, a Week after her Delivery, they took her Infant away; and, the 15th Day, confin'd her more closely, and us'd her with no less Severity than the other Prisoners; and carried on her Prosecution with the Artifices and Inhumanity common to the Inquisitors.

In this miserable State, her only Consolation was a young Woman, of great Good-Nature and Piety; whom the Inquisitors burnt some Time after, upon Pretence of her being a Heretic; she having before been tortur'd so cruelly,

elly, and reduc'd so very low, that she cou'd not move without feeling the sharpest Pains. Mrs. *Bohorquia* comforted her as well as she could, and behaved to her with the Tenderness of a Parent: Scarce was the young Woman recovered, but Mrs. *Bohorquia* herself was violently tortur'd, the Ropes having pierced quite to the Bones of her Arms, Legs and Thighs; she then was carried back to her Dungeon; throwing up great Quantities of Blood, which emaciated her to such a Degree, that she expired a Week after.

The Inquisitors were the more perplex'd on Account of her Death, since that, as she was a Native of the Town in question, it was necessary for the mock Holy-Office to give the Inhabitants some Account concerning her. Accordingly, in the next *Auto da Fé*, her Sentence was pronounc'd, to the following Purport, (Care being taken to suppress the Cause of her Exit:) " That

"That *Jane Bohorquia* was dead in
"Prison, and that the Inquisitors, af-
"ter reviewing her Prosecution, had
"found her innocent: That no far-
"ther Prosecutions wou'd be carried
"on against her; that she was resto-
"red to her Innocence and Reputa-
"tion; and therefore, that all her
"Possessions which had been confis-
"cated, should be restored to her
"Heirs."---How barbarous a Satis-
"faction was made to the Relations of
"this Lady, in thus declaring her in-
"nocent, after she had been put to
"a most cruel Death †!

Doctor *Isaac Orobio*, a Physician, is another Instance of the Barbarity and Injustice of the Inquisitors; this Gentleman tell us, that he was accus'd of *Judaism* by a *Moor* who had been his Servant, and whom he caus'd to be beaten for Theft. Dr. *Orobio*, after being kept three Years in Prison, and

† *Limborch*, Vol. II. p. 215, 216.

of the INQUISITION.

interrogated several Times; still persisted in denying the Crimes laid to his Charge; upon which he was tortured successively, in Manner following: First, they put him on a coarse linnen Coat, which the Tormentors strain'd so very tight, that his Breath was almost lost; when loosing it on a sudden, this instantaneous Motion put him to incredible Pain. They next tied his two Thumbs with small Cords, so very hard, that the Blood started from under his Nails. The third Torture was, the Tormentors seated him on a Bench, with his Back against a Wall, wherein little Iron Pullies were fixed; through these, Ropes were run, which took hold of several Parts of his Body, and particularly his Arms and Legs; then the Executioner, pulling these Ropes with all his Strength, drew the unhappy Victim's Back so close to the Wall, that his Hands and Feet, and particularly his Thumbs and great Toes, were squeez'd so violently, that he felt the most acute Pains, like to burning. In the Midst of these dreadful Agonies, the Bench was drawn suddenly from under him, so that the poor Gentleman hung by the Ropes; and being thus quite unsupported, the Weight of his Body drew the Knots of the Ropes still tighter.

This Torture was succeeded by another, *viz.* by an Instrument in Form of a little Ladder, cross'd by five Pieces of Wood, and made sloping before. This Instrument being set directly opposite to the Sufferer, he received, on a certain Motion, at one and the same Time, five dreadful Blows on the Cheek, which put him to such Pain that he fainted away. Recovering afterwards, the last Torture was inflicted. The Executioner fastned Ropes about Dr. *Orobio*'s Wrists; then wound them round his Body; after which he was laid upon his Back, with his Feet against a Wall: This being done, the

Execu-

Executioner drew him afterwards with all his Might, whereby the Ropes pierc'd quite to his Bones. This Torture was thrice repeated; the Ropes being fix'd round the Prisoner's Arms, not above two Finger's Breadth from the Wounds which the first Torture had made. And now the Ropes (at the second Torture) slid into the first Wounds, by the Violence of the Jerk; which occasioned so great an Effusion of Blood, that the Doctor seem'd expiring. The Physicians were then consulted, to know whether the same Torture might be practis'd a third Time, without endangering his Life. As These were not Enemies to Dr. *Orobio*, they answered that he might suffer it a third Time without the least Danger; and, by this Declaration, sav'd him from undergoing again all the various Sorts of Tortures abovementioned; his Sentence declaring, that he should suffer, successively, all these different Kinds of Torture, the

the same Day. Being tortur'd, for the last Time, he was remanded back to Prison, where he lay above seventy Days, before his Wounds were heal'd. He, at last, was banished for Life out of the Kingdom, for being suspected of *Judaism* †.

In 1559, a furious Persecution begun to break out, at *Seville*, against Hereticks. We are told, by *Thuanus*, that *Philip* II. upon his Return from the *Netherlands*, discovered an amazing Spirit of Cruelty. All Persons confin'd in the Prisons of the Inquisitions of *Spain*, who were sentenc'd for Heresy, were brought, by his Order, to *Seville* and *Valladolid*, to be executed in those Cities with great Parade. The first of those *Auto da Fé's* was exhibited, at *Seville*, *October* the 8th, of the same Year; on which Occasion *John Pontius de Leon*, Son to Count *Villalon*, was led in a kind of Triumph; and

† *Limborch*, Vol. II. p. 221, 222.

burnt

burnt as a *Lutheran* Heretic, with about thirty more Victims. The King affisted, in Person, at this cruel Ceremony. *Oct.* 8th following, those Persons, condemn'd at *Valladolid* as Heretics, were executed with no less Barbarity. Twenty eight of the principal Nobility of that Country were tied to Stakes, and burnt in Presence of King *Philip*. *Caranza*, Archbishop of *Toledo* was likewise impeach'd. This Prelate was famous for his Probity, his Learning and Piety; and yet lost all his Preferments, by the Sentence pronounced against him by Pope *Gregory* XIII. to whom he had appeal'd ‡.

In

‡ I cannot omit what Mr. *Bayle* observes concerning the Inquisition, in his Dictionary, under the Article of this illustrious Bishop, where he tells us, (after Count *de la Roca*, in his History of the Emperor *Charles* V.) that *the Populace had so great a Veneration for* Caranza, *that they paid the like Veneration to his Corps on the Day of his Interment, as to those of the greatest Saints.*—Mr. *Bayle*'s Reflections on the Inquisition are these: " 'Tis certainly a grateful
" Circumstance for us to hear, that the common
" People did Justice on this Occasion to persecuted
" Innocence.

In the same *Auto da Fé*, held at *Seville*, were burnt a Lady, and o-

"Innocence. And yet they perform'd but Part of
"their Duty; for they ought, at the same Time, to
"have vented their Indignation against this unjust
"Tribunal, (the Inquisition) for its so long perse-
"cuting an excellent Man; and shou'd, at least,
"have infisted that those iniquitous Judges might
"be branded with Infamy. For what can be more
"abominable, than to see a learned Prelate, against
"whom the Inquisitors had no Evidence, not get
"out of their Hands, till after he had suffered a long
"and severe Imprisonment; and then be releas'd
"with a Mark of Infamy, calculated merely to save
"the Honour of his detestable Accusers? In order to
"cloak the Injustice exercis'd against *Caranza*, it
"was necessary to declare that Presumptions had
"been entertained, of his being a Heretic; other-
"wise his Accusers wou'd have expos'd themselves
"too much to the Murmurs and Indignation of the
"Populace. Here they abus'd the Public, and the
"Public ought to have been properly offended a-
"gainst them for it. But this wou'd be requiring
"too many Things, at one and the same Time,
"from the Multitude. 'Tis the Business of wise
"Men to see thro' this double Iniquity, and hum-
"bly adore the Ways of Providence; not only for
"permitting the Tribunal of the Inquisition, (the
"true Abomination introduc'd into the holy Places)
"to triumph and reign in so many Parts of the
"Christian World; but also that it is suffer'd to
"lengthen, from Time to Time, its Phylacteries,
"and spread its Fibres and Roots every where.

thers.

thers. The Inquisitors seiz'd this Person, her two Daughters, and her Neice, who was a married Woman. As various kinds of Torture (which they suffer'd with Heroism) were inflicted, to no Purpose, in order to extort from them such a Confession as was agreeable to the Charge brought against them by the Inquisitors; and likewise to force them, by the Violence of the Torments, to betray one another; the Inquisitor ordered one of the young Ladies to be brought before him: He then examined her alone, and was very liberal of his Consolation. He afterwards sent for her several Evenings, on which Occasions he us'd to hold a long Conversation with her; affirming that he was greatly mov'd at her miserable Condition; intermixing, from Time to Time, his Discourse with Things indifferent and familiar. But now, having gain'd so mighty an Ascendant over the young Creature, as to strongly persuade her, that he was as much affected with her Misfortunes as if he were her own Father; and that, wou'd she consult him as such, her Mother, her Sister and Cousin, might be sure of his Protection; the Inquisitor having, by these specious Arts, impos'd upon the hapless young Creature, who had no great Share of Understanding; he then began to persuade her, that it was incumbent on her to discover what she knew concerning herself, her Mother, Sister, Cousin, as well as her Aunts, who were not yet seiz'd; he promising, with an Oath, that, if she wou'd make a general Confession of all she knew, he would find Means to procure them their Liberty, and send them all back safe to their House.

The young Maiden, unskill'd in the Artifices employ'd by these wicked Fathers, soon fell an easy Prey to the Inquisitor's Snare. She then disclos'd her Mind to him, with Regard to the holy Doctrine that had been taught her,

her, and on which (she said) they us'd to discourse in their Family. The Inquisitor, after these first Openings, made her a thousand Promises, in order to discover the Particulars of these pious Family Conversations. He then had her brought to the Audience, to give in her Deposition, pursuant to the Forms of Law; and repeated the Promises made by him before, of releasing her. Nevertheless, at the Time that this young Maiden was in Expectation of seeing all the Protestations made by the Inquisitor fulfill'd; he having now partly discovered, by his insidious Questions, what, till then, could not be extorted from her by Tortures; concluded, that it would be necessary to make her suffer them again, to force her to confess Particulars, which the Inquisitor imagin'd she, till then, had concealed. Accordingly she was tortur'd in the most cruel Manner ever heard of; till at last, overcome by extreme Anguish, she accus'd her Mother,

ther, her Sister, her Cousin, and many more Relations; who were all seiz'd, put to the Torture; and afterwards burnt alive, in the same Fire with the ill-fated Creature in question, spite of the solemn Promise made her by the Inquisitor †.

What can be more barbarous than such a Prosecution? 'What Right, ' (says Mr. *Bayle*) has any Body of ' Men to tyrannize over the Consciences ' of their Fellow Creatures? Who is it ' that appointed Parliaments supreme ' Judges of the Freedom of my ' Thoughts, in such a Manner that, ' if my Mind is not exactly of the ' same Cast with theirs; if I do not ' consider an Article of Faith in the ' same Light with them, they may ' order me immediately to the Gal-' lows? I confess, that the bare Re-' flection on this fills me with Hor-' ror. Let my Governors punish me

† Limborch, p. 158, 159.

' if

'if I injure my Neighbour in his Pof-
'feffions; if I abufe him, if I kill
'him, or make any Attempt againft
'the Government; but not to permit
'me to abftain from a Manner of ferv-
'ing God, which, to my Mind, ap-
'pears unlawful; not to allow me to
'worfhip him in that Way which, to
'my Confcience feems the beft, with-
'out dreading a Gibbet or a Stake;
'appears fo tyrannical, that this alone
'fufficiently perfuades me, that the
'Church of *Rome* is a very bad one;
'a Church, which, upon every Con-
'tradiction, deftroys thofe by Fire and
'Sword who take fuch a Liberty; a
'Church, which exerted its utmoft
'Endeavours to eftablifh the Tribunal
'of the Inquifition; the moft infer-
'nal, the moft execrable Manner of
'preferving its Authority that ever en-
'ter'd the Mind of Man; and which
'was never practis'd even in thofe a-
'bominable Heathen Religions, whofe
'Cruelty was fo extreme, as to prompt

Them

'Them to sacrifice Men to their Idols.
'That Embassador who, in a Speech
'to the Pope, call'd him *primatu Abel,*
'*gubernatu Noë, Ordine Melchisedech,*
'*dignitate Aaron*; and clos'd his Com-
'pliment with saying, *That he was the*
'*Grand Seignior of the Christians,*
'spoke more Truth than he himself
'imagin'd; for 'tis certain the *Popish*
'Religion conducts itself, with Regard
'to every other Christian Society, ex-
'actly as the *Turks* behav'd towards all
'Kingdoms and Commonwealths with-
'in their Reach. As these did not
'give Quarter to One, and all were
'forc'd to submit to the Yoke of their
'barbarous Government; so the *Ro-*
'*mish* Religion does not tolerate any
'other, but persecutes them round,
'and extirpates them when in its Pow-
'er; and (a still more shocking Cir-
'cumstance) gives no other Reason
'for this tyrannical Procedure, than
'its Infallibility. Any Person who re-
'fuses to believe this Church on its
bare

'bare Word; who presumes to argue
'with it; and does not extinguish all
'the Lights of Conscience and Judg-
'ment in its Favour, is, that Instant,
'delared a Rebel to God; an Enemy
'to Christ and his Church; is ex-
'communicated, put to Death, and
'damn'd †.

Gonsalvius gives us an Example, which shows that Vice is not the Object of the Inquisitors Hatred. A poor Inhabitant of *Seville*, who supported his Family by his daily Labour, had the Mortification to have his Wife kept forcibly from him by a Priest, which yet was winked at by the Inquisition, and every other Tribunal. As this Man was one Day discoursing concerning Purgatory, with some of his Acquaintance, he spoke in such Terms, as tho' he intended only to disburden his Mind: As to myself, (says he) I have my Purgatory in this

---

† *Critique generale de l'Histoire du Calvinisme de Mr. Maimbourg.* Tom. I. p. 316. & *seq. Ville Franche.*

World, by my Wife's being thus withheld from me by the Priest. These Words being told to the Ecclesiastic, he impeached the Husband to the Inquisition, as having advanced some Errors relating to the Doctrine of Purgatory. Hereupon the Inquisitors, without once reproaching the Priest for his Crime, seized the Husband. The latter then was imprisoned two Years; and, after walking in the Procession at the first *Auto da Fé*; and being sentenced to wear, during three Years, the *San Benito*†, in a private Prison; at the Expiration of that Term, he was ordered, either to be continued in Prison, or to be released, as the Inquisitors should see fitting. These carried their Cruel-

† Properly *Sanbenidos*. They are a sort of Scapularies, of yellow Linnen, having St. *Andrew*'s Cross painted before and behind. These sort of Scapularies are put on such Persons as have committed, or are supposed to have committed, Crimes contrary to the Christian Faith; whether such Persons are *Jews*, *Mohammedans*, Heretics, &c. who apostatize from the Christian Faith. *Histoire de l'Inquisition de Goa*. p. 150, 151. *Paris* 1688.

ties

ties to such lengths, as to confiscate, to the use of their Tribunal, the Little that this unhappy Creature had in the World, and permitted the Priest to still enjoy his Wife; the holy Lecher being passionately fond of her.

This Ecclesiastic acted agreeably to *Ignatius Loyola*'s supposed Instructions to his Brethren, the Jesuits:

Think not yourselves t' Austerities confin'd,
Or those strict Rules which other Orders bind.
To Capuchins, Carthusians, Cordeliers,
Leave Penance, meagre Abstinence and Pray'rs:
In Lousy Rags let begging Friars lie,
Content on Straw, or Boards, to mortify:
Let them in Sackcloth discipline their Skins,
And scourge them for their Madness and their Sins:
Let pining Anchorets in Grottos starve,
Who from the Liberties of Nature swerve:
Who mak't their chief Religion not to eat;
Place it in Nastiness, and want of Meat:
Live you in Luxury, and pamper'd Ease,
As if whole Nature were your Cateress.

Oldham. Sat. III.

⁽¹⁾ "To return: In the above Procession came forth likewise a rich Citizen of *Seville*, who was forced to walk without either a Cloak or a Hat, and carrying a lighted Torch. He was sentenced to this, only for saying, that the Sums expended in *Spain*, and in which its Inhabitants were more lavish than any other Nation, *viz.* for setting up, the *Thursday*, in Passion-Week, certain Knick-knacks, of Paper or Linnen, in honour of our Saviour, now in Heaven; as also those perform'd on *Corpus Christi* Day; that these Sums (I say) would be more grateful to God, were they employ'd in relieving the Poor, or in placing young Orphan-Maids in the Houses of good People, where they might be virtuously educated. For these just Reflexions, he was suspected of being a *Lutheran*; was forced, in order to recover his Liberty, to declare himself guilty of Heresy, and afterwards fin'd 100 Ducats, for the Benefit of the Inquisition.

Nicholas

Nicholas Burton, an *Englishman*, remarkable for his Piety, was seiz'd by the Inquisition of *Seville*; and afterwards burnt for adhering strictly to the Church of *England* Principles. The first Thing the Inquisitors did, was to seize the whole Effects brought by him into *Spain*; which was sold to the profit of their Tribunal. Among the Effects in question, were several belonging to another Merchant of *London*; and with regard to which, *Burton* acted only as Factor. The Merchant hearing of Mr. *Burton*'s Seizure, sent an Agent (one *Frontom*) into *Spain*, with a Letter of Attorney, and all other Powers necessary for him to recover his Effects. *Frontom* being come to *Seville*, and presenting the Inquisitors his Letter of Attorney, &c. they delayed him from time to time; and did all that lay in their Power to tire him out; putting him to very heavy Expences, in hopes of thereby forcing him to desist from his Claim. However, as he continued inflexible, they

they sent for him to the Inquisition, upon pretence of settling *Burton*'s Affair with him. *Frontom* was overjoy'd at the Message; fondly flattering himself that he shou'd now soon end this perplexing Business, and return to his native Country. However, the unhappy Man was greatly surpriz'd, when, instead of being conducted to *Burton*, he was led to a gloomy Dungeon, and confin'd there. Three or four Days after he was carried to the Audience, when, desiring that the Effects might be restor'd to him; he, instead of receiving a proper Answer, was commanded to say his *Ave Maria*; which he did accordingly (these concluding Words excepted) *Holy* Mary, *Mother of God, pray for us Sinners!* By this he plainly shew'd, that he did not approve of the Intercession of Saints; whereupon he was kept several Days in Prison; sentenc'd to walk in the Procession of the *Auto da Fé*; to have all

all his Effects confifcated, and to be imprifon'd a Year ‡.

The Author of the Hiftory of the Inquifition of *Goa* ‖, furnifhes us with another remarkable Inftance of the Injuftice of the Inquifitors. A very rich *Portugueze* Gentleman, of the Race of new Chriftians, nam'd *Lewis Peſſoâ d'Eça*, having drawn upon himfelf the Hatred of many Pèrfons, by the Lawfuit in which he had been involv'd; thefe thought the fureft way of taking Vengeance, wou'd be, to impeach him to the Inquifitors; and accordingly he was accus'd of practifing, fecretly the *Jewifh* Rites with his Family. Thereupon, on the fame Day, himfelf, his Wife, his two Sons, his Daughter, and fome other of his Relations who lived in the fame Houfe, were feiz'd and confin'd in the Prifons of the Inquifition at *Coimbra*.

‡ *Limborch*, Vol. II. p. 243, &c.
‖ Page 246, & *feq*. *Paris* 1688. 12*mo*.

Pessaá d'Eça was first examin'd about his Estate, amounting to above 30,000 *Livres* a-year; all which, together with his Goods, were seiz'd by the Inquisitors. He afterwards was order'd to tell the Cause of his Imprisonment; a Circumstance that was impossible, since he himself was quite in the dark, as to that Matter. The Inquisitors then had Recourse to every cruel Practice, usually employ'd by them to force Prisoners to plead guilty to the Articles of their Indictment, but in vain.

In fine, about 3 Years after, he was made acquainted with the Articles; and assur'd that the Proctor wou'd insist on his being put to death, in case he did not make a full Confession. However, the unhappy Victim, so far from accusing, endeavour'd to justify himself; protesting that the several Articles brought against him were so many Falsities; all which he refuted by solid Arguments. He then desired to see the

the Witnesses who had sworn against him; declaring that he cou'd easily convict them of Perjury. The Reasons alledg'd by him, to the Inquisitors, were sufficient to prove his Innocence, had they been inclin'd to give Attention to them; but they, utterly disregarding whatever he cou'd offer in his Justification, and finding him still persist in pleading not guilty, sentenced him to the Flames; informing him of his Sentence, pursuant to the Formalities of Law, a Fortnight before his coming out.

But now Duke *de Cadaval*, who had a great Kindness for the Prisoner, and was an intimate Friend of Duke *d'Aveira*, the Inquisitor-General; enquiring of the latter privately from time to time the Prisoner's Frame of Mind, Duke *d'Aveira* answer'd always, that he wou'd confess nothing; but that, being convicted, pursuant to the Proceedings of the Inquisition, it wou'd be impossible for him to escape the Flames,

Flames, unless he pleaded guilty before the Goal-delivery: This Circumstance greatly perplex'd Duke *de Cadaval*, who wou'd gladly have spoke himself, or have employ'd others, to speak to the ill-fated Gentleman, to exhort him to save his own Life, which yet was judg'd impossible. At last, Duke *de Cadaval* thought of a Thing, of which there had been no Precedent in *Portugal*; and this was, to insist on a Promise from the Inquisitor-General, *viz.* that if he cou'd prevail with *Peſſoá d'Eça*, to acknowledge his Guilt, even after he was come forth from Prison, in order to walk in the Procession, he shou'd not be put to death; tho' this was in direct Opposition to the Laws of the holy Office.

Duke *de Cadaval* having obtained this Promise from the Inquisitor-General; and being told the Day when the *Auto da Fé* would be solemnized at *Coimbra*, he got some Friends of his and *Peſſoá d'Eça*'s, to set out from *Lisbon*;

Lisbon; when these, placing themselves near the Gate of the Inquisition as the Procession was advancing, they drew near to their unhappy Friend, the Instant they saw him come forth.

As he was sentenc'd to die, a Stake had been prepared for him. He wore a *Carrocha* † and a *Samarra* ‡, painted

† This is a Paste-board Cap, pretty nearly in the Shape of a Sugar-Loaf. 'Tis painted full of Devils, and Flames, with an Inscription round it, answering to the Word *Wizard*; and is worn by such Prisoners, as are suppos'd to have been most addicted to Magic. *Relation de l' Inquisition de Goa*, p. 152, 153.—How cruelly stupid is this! to suppose such unhappy Creatures great Adepts in that pretended Science, *Magic*; and yet not to have Power to extricate themselves from the barbarous Hands of the Inquisitors.

‡ This is a Sort of Scapulary worn by those who are looked upon as convicted, and yet persist in denying the Articles of their Indictment, or have relaps'd. The Ground of this Scapulary is green; and on it, both before and behind, the Portrait of the sad Victim is represented, standing on burning Firebrands, with Flames rising upwards, and Devils around. The Name and Crime of the poor Sufferer is writ at the Bottom of the Picture. But those who accuse themselves, after Sentence is pronounced, before their coming out of Prison; and who have not

ed as ufual. His Sentence was writ at the Bottom, and the Confeffor walk'd by his Side. He was no fooner fpy'd by his Friends, than thefe, melting into Tears, flung themfelves about his Neck; they conjur'd him, in Duke *de Cadaval*'s Name, and all Things dear to him, to refolve to fave his own Life. They told him, that he wou'd certainly efcape the Flames, provided he did but make a Confeffion; adding, that he need not be difturbed with Regard to the Seizure of his Poffeffions, fince Duke *de Cadaval*, from whom they were fent, had charg'd them to affure him, that he wou'd beftow upon him more than he had loft. Yet nei-

relapfed, have painted, on their *Samarras*, Flames with the Points turn'd downward. *Inquifition de Goa*, p. 151. What dire Inventions have we here! Are fuch Practices, on haplefs human Creatures, worthy of Perfons who pretend to be as Angels of Light, and to copy the Conduct and Doctrine of Chrift! Wou'd One not rather conclude them to be the moft wicked Species of Devils; and think that they had ranfack'd every Part of the infernal Regions, for thefe diabolical Reprefentations!

ther thefe Reafons, nor the Sollicitations or Tears of his generous Friends, cou'd once move *Peſſoá d' Eça.* He ſtill continued to cry aloud, that he had ever been a Chriſtian, and wou'd die ſuch; and that all the Articles laid to his Charge were ſo many Falſities, invented by his Enemies; and liſtned to by the Inquiſitors, in no other View than to rob Him of his Eſtate. The Proceſſion being arrived at the fatal Spot, a Sermon was preach'd, and the Proſecutions were read; Abſolution was given to the Perſons whoſe Lives were ſpar'd; and Evening being come, the Proſecutions of thoſe to be burnt were upon the Point of being read. 'Twas then the Gentlemen, ſent from Duke *de Cadaval,* renewed their Intreaties; and, at laſt, prevailed upon their Friend to ſue to be admitted to Audience. At his riſing up he ſaid: "Well, I'll go and confeſs Falſities, "to ſatisfy my Friends." He then was permitted to come to Audience; which,

which, being ended, he was conducted back to Prison; but being called to the Table to make his Confession, at the Ending of the *Auto da Fé*, 'twas with great Difficulty he could prevail with himself to comply with their urgent Request; and was several Times upon the Point of having his Sentence confirm'd, after which he cou'd expect no Mercy. However, he at last did every Thing requir'd of Him, and sign'd his Confession. Two Years from thence, he was sent to *Evora*, where he walked in the *Auto da Fé*, wearing a *Samarra*, with the Flames pointing downwards; and, being confin'd five Years in the Prisons of the Inquisition, was sentenc'd to the Galley for five Years longer, and led thither next Mornning. 'Twas there (continues the Author of the Inquisition of *Goa*) I got acquainted with this Gentleman, and learnt the several Particulars told above.-----This ill-fated Person, who seem'd good natur'd, was inform'd, upon

upon his Releafe, that both his Wife and Daughter died in Prifon a little after their being thrown into it; but that his two Sons, having lefs Refolution than himfelf; and accufing themfelves foon after their Confinement, had been carried, fome Time before, to *Algarve*, whither they were banifhed for ten Years.---How fhocking is this Severity!

Gonfalvius Montanus gives us another Inftance of the Avarice and Cruelty of the Inquifitors. An *Englifh* Ship arriving in the Harbour of *Cales*, the Familiars of the pretended Holy-Office went, purfuant to their Cuftom, on board the Ship, to fearch for heretical Books, before any Perfon was come out of it. They feiz'd feveral *Englifhmen* who were in this Ship, and had given various Indications of their being Proteftants. In the fame Ship was a Boy, about eleven or twelve Years of Age, Son to a wealthy *Englifh* Merchant, who was Owner of the faid said Merchantman, and of the best Part of her Cargo. The Pretence of their seizing the Child in question was, for his having an *English* Psalter. Hereupon the Ship, and the whole Cargo, were confiscated: After which the Boy, with the rest of the *English*, were thrown into the Inquisition at *Seville*, and confin'd six or eight Months there. The Child, having been brought up with great Tenderness, fell dangerously ill; either from his long Confinement; from the noxious Damps of his Dungeon, or the unwholesomness of his Food. In a Word, he quite lost the Use of his Limbs, and what became of him afterwards was not known.

The Inquisition must necessarily be an abominable Tribunal, since even the *Jesuits* themselves thus characterize it in their *General* French *and* Latin *Dictionary*, printed at *Trevoux*, " 'Tis " a Maxim with the Inquisitors, to " employ, in their Prosecutions, all " Things

"Things which may strike Terror. Those who are seiz'd by them, are universally abandoned, not a Soul daring to open his Lips in their Favour; for the bare offering to do this, wou'd raise a Suspicion of Heresy. Persons may be inform'd against for Heresy, tho' of ever so long standing; and even the Dead are not exempt, their Carcasses being often impeached. 'Tis usual to make large Executions, in order that the considerable Number of Criminals may strike the greater Terror."

The succeeding Example shows the insatiable Avarice of the Inquisitors, who presume to extend their Jurisdiction even over the Effects of those Foreigners who come into the Countries where their Tribunal is settled. In *February* 1687, several Persons were imprisoned in the Inquisition at *Madrid*, upon their being charg'd with practising the *Jewish* Rites in secret.

Among these were *Diego* and *Anthony Daix*, and Don *Damiano de Lucena*. Their Possessions and Effects were first seiz'd, and at the Close of *August* 1688, Sentence was pass'd upon them, by which their Estates were confiscated; and themselves ordered to be sent to *Toledo*, where the Remainder of their Sentence was to be pass'd upon them. The Persons in question traded with *Peter Poulle*, a Native of *Holland*, and a Protestant, who had several Effects, in his Hands, belonging to these *Spanish* Merchants. The Inquisitors, in order to get Possession of them, discovered, privately by their Emissaries, that the abovementioned *Dutch* Gentleman traded with several other *Spanish* Merchants, who had many of his Effects in their Hands. Hereupon the Inquisitors commanded their Receiver of Confiscations, to seize the Goods in Question, to the Amount or Value of those which the *Dutch* Merchant had in his Hands, belonging to *Diego* and *Anthony*

Anthony Daix, and Don *Damiano de Lucena*. The Reasons alledg'd by them for this Act of Violence was, that the Persons imprisoned had a Claim on the *Dutch* Merchant's Effects, which devolved to the Inquisition; and consequently, that this Tribunal had an equal Right to seize the *Dutch* Merchant's Effects, in what Part of *Spain* soever they might find them; to indemnify themselves for the Possessions belonging to the Prisoner. Nevertheless, the Efforts employ'd by the Inquisitors were vain; because the *States General*, upon the Petition of the Merchants of *Amsterdam*, prevailed with the Court of *Madrid*, to cause the Effects in question to be restor'd to Mr. *Poulle* †.---
Justly, therefore, does the learned and ingenious Dr. *Trap*, in his *Popery truly stated, and briefly confuted*, exclaim thus against this wicked Tribunal. ' Now we are upon the Subject of

---

† *Limborch*, Vol. II. p. 18.

' Tortures,

'Tortures, (says he †) 'tis impossible to forget that Depth of Satan, the Inquisition. For Satanical it is, by the Conjunction of three Qualities; indefatigable Diligence, profound Subtlety, and inhuman Cruelty. Some of its Mysteries have been discovered to us; enough to show that the whole is a Mystery of Iniquity; and that Popery is rather a Scheme of Machivillian Politicks, than any Part of Christ's Institution.'

We find, by the following Instance, that no Person can safely trust the Promise, or even Safe-Conduct of the Inquisitors, especially where their Interest is concern'd; for then they never scruple to violate the most solemn Assurances, &c. given by them. This Example is furnished us by the Author of *the Inquisition of* Goa; he knowing very well the Person who is the Subject of it. 'I was acquainted,

† Page 130, 131. *London*, 1727. 12mo.

'says

'(says he ‡) in *Surat*, with a *Domi-*
'*can* Friar, Father *Hyacinth* by Name,
' who, several Years before, had quit-
' ted his Convent; and throwing off
' his Habit, led a dissolute and scan-
' dalous Life. Sometime after, a Wo-
' man he had long lov'd, and who
' had borne him several Children, hap-
' pen'd to die. Greatly afflicted at
' her Death, he resolved to change
' his Courses, and to return to his
' Convent in *Baçaim*. However, as
' all the *Portugueze*, and especially
' such Priests and Monks as have liv'd
' for some Time among the Heathens,
' are obliged, at their Return into the
' Dominions of the King of *Portugal*,
' to present themselves before the In-
' quisitors, and give a faithful Account
' of the Life led by them; the Friar in
' question, whose Conscience very possi-
' bly might sting him, and being in Fear
' of the Inquisition; he, before his

‡ Page 187, & *seq.*

' leaving

'leaving *Surat*, wrote to the Inquisi-
'tor at *Goa*, desiring a safe Conduct,
'in order that he might go and accuse
'Himself, which Request was instant-
'ly complied with. Thus furnished,
'he set out, and went to *Baçaim*,
'where he was not allowed to resume
'the religious Habit, till he shou'd
'first clear himself before the Inquisi-
'tors. For this Reason he went to
'*Goa*, when, presenting himself to
'the Audience, or Inquisition-Board,
'he was heard several Times. At last,
'after having been sufficiently inter-
'rogated, he was absolved and sent
'back to the Vicar-general of his Or-
'der, who permitted him to wear the
'Habit again; and restor'd him to his
'Functions of Preacher and Con-
'fessor.

'Our Friar now imagin'd that his
'Affair was compleatly settled; and
'accordingly was preparing to set out
'for his Convent in *Baçaim*. But,
'as he was stepping on board a Gal-
'liot,

'liot, he, to the great Surprize of all
'his Friends, was feiz'd and convey'd
'to the Prifons of the Inquifition, the
'Agent of which granted him Abfolu-
'tion, in no other View than to ftrike
'the furer Blow; for Father *Hyacinth*,
'impos'd upon by this feigned Pardon,
'had brought, from *Surat*, fome con-
'fiderable Effects, acquir'd by him
'there, all which were confifcated by
'the Inquifitors. This they cou'd
'not have done, without employing
'the Stratagem abovementioned; that
'is, by making him a Promife which
'they never intended to perform. How-
'ever, to prevent their being re-
'proached, with violating the Safe-
'Conduct fent him by them, they
'fpread, artfully, a Report, *viz*. That
'they, fince Father *Hyacinth*'s Abfo-
'lution, had difcovered Crimes of
'which he had not impeach'd him-
'felf."---'Tis plain that Father *Hyacinth* had not kept fufficiently upon his Guard, nor plung'd in Vice with

the Caution obferved by many of his Brethren, the Monks.

For each Thing fained, ought more warie bee;
There thou muft walk in fober Gravitee;
And feem as Saint-like as Saint Radegund:
Faft much, pray oft, look lowly on the Ground.
                    Spenfer's Mother Hubberd's *Tale.*

The Author of *the Relation of the Inquifition of* Goa, is look'd upon as a very faithful Writer. What Idea then does the above Story give us of the Inquifitors! It degrades them on this Occafion even below the moft capital Villains; Thefe, when forming Plots to rob or murder, (as the melancholy Accounts from *Tyburn* too frequently fhow) binding themfelves, by certain Articles or Conditions, (to which they all fwear) and which they think it incumbent on themfelves to comply with; at the fame Time that they declare War againft the reft of Mankind.

To the above Examples we will add another, of a different Sort, which

which shows, that the Inquisitors stretch their Authority so far, as often to abuse it for Trifles, greatly below the Notice of a prudent Judge. This Incident is borrow'd from *Gonsalvius*.

The Bishop of *Tarragona*, chief Inquisitor of *Seville*, went, with certain of the principal Officers of his Tribunal, to take the Diversions of the Country, for some Days, in certain beautiful Gardens situated by the Sea-side. As he was walking in them, with his Train, a Child of the Gardiner's, about three Years old, was seated by a Pond's Side, playing with a Switch or Stick, not far from where the Bishop stood. It happened that a little Page, belonging to the Bishop, forc'd the Stick out of the Gardiner's Son's Hand, which made the Latter fall a crying. The Father coming up, and being told the Cause of his Child's Tears, desired the Bishop's Page to return the Stick; which, the Latter refusing, with an Air of Contempt, the

Gar-

Gardiner endeavoured to force it from him; and as the Page held it with all his Might, the Gardiner began to be in a Passion; and pull'd it so hard before he could get it away, that the Knots of the Switch rais'd a little the Skin of the Boy's Hand, but without doing him any farther Harm. Immediately the Page flew crying to his Master, as tho' he had receiv'd a deep Wound. The Inquisitor, without making the least Enquiry into this Affair, order'd the Gardiner to be seiz'd; which done, he was carried to the Prison of the Inquisition, and, being loaded with Irons, was confin'd there nine Months. As the Man in question was but in very indifferent Circumstances, this Affair almost ruin'd him; so that his Wife and Children were reduc'd, during his Confinement, to the Extremes of Misery. Nevertheless, the Bishop, upon his releasing the Gardiner, wou'd fain have persuaded Him, that he had met with much

much more Indulgence than his Crime merited.

However, the Inquisitors have sometimes been treated with due Contempt, as appears from the following Example. In 1706, after the Battle of *Almanza*, a Body of *French* Troops, consisting of 14000 Men, march'd in order to conquer *Arragon*, whose Inhabitants had declared in Favour of the Archduke of *Austria*. The Corps in question was commanded by the Duke of *Orleans*, Generalissimo of the Army. The Duke, before he arrived at their Capital, was met by its Magistrates, who waited upon his Royal Highness, offering him the Keys of their City.--- The Duke refus'd them, declaring that he wou'd march in at the Breach, and was as good as his Word. He then treated the Inhabitants as Rebels to their lawful Sovereign.

After giving Orders, with Regard to Affairs both civil and military, he set out for the Frontiers of *Catalonia*, leaving

leaving Lieutenant-General *Jofreville* Governor of the City. This General, being of too gentle a Difpofition to levy the Contributions purfuant to the fevere Orders of the Duke,, was recalled to the Army, and Lieutenant-General *Delegal* appointed in his Stead.

The City in queftion was commanded to pay a thoufand Crowns, Monthly, for the Duke of *Orleans*'s Table; and every Houfe a Piftole, which amounted to 18000 Piftoles per Month, all which the Inhabitants were obliged, during eight Months, to furnifh. Farther, religious Houfes were order'd to give, by Way of Free-gift, a Sum proportionable to their Revenues; the *Jefuits* being tax'd at 2900 Piftoles; and the *Dominicans*, *Auftin* Friars, and *Carmelites*, at 1000 each. General *Delegal* fending to the *Jefuits*, with Orders for them to furnifh their Quota, they refus'd, pleading the Immunities of the Church. However, the General,

of the INQUISITION.

ral, being resolved not to be trifled with, sent four Companies of Granadiers, who were commanded to quarter, at Discretion, in their Houses. The Fathers dispatched immediately an Express to the King's Confessor, who also was a Jesuit, to complain of this Violence. But the Granadiers, plundering faster in Proportion than the Courier rode; the Fathers thought it prudent, in order to save their Treasures, and other Effects which had escaped hitherto, to wait upon General *Delegal* with the two thousand Pistoles.

The *Dominicans*, being all of them Familiars of the Holy Office, imagin'd that their Employment wou'd secure them from the Fury of the Soldiers. They excus'd themselves in the most polite Terms, assuring the General that they had no Money; and that, shou'd he insist upon the thousand Pistoles, they had no other Way of paying him, than by sending him the silver Statues

Statues of their Saints. The Monks imagined that General *Delegal* wou'd be satisfied, at once, with this Answer; resolving, on the other Hand, in case he dar'd to accept of them, to send away the Saints in Procession, and thereby stir up the Populace to cry out *Heresy*. Accordingly the Fathers prepar'd to go, in solemn Procession, with their Saints and lighted Wax-Tapers, and wait upon the Governor. The Instant the Latter heard their Design, he commanded four Companies of Granadiers to line both Sides of the Street leading to his House; and, with their Muskets on their Shoulders, and lighted Tapers in their Hands, to receive the Saints.

The General took the Saints, and sent them to the Mint, promising to pay back to the Fathers, the Overplus of the thousand Pistoles. The Projects of the Monks being thus defeated, they went to the Inquisitors, beseeching them to redeem their Saints, and

and excommunicate General *Delegal*. The Excommunication being inftantly drawn up and fign'd, they gave pofitive Orders to their Secretary, to go and read it to the General, which was done accordingly. The Governor, inftead of falling into a Paffion, receiv'd the Sentence of Excommunication very calmly from the Secretary; defiring him to tell the Inquifitors his Mafters, that he would fend in an Anfwer next Morning. The Secretary went away, highly fatisfied with General *Delegal*'s Civility, who, the Moment after, order'd his Secretary to take a Copy of the Excommunication, and to fubftitute the Names of the Inquifitors inftead of his.

At the fame Time he commanded four Regiments to hold themfelves in a Readinefs to march; and to go, on the Morrow, to the Inquifition, with his Secretary, who was ordered to read the Excommunication to the Inquifitors; and, in cafe they made

made the least Murmur, to turn them out of their House, release the Prisoners; and quarter two Regiments there. The Secretary obey'd his Master's Commands punctually. But now the Inquisitors were in the highest Consternation to hear a Person excommunicate them, who was unauthoriz'd for that Purpose, by the Church; upon which they, in order to raise a Mutiny, cried aloud; *Down with Delegal the Heretic! this is a public Insult on the Catholic Faith.* The Secretary said no more than this: " Holy Inquisitors, his ' Majesty has Occasion for your House to ' quarter his Soldiers in; and therefore ' I must desire you to quit it instantly.' The Inquisitors making a Clamour, he sent them, under a strong Guard, to another House. These religious Tyrants, finding themselves now subject to a military Power, desir'd Leave to carry off their Effects, which Request was immediately granted. They then set out, next Morning, for *Madrid,*

drid, where they complain'd to the King, who return'd them a very flight Anfwer, exhorting them to Patience: And accordingly they were forced to practice this Virtue, during the eight Months that General *Delegal* continued in *Arragon*.

The General's Secretary, purfuant to the Orders given him, fet open the Gates of all the Prifons; on which Occafion the wicked Actions of thofe Inquifitors were brought to Light, by the Releafe of four hundred Perfons, who difcover'd the numberlefs horrid Arts of thefe worft of Wolves in Sheep's cloathing.

The many Victims, among the moft eminent Literati, to the Inquifitors; and the Tyranny they exercis'd over the fineft of their Compofitions, prove them to be no lefs ignorant and barbarous, than the *Goths* and *Vandals*. Among other Victims (Men of Learning) to this horrid Tribunal, was the celebrated Mathematician *Galileo*. In 1615, he was cited, to *Rome*,

to appear before the Inquisitors, and charg'd with Heresy, for asserting the Earth's Motion. The Inquisitors declar'd as follows: I. *Solem esse in centro mundi, & immobilem motu locali, est propositio absurda, & falsa in philosophia, & formaliter heretica, quia est expressè contraria sacræ Scripturæ.* II. *Terram non esse centrum mundi, nec immobilem, sed moveri motu etiam diurno, est etiam propositio absurda, & falsa in philosophia:* ' I. To assert that the Sun
' is the Center of the Universe, and im-
' moveable as to local Motion, is an
' absurd Proposition, and false in Phi-
' losophy; and expresly heretical, as
' being directly contrary to Scripture.
' II. To assert that the Earth is not the
' Centre of the World, nor immovea-
' ble, but to have also a diurnal Mo-
' tion, is likewise an absurd Proposi-
' tion, and false in Philosophy.' He was confin'd in the Prison of the Inquisition, till *February*, 1616, on the 25th of which Month Sentence was
pro-

nounced upon him; the Inquisitors declaring, that he shou'd renounce his heretical Opinions; shou'd not defend them either by Word or Writing; nor infinuate them into the Minds of any Person whatsoever. He was not discharged till he had promised to conform himself to this Decree. Upon his publishing in *Florence, anno* 1632, his Dialogues concerning the *Ptolemaic* and *Copernican* Systems; *Dialogi delle due massime Sisteme dell' Mundo, Tolemaico & Copernicano,* he was again cited before the Holy-Office, by whose Command he was committed to the Prison of the Inquisition in *Rome*; and *June* 22. *N. S.* the Congregation assembled, and, in his Presence, pronounced Sentence against both himself and his Book; and forced him to abjure his Errors in the most solemn Manner; committing him to the Prison of the Inquisition during Pleasure; and commanding him, as a saving Penance, to repeat once a Week, during three
Years,

Years, the seven penitential Psalms; but reserving to themselves the Power of moderating, altering, and annulling, altogether, or in Part, the abovementioned Punishment and Penance. He was discharged from his Confinement in 1634; but, his Dialogues of the *System of the World*, were burnt at *Rome* †. *Galileo* was no less esteemed for his great Probity, than for his exalted Discoveries. What Idea are we to entertain of a Tribunal, which persecuted so excellent a Man, and so great a Genius!

'Twas therefore with great Reason that Mr. *Bayle* observes, in his Dictionary, under the Article of *Cornelius Agrippa*, that in all Places where the Inquisition settles, it banishes Learning. Mr. *Bayle* speaks this on Occasion of *Agrippa*'s leaving *Metz*, because of the Ignorance and Cruelty of the Inquisitors of that City, who had seiz'd a

---

† *Salusbury*'s Life of *Galileo Galilei*, Lib. 3. cap. 4.

poor Countrywoman. It appears that *Nicholas Savini*, Inquifitor of the Faith at *Metz*, wou'd have the Female Peafant in queftion put to the Torture, only becaufe fhe was Daughter to a Woman who had been burnt, upon the ftupidly villainous Suppofition of her being a Witch. *Agrippa*, as appears from his Epiftles, did all he cou'd to protect the Daughter, but cou'd not fave her from the Torture; tho' he afterwards prov'd her Innocence, and her Accufers were fin'd. This Punifhment, as Mr. *Bayle* takes Notice, was too gentle; *Agrippa* had remark'd, in the Clergy of *Metz* who were the principle Accufers, fo much Meannefs of Spirit, and fuch a perfect Ignorance in polite Literature and true Philofophy, that he brands *Metz*, in his Epiftle dated *June* 2d, 1519; by calling it the Step-Mother of Learning of every kind, and of all the Virtues, *omnium bonarum litterarum virtutumque noverca*. *Agrippa* promis'd to write a
Book

Book against the *Dominicans*, as these were the principal Managers of the Inquisition. *Agrippa* wou'd lose all Patience, whenever he perceived them so indulgent to the Errors of their Brethren, and so severe against the ambiguous Propositions of others. This Indulgence, (adds Mr. *Bayle*) wou'd have been less scandalous, had it been found in these Friars only; but, unhappily, the Vulgar are so stupid, that, at the same Time that they applaud the Zeal of an Inquisitor, who brands whatever he pleases as Heresy; they yet won't permit him to be reproached in his Turn, nor suffer his pernicious Doctrines to be publickly expos'd. We find, by *Agrippa*'s Works, that he intended to charge the *Dominicans* with the most horrid Crimes; such as their poisoning the Host, palming sham Miracles upon the World, poisoning Princes, betraying Governments, seducing the common People, and advancing Heresies. *Neque tamen putetis* (says
Agrippa

Agrippa to the Magistrates of *Colen* †) *hunc solum articulum apud illum reperiri hæreticum, sed alii multi quos cum hic nimis longum vobisque tædiosum foret, referre, enumerabo alibi, in eo scilicet Libro, quem de Fratrum Prædicatorum Sceleribus & Heresibus inscripsi, ubi infecta sæpius veneno sacramenta, ementita sæpissimè miracula, interemptos veneno reges & principes, proditas urbes & respublicas, seductos populos, assertasque hæreses, & cætera ejusmodi heroum illorum facinora flagitiaque in varias transfusa linguas, omnique populo expofita dilucidè narrabo.*

Persons who have the sad Fate to be seiz'd by the Inquisitors, shou'd naturally endeavour to extricate themselves as soon as possible, out of their tyrannical Hands. But this is not all; after they have once procured their Liberty, they ought to be as easy as they can, and check all Suggestions of Ven-

† *Agrip. Opr.* Tom. II. p. 1037.

geance, except they remove to Countries where the Horrors of this Tribunal have no Influence: Otherwise, fhou'd they vent their Indignation publickly, this wou'd be of the moft dreadful Confequence; as is but too fatally exemplified in *Lewis de Berquin*, a Gentleman of *Artois* in *France*. This Perfon, who was one of the Counfellors of *Francis* I. having fpoke very openly againft the Monks, and been engaged in a very warm Conteft with one *Bedda*, an Inquifitor, was feiz'd, tried, and fentenc'd to be burnt, except he would recant his Errors. Tho' *Bequin* refus'd to comply, he yet was releas'd by the Interpofition of Friends. He then profecuted his Accufers, but had the ill Fate to fall a Sacrifice to them; he being, at laft, ftrangled and burnt at the *Greve* in *Paris*. We find, by *Erafmus*, Epift. 4. Lib. 24, That he was a Man of good Morals, and obferv'd regularly the Injunctions of the Church. *Erafmus* adds, that his great
Crime

Crime was, the Hatred he profess'd openly against such Divines as were of a morose Temper; as well as against savage and ignorant Monks. *Erasmus*'s Words are very strong. *Hoc aiebant eo crimen esse gravissimum, quod ingenuè præ se ferebat odium in morosos quosdam theologos, ac monachos non minus feroces quam stolidos. In eos palam debacchabatur, nec stomachum suum dissimulare poterat.* *Berquin* had translated some Books of *Erasmus,* who had a very great Regard for him, and gave him excellent Advice: He observing, that *Bedda,* the chief Inquisitor, was a Hydra; that the Friars he contended with were very artful, and the most wicked of Mankind; that he fought with an immortal Enemy, and that a Faculty or Community never dies: *Erasmus* advised him not to trust to the Favour of Kings, an Informer having often an Opportunity of changing their Minds; that the Awe in which Monarchs stand of Churchmen, and
the

the Desire which the Former have, of being freed from their importunate Solicitations, often force them to comply with the Desires of those wicked Men. Let us hear *Erasmus: Etiam atque etiam cogitaret, qualis excetra esset* Bedda, *quotque capitibus efflaret venenum: Tum expenderet sibi cum immortali adversario rem esse; facultas enim non moritur: simul illud cogitaret, qui cum tribus monachis, belligeratur, eum cum multis phalangibus habere rem, non solum opulentis ac potentibus, verùm etiam improbissimis, & in omni malarum artium genere instructis. Illos non conquieturos donec ei procurassent exitium, etiamsi causam haberet meliorem quam habuit Christus: neque plus satis fideret Regis præsidio, Principum enim favores esse temporarios, ac delatorum artibus facilè in diversum trahi illorum affectus. Postremò, ut nihil horum accidat, magnos etiam Principes vel*

vel delassari talium improbitate, vel metu nonnunquam cogi, ut cedant †.

Laurentius Valla, born at *Rome*, in 1415, was very famous for his Skill in the *Belles Lettres*, as well as for his Criticism on them. But presuming afterwards to censure the *Romish* Clergy, &c. he was obliged to leave his native Place, and to retire to the Court of *Alphonso* King of *Naples*, a great Patron of Men of Letters. As *Valla* still continued to write against the Churchmen, they prosecuted him with so much Virulence, that, had he not been protected by King *Alphonso*, they wou'd have burnt him alive; and 'twas very happy for him that he escaped with only a Whipping round the Cloister of the *Dominicans*. *Valla* had the Courage to refute a Tradition, highly priz'd by the Court of *Rome*, viz. the pretended Donation of *Constantine*. 'Tis thought that this Circumstance serv'd

† *Erasmi Epist.* 5. *Lib.* 24.

as a Handle for the Profecution carried on againſt him by the Inquiſitors; but that the real Cauſe of it was his Cenſure of them. The Inquiſitors were exaſperated at his perſonal Reflections; after which they endeavoured to make him fall a Sacrifice, by charging him with Hereſy. The better to ſatiate their Vengeance, they declared that he was a Heretic, with Regard to ſeveral important Articles, ſuch as the Myſtery of the Trinity, the Doctrine of Free-will, Vows of Continence, &c. *Spondanus* † informs us of ſome of the above Particulars; *Laurentius Valla Neapoli exiſtens, cùm quaſdam propoſitiones hæreticas aſſeruiſſet, delatus ad Inquiſitores, et in carcerem truſus, damnatuſque pro hæretico, beneficio Alfonſi Regis pœnam ignis evaſit, propoſitionibus tamen publicè ejuratis, virgis, privatim per clauſtra Monaſterii prædicatorum manibus revinctis cæſus.*

† *Ad annum*, 1446, num. 10. pag. m. 3.

Valerius

Valerius Andreæ, in his *Bibliotheca Belgica*, printed at *Louvain*, mentions an Inquifitor, of whom a moft difadvantageous Picture is given, in *Jo. Henricus Majus*'s Oration on the Life of the celebrated *Reuchlin*. The Name of this *Dominican* is *Hochftratus*. He was Prior of the Monaftery of *Colen*; Doctor and Profeffor of Divinity, and Inquifitor in the three ecclefiaftical Electorates. No Man was ever rais'd with greater Propriety to the laft mentioned Employment; he having an ample Provifion of thofe wicked Qualities, which conftitute an Inquifitor and Informer. *Hochftrat* was furious in his Temper; impeach'd on the flighteft Sufpicion; wou'd be both Judge and Party; gave unfaithful Extracts of the feveral Books or Propofitions animadverted upon by him; wou'd never own his being a Slanderer, tho' legally proved fuch; and advanced, with Impunity, Herefies, in which he himfelf pretended to refute Heretics, as appears from an Epistle of *Cornelius Agrippa* †. He, nevertheless, was once obliged to give Satisfaction to a very worthy Gentleman whom he had slandered; but, to force him to this, it was necessary to have Recourse to a remarkable Expedient, which was, to deprive his Convent of the Benefits arising from begging. *Hochstrat* was obliged to go to *Rome*, on Occasion of a Contest between Him and *Reuchlin*, when he narrowly escaped losing his Cause. He was one of the first who took up the Pen against *Luther*, and was likewise a Persecutor of *Erasmus*. In a Word, any Person who was an Enemy to the Jargon of the Schools, was instantly hated by *Hochstrat*. Those who judg'd in *Rome*, by the Pope's Order, the Contest between *Reuchlin* and *Hochstrat*, wou'd have decreed in Favour of the Former,

† Epist. 26. Lib. 7. Oper. Tom II. Page 1037.

had not the Latter obtained a Command from the Pontiff to fuperfede the Affair. ' This (as Mr. *Bayle* obferves)
' is an authentic Inftance of the migh-
' ty Power of the Inquifitors. If they
' cannot gain their Caufe; if it is fo
' palpably bad, as makes it impoffible
' for them to obtain a favourable Sen-
' tence, they yet have Credit enough
' to efcape Condemnation: They ob-
' tain all the Delays requifite for their
' Purpofe, and pretend this to be an
' Advantage; it being a Maxim
' with the Inquifitors, and fuch like,
' to never own their being in the
' Wrong." The following Epitaph was writ for *Hochftrat:*

Hic jacet Hochftratus, viventem ferre patique
    Quem potuere mali, non potuere boni.
Crefcite ab hoc taxi, crefcant aconita fepulchro,
    Aufus erat fub eo, qui jacet, omne nefas.

Imitated.

Imitated.

Here Hochstrat *sleeps; to all the Worthless, dear:*
At whose bare Sight, the Virtuous dropt a Tear.
Spring forth, Yew, Wolfbane; round his Ashes rise;
All Crimes he dar'd, whose Corps here mould'ring lies.

Here a turbulent, worthless Friar comes off with Impunity in *Rome*, whilst the calm and patient *Molinos*, a *Spanish* Priest, is thrown into the Inquisition there, for writing a Book entitled, *The Spiritual Guide*, (*Il Guida Spirituale*.) ' The Substance of the whole
' Treatise (says Bishop *Burnet* †) is re-
' duced to this; That in our Prayers
' and other Devotions, the best Me-
' thods are, to retire the Mind from
' all gross Images, and so to form an
' Act of Faith, and thereby to pre-

† *Some Letters, containing what seemed most remarkable in* Italy, Switzerland, *&c.* p. 197, 198. *Rotterdam*, 1686, 12mo.

' sent

'sent ourselves before God; and then
' to sink into a Silence and Cessation
' of new Acts; and to let God act up
' on us, and so to follow his Conduct.
' This Way *Molinos* prefers to the
' Multiplication of many new Acts, and
' different Forms of Devotion; and
' makes small Account of corporal
' Austerities, and reduces all the Ex-
' ercises of Religion to this Simplicity
' of Mind. He thinks that this shou'd
' be proposed, not only to such as live
' in Religious Houses, but even to
' 'secular Persons; and by this Means
' he hath proposed a great Reforma-
' tion of Men's Minds and Manners.
' He hath many Priests in *Italy*, but
' chiefly in *Naples*, who dispose such
' as confess themselves to them, to fol-
' low his Methods. The *Jesuits* have
' set themselves much against this
' Conduct; as foreseeing that it may
' much weaken the Empire, which
' Superstition hath over the Minds of
' People; that it may make Religion

be-

' become a more plain and simple
' Thing, and may also open a Door
' to Enthusiasm; and they likewise
' pretend, that his Conduct is factious
' and seditious, and may therefore breed
' a Schism in the Church. *Pasquin*
' said a pleasant Thing on this Occa-
' sion. In one Week a certain Man
' had been condemned to the Gallies
' for somewhat he had said; another
' had been hanged for something he
' had writ; and *Molinos* was clapt in
' Prison, whose Doctrine consisted
' chiefly in this; That Men ought to
' bring their Minds to a State of in-
' ward Quietness, from which the Name
' of *Quietists* was given to all his Fol-
' lowers: The Pasquinade upon all
' this was, *Si parliamo, in Galere; si
' scrivemmo, impiccati; si stiamo in quie-
' te, al Sant' Officio: & che bisogna
' fare?* If we speak we are sent to
' the Gallies; if we write we are hang-
' ed; if we continue quiet we are clapt
' up

'up in the Inquisition: What must
'we do then?'

The tyrannical Conduct of *Hannibal Grifon*, an Inquisitor over the Districts of *Pola* and *Capo d'Istria*, in *Italy*, well deserves a Place here. The *Romish* Bishop of *Pola* being persuaded of the Truth of the Protestant Doctrine, and inculcating it from the Pulpit, the Monks impeach'd him to the Inquisition. Upon this *Hannibal Grifon* behav'd towards the Inhabitants of the Diocese of *Pola* in Manner following: He us'd to enter their Houses, in order to search for suspected Books; wou'd excommunicate all Persons who did not inform against such as were suspected to imbibe the *Lutheran* Principles; he promised to mitigate the Punishment of those who might renounce their Heresy, and come and ask his Pardon; but threatned to burn such as shou'd be impeach'd before they anticipated the Informers, by an humble Confession of their Crimes. He wou'd go from Door to Door, and vent these Menaces, and thus spread Terror universally; upon which some accused themselves. He inveighed very strongly against all who confess'd their reading the Bible in the vulgar Tongue, and commanded them to look into it no more. Soon after this, nothing but Informations were talk'd of; all Persons concerning themselves in them, without any Regard to the Ties of Blood, or those of Gratitude. A Woman did not spare her Husband; a Son his Father; nor a Vassal his Lord: People were impeach'd for mere Trifles; those, for Instance, who dar'd to censure Bigottry in others. *Deinde promiscua multitudo, timore perculsis animis, deferebant quosque certatim, nulla neque propinquitatis neque necessitudinis aut beneficiorum habita ratione: non parenti filius, non uxor marito, non cliens patrono parcebat. Delationes autem erant plerumque de rebus frivolis; ut quisque forte aliquid ob superstitionem in aliquo repre-*

reprehenderat. These are *Melchior Adamus's* Words †. What follows is cruelly whimsical, and shows the Ascendant which the *Roman* Prelates have over the Minds of the Vulgar. 'The
'Inquisitor abovementioned, after so-
'lemnizing Mass, on a certain high
'Festival, in the Cathedral of *Capo*
'*d'Istria,* spoke thus to his Congrega-
'tion : *You have laboured, within these*
'*few Years, under many Calamities ;*
'*sometimes your Olive-trees and Vines*
'*are barren ; and, at other Times, your*
'*Harvests are unfruitful ; at other*
'*Times again a Mortality reigns a-*
'*mong your Cattle. Know that these*
'*Evils arise from your Bishop and the*
'*rest of the Hereticks ; and expect not*
'*to be eased of these Calamities, unless*
'*you take Care to root the Hereticks*
'*out : Rush therefore instantly upon*
'*them, and put them to Death* ‡.' Was

† *In vitis Theol. Exter.* pag. 119.
‡ *Sleidan,* lib. xxi. *Folio m.* 589, *ad ann.* 1548.

not this Inquisitor a faithful Disciple of our Saviour, who declares the Essence of his Religion to be Love for our Fellow Creatures?

After the many Examples given above, is it surprizing that a Tribunal so remarkable for its Injustice and Cruelty, shou'd have been inveighed against by a *Mahommedan*, who came from *Morocco* to *Seville*, purposely to embrace the Christian Religion? This Man cou'd not forbear crying out, when he had pass'd some Time among the Christians, that they were more vicious and corrupt than his Countrymen, the *Moors*. For these Reflections he was thrown into the Inquisition, and treated with so much Barbarity, that he declar'd to all who came near him (during his Confinement) that he never repented his turning *Christian*, till his Imprisonment in the Inquisition, where the utmost Efforts of Cruelty and Injustice had been exercis'd upon him.

I shall

I shall close this Part, with some Examples copied from a Gentleman equally conspicuous for his very extensive Knowledge and Candor; I mean the late Mr. *la Croze*, Librarian and Antiquary to his *Prussian* Majesty.

The Name of *New Christians* (says this excellent Writer) is ignominious both in *Spain* and *Portugal*; in the *East-Indies*, as well as in *Europe*. A Heathen who lives with Honour in his own Country, becomes odious to his Relations the Instant he is converted to Christianity by the *Portugueze*; who, on the other Hand, look upon him, during his whole Life, with Suspicion and Contempt. *Tellez*, in his History of *Ethiopia* (pag. 114.) reproaches the *Abyssinian* Christians, for their not thinking it shameful to descend from *Mahommedans*. The new Converts, besides this Ignominy, become, by their Baptism, subject to the Inquisition; that is, TO THE MOST UNJUST AND

MOST

MOST CRUEL TRIBUNAL EVER ESTABLISHED UPON EARTH. Is not all this more than sufficient to deter these poor Heathens from embracing Christianity?

'Tis certain that a Spirit of Violence and Persecution, is the great stumbling Block which has made both the *Portugueze* and their Religion odious and detestable to all the *Indians*. This is an Article of so much Importance, that it justly merits to be expatiated on. The true Spirit of Christianity was not well known, nor is yet, by such Persons as sought, or still seek, to establish and preserve it by Violence and Cruelty. To prevent the Recriminations, which are usually made by those who are for authorizing and supporting these destructive Methods; it must be observed, that I here apply all that is here said, to every Sect and Communion without Exception.

Most Authors who have treated of the *Mahommedan* Religion, declare, that

of the INQUISITION.

that it was established by Force of Arms, and supports itself wholly by Violence. This Accusation is unjust, especially in a *Romanist*. The Methods by which the Protestant Religion was prevented from spreading in *Spain* and *Italy*; as well as the dreadful Cruelties exercis'd in those Countries, are well known. The Barbarity was carried to such a Height in *Italy*, that Hereticks, as they are term'd, were saw'd in two; as is affirm'd by a *Romish* Writer, who liv'd in those Times, and whose Veracity cannot be suspected. The Author I mean is *Tomaso Costo*, in his Supplement to *Colanello Pacca*'s History †. This Writer relates, that the Inhabitants of *la Guardia* and *Sisto*, two Towns in *Calabria*, having been seiz'd, upon Account of their professing the Protestant Religion, were all butcher'd *anno* 1561. *T. Costo*'s

† *Seconda parte del Compendio dell' Istoria del Regno de Napoli*, pag. 257.

Words are these: *Furon tutti, chi scannato, qual segato per mezo, e qua'l altro buttato giù da un altissima balza; fatti crudele, ma meritevolmente morire. Stranissima cosa à udire fu l'ostinazione di costoro, che mentre il padre vedeva dar morte al figlivolo, e'l figlivolo al padre, non pur non ne mostravan dolore, ma lietamente dicevano, che sarrebono Angeli di Dio, tanto il Diavolo, à chi s' erano dati in preda, gli havev' acciecati*; i. e. 'Some had their Throats
'cut, others were saw'd in two, and
'others again were hurl'd from Preci-
'pices: In fine, all of them were cru-
'elly put to Death, but they deserved
'it. Nothing could be more amaz-
'ing than to see and hear their Obsti-
'nacy. A Father wou'd behold, with-
'out the least Concern, his Son mas-
'sacred, and a Son his Father. All
'these wou'd declare, with Joy in
'their Countenances, that they shou'd
'be Angels of God; so strangely were
'they blinded by the Devil, whose
Prey

Prey they had made themselves.' According to this ignorant and superstitious *Italian* Author; whoever preferr'd the Gospel to the vain Traditions of the Pope, abandonned himself to the evil Spirit.---Horrid Blindness sure!

In *Spain* a numberless Multitude of Persons, of both Sexes, and of every Age, were put to Death; for no other Crime than their turning Protestants, after their being fully convinced of the horrid Abuses of the Religion in which they were born and educated. The *Romish* Religion in *Spain* owes its whole Support to Violence, and the most barbarous Cruelties; a Circumstance acknowledged by the most superstitious Writers of that Nation. Doctor *Illescas*, in his Pontifical History, (a Work greatly esteemed in *Spain*) after speaking of Dr. *Caçalla* and *Constantine de la Fuente*, the former Preacher, and the latter Confessor to the Emperor *Charles* V. Both of whom were seiz'd by Order of the Inquisitors, and lost their

Lives for the Truth; *Conſtantine de la Fuente* dying in Priſon; and *Caçalla*, a Man of ſingular Learning and Piety, being burnt at *Valladolid*, together with his Mother, five of his Brothers, and ſome of his Siſters; Doctor *Illeſcas*, (I ſay) adds theſe very remarkable Words: *Huvo entre los quemados algunas Monias bien moças y hermoſas, las quales no contentas con ſer Lutheranas, avian ſido dogmatizadoras de aquella maldita dotrina. Eran todos los preſos de Valadolid, Sevilla, y Toledo, perſonas harto calificadas. Eran tantos y tales, que tuvo creydo, que ſi dos o tres meſes mas ſe tardaran en remediar eſte danno, ſe abraſara toda Eſpana* †. *i. e.* "A-
"mong thoſe burnt, were ſome young
"and beautiful Nuns, who, not ſatiſ-
"fied with being *Lutherans*, taught
"and inculcated their curſed Doctrine.
"All the Priſoners of *Valladolid*, of
"*Seville*, and of *Toledo*, were Perſons

† Apud Cyprianum de Valera, pag. 266.

"of

" of great Diftinction. They were fo
" numerous, and of fuch exalted
" Rank, that 'tis thought, had the
" Government delay'd applying a Re-
" medy to this Evil, only two or three
" Months longer, all *Spain* wou'd
" have been loft to the Catholic Faith."
'Tis, therefore, to Fire, and to the infinitely barbarous Cruelties of the Inquifitors, that the Church of *Rome* owes
its Prefervation. Doctor *Illefcas* is not
the only Author, who confeffes this
Truth; all the *Spanifh* and *Portugueze* Writers owning, and thofe of
Italy not prefuming to deny it. Here
follow fome remarkable Words, delivered by a *Portugueze* Preacher, Commiffary of the Holy Office, and Prior
of the *Dominicans* in *Evora*; in a
Sermon preach'd by him, at an *Auto
da Fé* folemnized in the fame City,
14th *June* 1637. *Demos meus Portu-
guezes muitas graças a o Ceo, que nos
fez tam grande merce de nos dar efta
Tribunal fanto, porque a nos faltar,*

A a *efta-*

estevera o nosso Reyno feito hum mato sem flor, nem fruto. Vamos com a consideracam a Inglaterra, França, Alemanha alta & baxa, & vejamos a altura em que estam as heresias por falta de Inquisiçoems, &c. † *i. e.* 'Let us return the
'greatest Thanks, my beloved *Portu-*
'*gueze*, to Heaven, for its signal Good-
'ness in giving us this holy Tribunal.
'Had we been depriv'd of it, our
'Kingdom wou'd have become a mere
'Shrub, without Flowers or Fruits,
'fit only to be burnt. Let us take
'a View of *England, France, Germa-*
'*ny* and the *Netherlands*; and reflect
'on the mighty Progress which Here-
'sy has made in them, for want of
'an Inquisition. 'Tis plain we shou'd
'be like those Countries, had we not
'been favour'd with so great a Bles-
'sing.' I know not what we are to think of such Confessions, which the

† *Sermam do Padre Frey Antonio Coutinho, im:presso em Lisboa. anno de* 1638, *folio verso.*

of the INQUISITION.

Force of Truth extorts from these heedless Writers, who don't consider the horrid Consequences that may be drawn from them. If the *Romish* Religion, even after its being long settled in a Country, can support itself only by inflicting the most cruel Punishments; and by a Tribunal [the Inquisition] which openly violates all the Laws of Justice, and the natural Rights of Mankind, what can the Heathens think of it? What will the *Chineze* and *Tartars* say, when they shall be told these Things?

The same Methods are employ'd in the *East-Indies*, for the Conversion of the Heathens, whenever they can be practic'd with Safety. This is the ultimate Aim of the *Romanists*, when they imagine themselves sure of attaining it. *Francis Xavier*, of whom so many wonderful Things are told †, us'd to say, (according to the *Jesuits* his Bre-

† Navarrete, Treatise 6. pag. 436, col. 6.

thren) *That the Christian Religion cou'd not be planted among the Heathens, so as to last any Time, unless the Auditors were within Musquet-Shot.* Father *Tellez* ‡, does not scruple to own this: 'Our Friars (says he) were always of 'Opinion, that the Catholic Religion 'wou'd never be of long Duration in '*Ethiopia*, except it shou'd be sup-'ported by Force of Arms.' This Reflection is so often repeated in Father *Tellez*, that there is no Room to doubt but 'tis the common Opinion, and the constant Practice of the Missionaries; and particularly the *Jesuits*. The like Particular is met with in a Letter written from *Ethiopia* to Pope *Paul* V. by the Patriarch *Andrew Oviedo*, a *Jesuit*; and in that of *Emanuel Fernandez*, another *Jesuit*, to the Provincial of the *East-Indies:* 'Is it surprizing that we shou'd desire 'the Aid of Soldiers, to support our

‡ History of Ethiopia, Lib. IV. cap. 3.

'Mission;

' Miſſion; *ſince the Prelates, even in* ' Portugal, *cannot diſcharge the Duties* ' *of their Function, without calling in* ' *the ſecular Arm?* §.'

'Tis therefore a certain Truth that the *Jeſuits*, and other Miſſionaries of the *Romiſh* Communion, have recourſe to Guns and Swords, to eſtabliſh their Religion, whenever this is practicable; and that, when 'tis not, they endeavour it as ſoon as poſſible, by the Increaſe of their new Converts. Father *Couplet*, a famous *Jeſuit* Miſſionary, was not aſhamed to own this Circumſtance, in a Piece preſented by him, *anno* 1681, to the College *de propaganda fide*: " How
" glorious, (ſays he) will it be for the
" Church of *Rome*, and for the Col-
" lege *de propaganda Fide*, ſhou'd the
" Miſſion of *China* obtain, one Day,
" this Privilege above the reſt; I
" mean, ſhould extend itſelf, ſo far
" and wide, by Means of the Prieſts

§ Apud Tellez. pag. 192.

"born in the Empire, that the Increase of the Faithful may terrify the Emperors of *China*, and the Heathen Princes? ||"

From what has been related above it appears, that the Hatred the *East-Indians* harbour against all the Christian Nations of *Europe*, whom they call *Franks*, is levelled chiefly at the *Portugueze*; which Abhorrence does not arise so much from the little Care these *Europeans* take, to keep at a Distance from the lowest and most infamous *Castes* or Tribes in *India*; as from the Knowledge the Heathens in question have, of the Cruelty of these Christians; of their domineering Spirit, even in preaching the Gospel; and of the vicious Lives they lead. If this were not the true Cause of the Hatred of

---

|| Bibliotheque Hist. & Crit. de Bréme, Part IV. Class V. pag. 646. See also, Travels of the Jesuits into various Nations of the World, with Notes Historical and Critical. Printed for J. Noon in the Poultry.

the *Indians*, these wou'd not entertain so much Reverence for their *Gnanigueuls*, or spiritual Men, who laugh at such superstitious Distinctions; nor bear a greater Aversion to the *Portugueze*, than to the *Mahommedans*, of whom they speak with Esteem enough, as is evident from the Writings of the Missionaries of *Tranquebar*. Farther, tho' there is no Distinction of *Castes* in *China*, yet its Inhabitants despise the *Portugueze* still more. The Mandarin of the Capital of the Island where stands *Macao*, a City of *China*, in which the *Portugueze* have been settled, ever since the 16th Century, treats them with supreme Contempt; as is evident from Father *Navarrete*, one of the sincerest and most famous Missionaries who have wrote on this Country:

'When the Citizens of *Macao* have
' any Business to transact, they send
' Deputies, who go in a Body, with
' their *Varas*, or Staves in their Hands,

'Hands, to wait upon the Mandarin
'of the Island, which is scarce a
'League from *Macao*; and always
'address him, upon their Knees, with
'their Memorials in their Hands. When
'the Mandarin gives them their An-
'swer, Part of it runs in the following
'Style : *This barbarous and brutal Na-
'tion deserves such and such a Thing.
''Tis granted or refused.* The *Portu-
'gueze*, thus dispatch'd, return to their
'City with the utmost Gravity. Some
'of these Deputies were Knights of
'the Order of Christ, which they wore
'on this Occasion, on their Breasts †.'
Such is the Contempt in which all the
Agents of the Church of *Rome*, especially those of the Inquisition ought to
be held in every Place.

The various Instances given above,
all of them compiled from Authors of

---

† Navarrete, Tom. I. Treatise 6. pag. 366. n. 23. quoted in Histoire du Christianisme des Indes, par Mr. V. La Croze, Livr. VII. pag. 524, & seq; Haye, 1724. 12mo.---This is an excellent Work.

ap-

approved Veracity, sufficiently show, that the Inquisition is the most iniquitous, and most inhuman Tribunal on Earth; opposite, in every Respect, to the gentle Spirit of Christianity; and to the uninterrupted Practice of the primitive Church, in its Conversion of Hereticks, as we shall now show.

PART

PART V.

Practice of the primitive Church, in bringing over Hereticks, compar'd with that of the Inquisition.

FRom the Infancy of the Church, to this Time, new Heresies and Hereticks have continually been starting up; but 'tis certain that the Rise of the Inquisition is not of older Date than the 12th Century.

Tho', so early as the Time of the Apostles, many Hereticks oppos'd their Doctrines; it nevertheless appears that these holy Men employ'd no other Weapons, in order for winning over these Hereticks, than Gentleness and Persuasion; and, at last, Excommunication, and cutting them off from

all

all Commerce with the reſt of Society. When a Heretic (ſays St. *Paul* in one of his Epiſtles) ſhall have been admoniſh'd once or twice; if he does not amend, ſhun all Communication with him. And, in another Place, St. *Paul* even forbids our eating with ſuch a one.

Thus the Apoſtles behav'd towards Hereticks; and ſuch was the Uſage they met with, till the Reign of *Conſtantine* the Great, which was in the fourth Century. All who ſucceeded them, as Preachers of the Goſpel, own, that it is juſt to have the Enemies of God in Abhorrence; but declare, that they muſt not be treated with Violence, or perſecuted: 'It becomes,
' (ſaid they) only *Gentiles*, who know
' neither God nor Chriſt, to uſe them
' cruelly.' Hereticks muſt be exhorted to Repentance, this being the Method which Heaven itſelf often employs in converting them.

'Twas

'Twas not till after the Conversion of *Constantine*, and till his Successors publickly professed the Christian Religion, that the Christians began to appoint Tribunals, Magistrates and Prisons, for all such as might infringe the Laws whether divine or human. 'Twas then the Face of Things began to be very much changed; Persons in Power declaring it as their Opinion, that if Thefts and Murders ought to be punished; 'twas not fit that Blasphemers, False-Swearers and Hereticks shou'd be permitted to proceed with Impunity.

'Twas now that Hereticks were punished; but with this Difference, that as the Emperors were persuaded, it was their indispensible Duty to maintain the Purity of Doctrine, and the Peace of the Church; they never failed to address themselves to the Bishops, in order to enquire what Idea these might entertain of a new Opinion; and whether it was heretical or otherwise. And, in case the Bishops cou'd not agree,

gree, the Emperors then fummon'd Councils, either national or provincial, to take Cognizance of fuch Opinions.

This is evident from the general Councils held under *Conftantine*, *Theodofius* the Great, *Theodofius* the Younger, and feveral other Emperors, who condemn'd the Herefies of *Arius*, *Macedonius* and *Neftorius*. 'Twou'd be deviating too far from our Subject, fhou'd we quote all the Inftances furnifhed, by Hiftory, for this Purpofe.

At the Time that *Charlemagne* fway'd the *Gallic* Scepter, and fome Years before he was proclaimed Emperor of the *Weft*, he obferv'd the fame Maxim with Regard to Hereticks. He convened, at the Requeft of Pope *Adrian* I. two Councils; the one at *Ratifbon* in 792, and the other at *Franckfort* in 794, to enquire into the Herefy of two Bifhops, who had revived, in *Spain*, the Errors of *Neftorius*. Both thofe Bifhops were condemned as Hereticks.

'Tis manifest, from what is here observed, that the Court of *Rome* and its Adherents, assert, without Foundation, that the Pope and the See of *Rome*, have a peculiar Right to take Cognizance of Heresies, and to condemn them. For if it was their Right, why did they, during above ten Centuries, leave such Enquiries to general or provincial Councils; without once complaining that this was an Infringement of their Privileges?

'Tis therefore a certain Truth, that the Church, in the Business of Opinions, always judg'd whether they were heretical or not; and that, after such Judgment, 'twas then the Affair of Princes, and Lay Magistrates, to take Cognizance with Regard to the Fact, and to pronounce Sentence.

It must be confess'd, indeed, that the Church, when it condemned Heresy condemned also the Authors of it, or such as were convicted thereof; but then, the Sentence went no farther than ecclesiastical

ecclesiastical Punishments; that is, the Laity were excommunicated; and the Clergy excommunicated; and likewise deprived or removed. But when Corporal and Civil Punishments were to be inflicted, the Person who was convicted of Heresy, and incurr'd the Punishment decreed by the Laws, receiv'd the Sentence whether of Absolution or Condemnation, from the Lay-Magistrates, to whom only this Right belonged; the Church never concerning itself any farther in these Matters, than merely to admonish the Magistrates to do their Duty; and to exert their Authority, in order to check the Progress of Heresy, and the Licentiousness of Hereticks.

When Magistrates prosecuted Hereticks, they did not do it as deriving their Authority from the Church; or as Executors of its Judgments, tho' the Adherents of the Court of *Rome* now pretend this; but by an Authority no less peculiar and natural to them, than

than that they enjoyed, with Regard to the punishing of other Criminals. A sufficient Proof of this is, the Laws enacted by the Emperors themselves against Hereticks, some whereof we shall quote here. 'Twill thence appear, that Princes act, on these Occasions, in Quality of Sovereigns; and not as tho' the Authority exerted by them, was only subordinate and borrowed.

Constantine, who was the first Christian Emperor, first enacted Punishments against Hereticks, which went no farther than Banishment; nor were all Hereticks condemned indiscriminately; none but Heresiarchs being punished; and this only to prevent their seducing the People, and disturbing the Peace of the Church.

Constantius his Successor, tho' not so favourably inclin'd to the Christian Religion; he nevertheless, in his Punishment of Hereticks, proceeded no farther than to banish them; not to mention that none but Bishops and the chief Clergy were sent into Exile.

Julian the Apostate publickly renounced the Christian Faith, and cruelly persecuted its Professors; but whether it were owing to his having been educated in their Religion, or from Political Views; he studiously endeavoured to have it imagin'd that Religion was no Ways concerned in the Punishments inflicted by him, but that the Sufferers were condemned for other Crimes. The Inquisitors are perfect Copists of *Julian*'s Policy, on these Occasions.

Theodosius the Great, decreed no greater Punishment against Hereticks, than a pecuniary Fine. *Gratian, Valentinian,* and *Theodosius,* his immediate Successors, increas'd the Punishment against Hereticks, which yet did not touch their Lives. The *Manichees,* the *Donatists* and *Samaritans,* were banish'd, and their Possessions confiscated; they were rendered incapable of being Witneſſes or Heirs; they were not allowed to buy, ſell, or enter into any Sort of Contract; and their Puniſhment extended even beyond Death. In a Word, the ſame Law enacted, that all the Fautors of ſuch Hereticks, or who might ſhelter them, ſhou'd be ſubject to the like Puniſhments. 'Tis from theſe Emperors that the Inquiſitors have borrow'd many unjuſt Practices, which they exerciſe againſt all Perſons, tho' ever ſo innocent, who have the ſad Fortune to fall into their Hands; and extend their Cruelties even beyond the Grave.

The firſt Emperor who ſentenc'd Hereticks, capitally, was *Maximus*, Uſurper of the Empire of the Weſt, after *Gratian*'s Demiſe. He put ſeveral to Death, which Puniſhment was thought too cruel; and yet he was imitated, in this Particular, by ſome of his Succeſſors. *Theodoſius*, among others, condemn'd to Death thoſe *Manichees*, who, after having been Chriſtians,

Christians, return'd to their Heresy. But, on these Occasions, it was necessary that there shou'd be some peculiar Reason drawn from the Nature of the Heresies, such as their containing certain blasphemous Tenets, injurious to the most sacred Mysteries; or that such Hereticks acted seditiously: for there are Proofs that *Nestorius*, tho' an Heresiarch, was sentenc'd only to Banishment.

The Emperor *Justin* sentenc'd *Severus* to have his Tongue cut out, for his Blasphemies.---Such were the Punishments inflicted, by the *Roman* Emperors, on Hereticks, till near *Anno* 800, about which Time the two Empires were separated.

After this Separation, Hereticks were proceeded against, in like Manner, in the Empire of the East; that is, the Church always took Cognizance of Heresy; and the Emperors, and Lay-Magistrates, pronounced the Sentence of Absolution or Condemnation.

In the Western Empire, after *Anno* 800, we find few Laws decreed against Hereticks; and indeed such were not necessary, since very few started up, during three hundred Years; and when any happen'd to rise, the Bishops proceeded against them, pursuant to the Practice of the Church; but if the Hereticks deserv'd more severe Punishments than those enacted by the Canons; in this Case the Bishops were obliged to have recourse to the secular Magistrates, who exercis'd, with regard to them, the Right or Authority which devolved to them from their Prince, *viz.* the restraining Hereticks by Punishments.

The Church contented itself with employing, with respect to the unhappy Persons in question, the Gentleness and Moderation which the Gospel enjoins, by interceeding with the narch in their Favour.

If we weigh a little the Opinion entertained by the Fathers of the Church,

con-

concerning the Punishments due to Hereticks, we shall be fully persuaded that they were truly animated by the Spirit of the Gospel; a Spirit directly opposite, in all Respects, to that which fires those, who form the cruel and barbarous Tribunals of the Inquisition.

St. *Athanasius*, in his Epistle to the *Anchorets*, complaining of the Persecutions carried on by the *Arians* against the other Christians.--- ' Satan, (says
' he) because he has not Truth on his
' Side, has recourse to Violence, and
' causes himself to be received by Force.
' Whereas our Saviour says: If any
' Man will be my Disciple, let him fol-
' low me. He does not constrain any
' One; he does not break open the
' Doors of those in whose Houses he
' is desirous of entring; but knocks
' gently; and employs, in order to
' procure Admittance, none but the
' mildest Words. Open the Door (says
' he) Sister. If the Door be open'd,
' he

' he enters; if it be not open'd, he
' retires; for Truth does not gain Ad-
' mittance by Force and Violence, but
' by Gentleness and Perswasion.'---And
' a little lower. --' This Sect (says he)
' shows, by its violent Conduct, that
' it is not from God, and cannot be the
' true Religion, which employs only
' Perswasions, and never has recourse to
' Violence. *If any one be my Disci-*
' *ple* (these are Christ's own Words) *let*
' *him follow me.* He even permits his
' Apostles to leave him, after they had
' begun to follow him: *Will you* (says
' he to his Apostles) *go also?*

 St. *Ambrose*, speaking of the Apostles who were the first Preachers of the Gospel: " The Lord (says he) sent " them to sow the Seeds of Faith in " the Heart; to teach, and not to " force; to preach a Doctrine of Hu-" mility, and not to exercise, haugh-" tily, their Power." He afterwards relates what pass'd between our Saviour and his Apostles, when these besought
him

him to call down Fire from Heaven, to confume the *Samaritans*, who had refus'd to receive him.--- " The Lord " (fays he) reprimanded them, faying, " You don't yet know what Spirit you " ought to breathe; nor do you con- " fider, that the Son of Man did not " come to deftroy, but to fave."---It cannot here be objected, that the Fathers of the Church fpake thus, only becaufe they were perfecuted; were the weakeft; and that the Emperors did not fide with them. Thofe Fathers always entertained fuch Sentiments, even when they might have taken Advantage of the Credit and Favour they enjoy'd with the Emperors, in order to perfecute Hereticks, as is evident from what follows.

Prifcillian having fpread, about the clofe of the fourth Century, a very pernicious Herefy in *Spain* and *Gaul*; a *Spanifh* Bifhop named *Ithacius*, either from a falfe Zeal, or from fome other Motive, refolved to profecute him;

him; and not ceafe purfuing him, till he had taken away his Life. For this Purpofe he obtained of *Maximus*, who had feiz'd on the Weftern Part of the *Roman* Empire, Permiffion to affemble a Council in *Bourdeaux*. Hither *Prifcillian*, and his Brother Herefiarchs were fummoned, on which Occafion One of them was depos'd; when *Prifcillian*, who forefaw that the like Sentence wou'd be pafs'd upon him, refus'd to obey the Council, and appealed from it to the Emperor. His Appeal being admitted, he was conducted to *Maximus*, followed by the two Bifhops, *Ithacius* and *Idacius*, his Accufers.

St. *Martin*, Bifhop of *Tours*, oppofed, with his utmoft Efforts, *Ithacius*, who was moft exafperated againft them. He was for ever intreating him to quit the Profecution; and befought the Emperor not to imbrue his Hands in the Blood of thefe unhappy Men. St. *Martin* declar'd, that 'twas enough they

they had been punished by the Canons; and were remov'd, by the Sentence of the Bishops, from their Sees.

But all these Remonstrances made by St. *Martin*, and his other Endeavours, in Favour of the ill-fated Hereticks in question, were fruitless. *Ithacius* prevailed; and was so urgent with *Maximus*, that *Priscillian* and four of his Companions were sentenc'd to die, as having taught abominable Doctrines.

How guilty soever *Priscillian* might be, yet this Action of *Ithacius*, in thus folliciting his Death, was censur'd by all the Bishops, who resolved to punish him for it; they justly considering him as a bloody-minded Man, who had defil'd the Church by this cruel Prosecution. These Bishops thought it, therefore, their Duty to chastise him; and to evince to the whole World, that the Church did not approve of what *Ithacius* had done; but, on the contrary, that its Sentiments, with regard to Hereticks, were temper'd with Gentleness and Moderation.

Nevertheless *Ithacius*, having a Genius for Caballing and Intrigues, and Time to ward off the Blow, secur'd himself from it entirely, by throwing the Blame on other Persons. One of these, tho' less guilty than *Ithacius*, was depos'd and degraded; and the Church thereby clear'd itself from all Suspicions which might otherwise have been entertained, *viz.* of its approving the sentencing Hereticks to Death.

It appears, from History, that this *Ithacius* was a Man of a very black Character; vain, insolent, dissolute, and an Enemy to Letters. *Secuti etiam accusatores Idacius & Ithacius Episcopi; quorum studium in expugnandis hæreticis non reprehenderem, si non studio vincendi plus quam oportuit certassent. Ac mea quidem sententia est, mihi tam reos quam accusatores displicere. Certe Ithacium nihil pensi, nihil sancti habuisse definio. Fuit enim audax, loquax, im-*

impudens, sumptuosus, ventri & gulæ plurimum impertiens. Hic stultitiæ eo usque processerat, ut omnes etiam sanctos viros, quibus aut studium inerat lectionis, aut propositum erat certare jejuniis, tamquam Priscilliani socios aut discipulos, in crimen arcesseret. Ausus etiam miser est, ea tempestate Martino episcopo, viro planè Apostolis conferendo, palam objectare hæresis infamiam. Namque tum Martinus apud Treveros constitutus, non desinebat increpare Ithacium, ut ab accusatione desisteret: Maximum orare, ut sanguine infelicium abstineret: satis superque sufficere, ut episcopali sententia heretici judicati ecclesiis pellerentur †.

The above Incident may suggest a Variety of Reflexions, to strongly corroborate our Argument. First, we may consider it as a Proof, that all the Churches of *Gaul* and *Spain*, did not

---

† Sulpic. Severus, Hist. Sacræ, Lib. II. p. 168, 169.

approve of putting Hereticks to Death; at least that the Bishops and the Clergy shou'd follicit this: Much less wou'd those Churches have been pleased to hear ecclesiastical Judges pronounce such Sentences. Secondly, No one, in in those Ages, thought it improper that the Prosecution of Hereticks shou'd be brought before Monarchs and secular Magistrates; whereas the Court of *Rome*, and the Inquisitors hate to have the former concern themselves, in any Manner, with their Sentences, except as Executors of them. Thirdly, we find, by the above Relation, that the Right of inflicting Punishments, both ecclesiastical and temporal, on Hereticks, belong'd indisputably to Kings, and lay Magistrates. Finally, That though Hereticks have sometimes been treated with great Severity by Monarchs, yet this is no Proof that the Church breath'd the same cruel Spirit.

This is evident from the Writings of the Fathers. St. *Chrysostom*, speaking of of the Correction due to thofe who offend thro' Error, or otherwife, fays: "That we muft reprove them, left "God, who will judge Us, fhou'd "require them at our Hands; but "that, in correcting them, Patience "and Moderation are to be intermix'd: "That we muft be careful, above all "Things, not to hate fuch as we cor- "rect; and never to treat them with "Force or Violence."

St. *Auftin*, who has engag'd more deeply in this Subject than any other of the Fathers, is the laft we fhall cite on this Occafion. 'Tis certain he was long of Opinion, that not the leaft Reftraint or Violence ought to be employ'd againft Hereticks; which made him obferve, "That fuch only ufe "them with Severity, as know not "how difficult it is to difcover Truth, "and efcape Error." He adds ;--- "None but thofe behave with Ri- "gour towards them, who don't know "how difficult it is to conquer the
"Pre-

"Prejudices of Birth and Education:
"But far be it from us (continues he)
"to treat in this Manner, Persons who
"are divided from us, not by Errors
"which they invented, but by per-
"mitting themselves to be misled by
"the Mistakes of others. On the con-
"trary, we offer up our Prayers to
"Almighty God; in order that he,
"by refuting false Opinions, may gra-
"ciously be prevailed on to inspire us,
"on these Occasions, with a Spirit of
"Peace; such a Spirit as may yield to
"no other Impressions than those of
"Charity or Love; no other Interests
"than those of Christ Jesus; and no
"other Desire than that of converting
"Hereticks.

'Tis certain that, if St. *Austin* breath'd these Sentiments of Moderation with regard to the Manichees, an abominable Sect, who practis'd, in their Assemblies, the most infamous Acts; and whose Rites were scandalous and supremely wicked; he doubtless must have

have had more Favour for all other Hereticks, whose Opinions were less criminal, and consequently less distant from those of the Church of Christ. This he himself tells us, in one of his Epistles: 'My first Opinion (says he) 'was, that no Person ought to be 'compell'd to come into the Church; 'that no other Weapon but the Power 'of Words shou'd be exercis'd against 'Hereticks; that These must be com- 'batted by Arguments, and vanquished 'by Reason; lest, the forcing them 'into the Church, shou'd fill it with 'Hypocrites, false Christians and dis- 'guis'd Enemies; who are worse, and 'much more to be dreaded, than those 'who are openly such.

Hence we find St. *Austin*'s first Opinion was, that Hereticks shou'd not be proceeded against by Violence. He yet chang'd his Mind afterwards; and thought that it was, sometimes, of Advantage, to treat them with moderate Severity. He gives two Reasons for

for this Change of Opinion. *First*, the great Numbers of Converts won over daily, by Means of the Edicts which the Emperors published against Hereticks and Schismaticks, and the Punishments decreed against them. ' I
' was induced (says he) to alter my
' Opinion; upon my perceiving that
' Conversions, tho' brought about by
' the Dread of the Imperial Laws,
' were yet very sincere †."

The second Reason he gives for his Change, is, the Violence and Fury of the *Donatists*; and the Necessity there was for checking their ill Treatment of the Christians. ' They us'd to plun-
' der and carry off (says St. *Austin*) the
' Church Ornaments; wou'd lay Snares
' for the Bishops and Pastors of the
' Church, and sometimes beat them
' to Death: They dragg'd Priests thro'
' the Mire; ran up and down, in

---

† With Submission to St. Austin, how cou'd he be perfectly sure of this?

' Troops,

'Troops, to plunder Houses; they
'wounded the Christians, and often
'the Bishops themselves; and their
'Rage rose sometimes to so great a
'Height, as even to put them to a
'cruel Death.

'Cities were become Scenes of
'Slaughter; the Plains were uninha-
'bited; and the Woods serv'd only as
'Asylums to Assassins. The high
'Ways were now become so dange-
'rous, that there was no travelling
'with any Safety in them. The Cru-
'elty of the *Donatists* was so extreme,
'that they chopp'd off the Hands of
'the Bishops; cut their Tongues out,
'and afterwards left them in this sad
'Condition.'

After such Barbarities, 'tis no wonder St. *Austin* shou'd alter his Opinion; and declare that Persecution must be repuls'd by Persecution; and that these bloody-minded Schismaticks ought to be check'd, since otherwise their Rage might prove equally fatal to the
Christians,

Chriſtians, and to the Imperial Authority. This obliged the Emperor to publiſh an Edict, wherein the *Donatiſts* were commanded to be ſuppreſs'd, in order to put a Stop to their enormous Actions †.

But St. *Auſtin*, to evince how little the Church was inclined to lay aſide its Spirit of Gentleneſs and Moderation with Regard to Hereticks; adds: 'That 'Perſons were deputed to the Empe-'ror, to beſeech him, in the Name of 'the Church, not to force Hereticks 'to turn to the Faith; but to im-'plore that Monarch, not to let thoſe 'Hereticks perſecute the Chriſtians, and 'put them to Death.' Such was the 'Moderation of the Church during 'the firſt Centuries.

St. *Auſtin*, to ſhow that Monarchs, when they treated Hereticks with Se-

† *Religion* need not be introduc'd on this Occaſion. The *Donatiſts*, according to the above Relation, were become a Terror to Society, and conſequently ought to have been extirpated (for Its Sake) whatever might have been their religious Principles.

verity,

verity, were not animated thereto by the Church, but only by a necessary Policy, adds; --- ' That the Emperor
' paid no Regard to the Remonstran-
' ces of the Persons deputed by the
' Church; that nevertheless, in order
' to keep within the Bounds of Chris-
' tian Moderation, even with Regard
' to those Hereticks who did not de-
' serve it, he wou'd not sentence them
' to die, but only fined them; and ba-
' nish'd their Bishops, and other Clergy.

'Twas therefore St. *Austin*'s Opinion, that Hereticks might justly be punish'd, provided this was done with Gentleness, and without shedding their Blood or putting them to Death; and their wicked Actions be so restrained, as that the Offenders might be permitted to live, in order to repent of their Crimes.

But St. *Austin* must necessarily have disapprov'd of the putting Hereticks to Death; since he wou'd not even allow Excommunication to be pronounc'd against them, except with the greatest Precaution and Reserve †.

'Twere needless to add a greater Number of Authorities; those instanc'd by us being sufficient to prove, to all Persons of good Sense and Humanity, that the primitive Church exerted a Spirit of Gentleness and Moderation towards Hereticks. This Spirit prevail'd till the twelfth Century, when that Monster of Iniquity, the Inquisition, first began to put forth its horrid Head.

It may be inferr'd, from the several Particulars related above, that the Practice of the Inquisition, in all Places where this Tribunal is established, is diametrically opposite to the Spirit which the Church of Christ breathed, during above a thousand Years.

---

† St. Austin's Lenity, with regard to such Opinions or Doctrines as are not destructive to Society, is highly commendable. None but the worst of Wretches call out for Punishments on these Occasions.

The

The Church always difcovered, for above ten Centuries, a Spirit of Mildnefs, with Regard to all Hereticks; thofe efpecially who did not difturb the Peace of the Church, nor perfcute the Chriftians.

But in every Country where the Inquifition is fettled, all Perfons whom it confiders as Hereticks, are treated with the utmoft Barbarity. Such Hereticks are fought for with uncommon Diligence, and profecuted till they are brought to a cruel End.

In the firft Ages, 'twas with Regret, that the Church faw itfelf obliged to impeach Hereticks to the Tribunals of Monarchs and Lay Magiftrates; and when the Church thought it neceffary to proceed to fuch lengths, it always interceeded very kindly for them; us'd every Endeavour to get their Lives fpar'd; and to foften the Rigours of their Punifhment.

On the contrary; in the feveral Countries where the Inquifition prevails, thofe called Hereticks are imprifoned, tortured, and often put to a moft barbarous Death. 'Tis an inflexible Tribunal, whofe Severities nothing can alleviate; and fhou'd the Magiftrates, whofe Aid it implores, in order for burning Perfons, attempt to foften this Punifhment, they themfelves wou'd be look'd upon as Fautors of Herefy and Hereticks; wou'd become obnoxious to the fharpeft Cenfures of the Church, not excepting the Thunders of Excommunication.

The Church, during the twelve firft Centuries, had neither Judges, Officers, Tribunals, Prifons, Dungeons, Tortures, or Executioners; the Spirit of Gentlenefs profeffed by it, gave no room for fuch Inventions: it leaving, to the Tribunals of Kings and Lay Magiftrates, all the dreadful Articles abovementioned; in order for them to reftrain the Wicked, and to maintain Unity, Peace and Regularity in Society.

The

The Inquisitors, on the contrary, are ever furrounded with thefe Objects of Terror; and profecute peaceable Hereticks, with no lefs Rigour than fuch as are moft feditious and turbulent. The Inquifitors take Cognizance of Crimes of every kind, upon pretext of Herefy.

Under the antient Church, the only Inquifitors were the Bifhops and their Officials. Whenever rigorous Punifhments were to be inflicted, or Perfons fentenc'd to Death, the Bifhops addrefs'd the Magiftrates, whofe Right this was.

But in all Places where the Inquifition is fetled, Bifhops have the leaft Share in the Judgment of Hereticks; and moft Inquifitors are Friars, whofe inftitution is very fevere; and who, tho' they outwardly profefs a Life of the greateft Regularity and Piety; are often, in private, the moft wicked and debauched of Men; according to an obfolete Epigram quoted by *Hofpinian*:

*Vos Monachi vestri stomachi sunt amphora Bacchi:
Vos estis, Deus est testis, deterrima pestis.*

The Sense is:

*Your Paunches (Monks) are mighty Tuns confest:
Sure, of Mankind, ye are the deadly Pest.*

The Inquisitors have divested Magistrates of the Power, of taking Cognizance of their Judgments. The only Privilege left them (of those they enjoyed antiently) is, to be merely as Witnesses and Executors of the Inquisitors Sentences; but they are not allowed to concern themselves, in any Manner, in the Examination of Prisoners.

Antiently Hereticks us'd to be judg'd like other Delinquents; there was no Difference in the Formalities; the Prosecutions were the same; and the like Indulgence was shewn them, in order for them to make their Defence; they were confronted with their Witnesses, and cou'd challenge any, or all of them:

them: In a Word, the Means of juftifying themfelves were equally open to them, as to all other Prifoners.

But 'tis the very contrary in the Inquifition; its Profecutions varying, and its Formalities being quite new: The Witneffes never appear; a Prifoner muft guefs at the Crime he is accufed of, as well as the Perfons who fwear againft him: Nothing is eafier than to find Means to deftroy a Perfon impeach'd; and, on the other Hand, nothing fo difficult as for fuch a one to hit upon Ways to juftify himfelf.

Antiently, when a Heretic repented of his Errors, and fubmitted to the Penance and Correction of the Church, he was always received again into its Bofom with Joy.

But 'tis not fo in the Inquifition. Its Profecutions (as has been inftanc'd) are carried on even after the Death of a Perfon: The fame Rigours are exercis'd on his Bones, and on the Image of Him, as wou'd have been employ'd againft his living Body.

Body. Time cannot blot a single Circumstance from the Memory of the Inquisitors; they remembring as perfectly a Crime, many Years after its being committed, as if it had happen'd but the Day before.

In other Tribunals, a Son wou'd not be thought guilty of a Crime, for concealing his Father, when sought after, in order for his being put to Death; a Wife is not considered as guilty, for endeavouring to save her Husband in such extreme Danger; these kind Offices being look'd upon as Duties to which Nature strongly prompts all Mankind.

But in every Country, where the Inquisition prevails, all these natural Duties are strictly forbid; and a Person who is impeach'd to that Tribunal, is abandonn'd universally, even by his nearest Relations; upon Pain, shou'd these do him the least Service, of becoming obnoxious to all the Rigours of
the

the Inquifition, as being Fautors of Hereticks.

In all other Tribunals, Perfons who have been accus'd falfely; imprifon'd without a Caufe; or tortur'd undefervedly, are permitted to publifh their Innocence, and glory in it: Prifoners may complain, and their Murmurs are not thought a frefh Crime, for which a Perfon fhall be liable to be feiz'd anew: The Judges don't fcruple to own their being miftaken; and are the firft in declaring fuch to be innocent as are really fo.

But nothing like this is feen in the Inquifition; its Judges never confeffing their having been in an Error, but pretend they are always in the Right. And fhou'd an innocent Man, after he had been releas'd from their Prifons, prefume to publifh his Wrongs, and make a Merit of them; the Inquifitors wou'd certainly feize him again; and punifh Him, for having defam'd, as they term it, the Holy Office.

All

All unhappy Criminals, except those sentenc'd by the Inquisitors, when going to Execution excite the Pity of the Spectators in general, who sadly sympathize with them, and sincerely bewail their dire Fate.

But in the several Countries where the Inquisition is setled, its Executions are like so many Festivities; and the greater the Number of Victims, the more gay and splendid is the Solemnity.

What has been here related concerning the Inquisition, may seem incredible to those who inhabit the Countries where it is not admitted; but all Persons who have visited many Parts of *Italy*, or liv'd in *Spain* or *Portugal*, know the Truth of the Particulars asserted above.

Hence 'tis manifest, that the Tribunal in question assumes, very unjustly, the Title of Holy Office; since its Conduct is directly contrary to that which the ancient Fathers of the Church

of the INQUISITION.

Church employed againſt Hereticks; and quite repugnant to the Spirit of Gentleneſs and Love, which our Saviour breath'd, not only with Regard to Hereticks, but even for Perſecutors. This Tribunal, therefore, ſo far from meriting the Title of Holy, is a Scandal to Human Nature, and the higheſt Affront to the Almighty; eſpecially as its abominable Miniſters pretend to act under His Influence and Direction.
' The *Popiſh* Inquiſitors (ſays one † of
' the Writers of a noble Sett of Papers)
' while they deliver over to the Flames
' a poor Wretch, already half dead
' with Fears, Famine, and Torture,
' beſeech and adjure the civil Magi-
' ſtrate, who muſt ſee it done, by
' the Love of God, and the Bowels of
' Jeſus Chriſt, not to hurt his Life or
' Limb.' How ſhocking is this Gri-

---

† Mr. Trenchard, who, in Conjunction with Mr. Gordon, wrote CATO's LETTER'S. See Vol. I. pag. 43. 5th Edit.

mace,

mace, how blasphemous this Hypocrisy!---May Providence keep, for ever, this horrid Tribunal at the farthest Distance from *Great-Britain*; and Liberty shield it to latest Ages!

Oh LIBERTY, *thou Goddess heavenly bright,*
Profuse of Bliss, and pregnant with Delight!
Eternal Pleasures in thy Presence reign,
And smiling Plenty leads thy wanton Train;
Eas'd of her Load Subjection grows more light,
And Poverty looks chearful in thy Sight;
Thou mak'st the gloomy Face of Nature gay,
Giv'st Beauty to the Sun, and Pleasure to the Day.

Mr. Addison's *Letter from* Italy, *to Lord* Hallifax.

FINIS.

[This text appeared in the original publication.]

Colophon

THE SUFFERINGS OF JOHN COUSTOS

Twelve hundred and fifty copies of this limited edition were manufactured by Pantagraph Printing Company and Illinois Graphics, Inc., of Bloomington, Illinois, the former doing the composition and binding, and the latter the presswork.

The type faces used are of the Janson and Garamond families. The facsimile pages were reproduced from the first English Edition of "The Sufferings of John Coustos," now in the Scottish Rite Masonic Museum and Library, Lexington, Massachusetts.

The text paper is Bookmark 555 manufactured by International Paper Company. The book covers are made of Holliston Sturdite over board stamped in gold.

All volumes issued by The Masonic Book Club are designed and prepared by Louis L. Williams, Alphonse Cerza and Fred Dolan.

Related Titles from Westphalia Press

Ancient Mysteries and Modern Masonry: The Collected Writings of Jewel P. Lightfoot, Edited by Billy J. Hamilton Jr.

Jewel P. Lightfoot. Former Attorney General of the State of Texas. Past Grand Master of the Masonic Grand Lodge of Texas. From humble beginnings in rural Arkansas, he worked to become an educated man who excelled in law and Freemasonry. He was a gentleman of his time, well-known as a scholar, public speaker, and Masonic philosopher.

Essay on The Mysteries and the True Object of The Brotherhood of Freemasons
by Jason Williams

This isn't a reprint of a classic. It's a new rendition with new life breathed into it, to be enjoyed both by the layperson trying to understand the Craft and Masonic scholars taking a deeper dive into the fraternity's golden years—when the concepts of liberty and equality were still fresh.

Female Emancipation and Masonic Membership:
An Essential Collection
By Guillermo De Los Reyes Heredia

Female Emancipation and Masonic Membership: An Essential Combination is a collection of essays on Freemasonry and gender that promotes a transatlantic discussion of the study of the history of women and Freemasonry and their contribution in different countries.

Freemasonry, Heir to the Enlightenment
by Cécile Révauger

Modern Freemasonry may have mythical roots in Solomon's time but is really the heir to the Enlightenment. Ever since the early eighteenth century freemasons have endeavored to convey the values of the Enlightenment in the cultural, political and religious fields, in Europe, the American colonies and the emerging United States.

Freemasonry: A French View
by Roger Dachez and Alain Bauer

Perhaps one should speak not of Freemasonry but of Freemasonries in the plural. In each country Masonic historiography has developed uniqueness. Two of the best known French Masonic scholars present their own view of the worldwide evolution and challenging mysteries of the fraternity over the centuries.

Worlds of Print: The Moral Imagination of an Informed Citizenry, 1734 to 1839
by John Slifko

John Slifko argues that freemasonry was representative and played an important role in a larger cultural transformation of literacy and helped articulate the moral imagination of an informed democratic citizenry via fast emerging worlds of print.

Why Thirty-Three?: Searching for Masonic Origins
by S. Brent Morris, PhD

What "high degrees" were in the United States before 1830? What were the activities of the Order of the Royal Secret, the precursor of the Scottish Rite? A complex organization with a lengthy pedigree like Freemasonry has many basic foundational questions waiting to be answered, and that's what this book does: answers questions.

The Great Transformation: Scottish Freemasonry 1725-1810
by Dr. Mark C. Wallace

This book examines Scottish Freemasonry in its wider British and European contexts between the years 1725 and 1810. The Enlightenment effectively crafted the modern mason and propelled Freemasonry into a new era marked by growing membership and the creation of the Grand Lodge of Scotland.

Getting the Third Degree: Fraternalism, Freemasonry and History
Edited by Guillermo De Los Reyes and Paul Rich

As this engaging collection demonstrates, the doors being opened on the subject range from art history to political science to anthropology, as well as gender studies, sociology and more. The organizations discussed may insist on secrecy, but the research into them belies that.

A Place in the Lodge: Dr. Rob Morris, Freemasonry and the Order of the Eastern Star
by Nancy Stearns Theiss, PhD

Ridiculed as "petticoat masonry," critics of the Order of the Eastern Star did not deter Rob Morris' goal to establish a Masonic organization that included women as members. Morris carried the ideals of Freemasonry through a despairing time of American history.

Brought to Light: The Mysterious George Washington Masonic Cave
by Jason Williams MD

The George Washington Masonic Cave near Charles Town, West Virginia, contains a signature carving of George Washington dated 1748. This book painstakingly pieces together the chronicled events and real estate archives related to the cavern in order to sort out fact from fiction.

Dudley Wright: Writer, Truthseeker & Freemason
by John Belton

Dudley Wright (1868-1950) was an Englishman and professional journalist who took a universalist approach to the various great Truths of Life. He travelled though many religions in his life and wrote about them all, but was probably most at home with Islam.

History of the Grand Orient of Italy
Emanuela Locci, Editor

No book in Masonic literature upon the history of Italian Freemasonry has been edited in English up to now. This work consists of eight studies, covering a span from the Eighteenth Century to the end of the WWII, tracing through the story, the events and pursuits related to the Grand Orient of Italy.

westphaliapress.org

Policy Studies Organization

The Policy Studies Organization (PSO) is a publisher of academic journals and book series, sponsor of conferences, and producer of programs.

Policy Studies Organization publishes dozens of journals on a range of topics, such as European Policy Analysis, Journal of Elder Studies, Indian Politics & Polity, Journal of Critical Infrastructure Policy, and Popular Culture Review.

Additionally, Policy Studies Organization hosts numerous conferences. These conferences include the Middle East Dialogue, Space Education and Strategic Applications Conference, International Criminology Conference, Dupont Summit on Science, Technology and Environmental Policy, World Conference on Fraternalism, Freemasonry and History, and the Internet Policy & Politics Conference.

For more information on these projects, access videos of past events, and upcoming events, please visit us at:

www.ipsonet.org

www.ingramcontent.com/pod-product-compliance
Lightning Source LLC
Chambersburg PA
CBHW051522020426
42333CB00016B/1732